Divining Desire

Divining Desire

Focus Groups and the Culture of Consultation

Liza Featherstone

OR Books

New York · London

Published for the book trade by OR Books in partnership with Counterpoint Press. Distributed to the trade by Publishers Group West

All rights information: rights@orbooks.com

First printing 2017

Cataloging-in-Publication data is available from the Library of Congress. A catalog record for this book is available from the British Library.

ISBN 978-1-944869-48-9

Text design by Under|Over. Typeset by AarkMany Media, Chennai, India. Printed by Berryville Graphics, Berryville, Virginia

10 9 8 7 6 5 4 3 2 1

Table of Contents

Introduction: Dichter's Egg

Ernest Dichter, a famous mid-century market researcher, was assigned to solve a problem for the Betty Crocker company. Housewives liked the idea of cake mix, but in reality, they weren't buying it. Dichter's focus groups revealed why: women felt guilty that they were not doing the work of baking the cake for their families.[1]

Dichter's findings here were not at all unusual: other market researchers of the nineteen fifties also revealed great reserves of female ambivalence about prepared foods.

Industry was determined to push ready-made food. Many products had been developed during wartime for soldiers. After the war, industry sought to drum up consumer peacetime demand, even for foods specifically associated with the front, like Spam.[2] During the war, frozen foods got a big boost because of tin rationing, and industry continued to promote them after the war. Orange juice and lemonade were popular, and 30 million fish sticks were sold in 1954.[3] Frozen dinners were introduced in 1952.[4] More women were working outside the home, making the convenience of such products especially appealing. Additionally, in this postwar period, incomes rose, giving families more money to spend on conveniences and on trying out new products. But cooking was seen as so central to the role of wives and mothers that such products were viewed with unease.

Focus groups could illuminate the psychological complexities. In one focus group from this period, a woman made a Freudian slip: "Especially when I'm in a hurry, I like foods that are time-*consuming*." The slip of the tongue, as well as the context of the conversation, revealed the woman's conflicted feelings about convenience foods, even though she seemed to embrace them. Her mistake inspired the other women in the group to talk more openly about how guilty they felt about serving prepared foods to their families.[5]

Dichter was creative at coming up with solutions to the problems that focus groups revealed. As Bill Schlackman, vice president of Dichter's Institute of Motivational Research, would recall years later, the solution was to assuage the housewives' guilt by giving them more of a "sense of participation. How to do that?" He smiled, "By adding an egg." (Dichter added his own, more idiosyncratic spin: she would then be symbolically giving her own eggs to her husband.) It might sound off-the-wall, but sales of cake mixes took off—and it was an early focus group marketing triumph.[6]

This anecdote has been used to show how clever Dichter was, and how psychologically insightful early market research could be.[7] But it also offers a telling metaphor. Like Dichter's egg, the focus group itself has given us the feeling that we are participating.

Sociologist Erving Goffman wrote in 1959, "[S]ocieties everywhere, if they are to be societies, must mobilize their members as self regulating participants in social encounters. One way of mobilizing the individual for this purpose is through ritual . . ."[8] For our market democracy, the focus group is a fitting ritual, teaching us to reveal just what the corporate and political elites need us to reveal. It also helps us to play our assigned roles in a society where only a few people hold real power.

As Goffman observes, too, rituals contain as well as nurture. While focus groups sometimes look and feel empowering, they have also been part of a process in which citizenship has been reduced to consumerism, a set of choices, made passively under serious constraints, from our own access to money and time, to the narrow range of political parties with the resources to participate. In layperson's terms, the word "ritual" can sound dismissive. "This is just an empty ritual," we might say, especially if we are not religious. But social scientists like Goffman have long understood

A photo of Ernest Dichter, founder of motivational research and early pioneer of the focus group, who died in 1991, greets visitors to the focus group facilities at a company bearing his name, the Zurich-based Dichter Research AG. Reprinted with permission from Dichter Research AG.

that rituals have power. Focus groups, as rituals, not only reveal our desires—for a better life, for participation, for power, to be heard—they also limit them. We talk, we feel maybe someone has listened, and we demand nothing more.

Though they have received little serious discussion, focus groups came, over the course of the last century, to shape almost every aspect of our lives, from cake mix to Barbie dolls. They affect the toothpaste we use, the soap operas we watch, the news media we consume, the video games we play, and even the political discussions that ultimately determine what kind of society we have. Focus groups have also helped to create and nourish a seemingly boundless culture of consultation, in which ordinary people weigh in on just about everything before the folks in charge make a decision. Aided by technological innovations like Facebook, the scope of such consultation has, in recent years, expanded its reach with breathtaking speed. As Americans, our feelings about this reflect our feelings about democracy and consumerism, and expose the tension between populism and expertise.

The demographic depends on the target market—for the product or campaign under discussion—but often, focus groups attract, and include, working-class people. This is particularly striking in groups in Manhattan, a place where the working class is less and less visible. Yet even in Midtown, focus groups attract construction and clerical workers, lady truck drivers and city workers, as well as out-of-work actors and artists.

Whatever the topic—travel to Las Vegas, laundry detergent, or breast cancer—the focus group has certain commonalities. It is a discussion among a small group of anywhere from three to fifteen people (though the usual size is eight to twelve). Led by a trained moderator, the conversation is intended to answer specific questions for a client: hence the term "focus." Even if it appears to be free-wheeling, or to wander off-track, the moderator usually knows where it's going. Often, the client is observing through a one-way mirror from the next room. Indeed, the moderator may receive notes from the client throughout the discussion—perhaps demanding that she get the conversation back on track, or that she probe a little bit harder: how do those present *really feel* about brewing instant coffee in the privacy of their own homes?

In the United States, there are about 750–800 focus group facilities, especially equipped with audiovisual equipment and one-way mirrors so that a client can observe without disrupting the conversation.[9] Most cities have such facilities, and since the nineteen eighties, most focus groups have been conducted in such settings. For convenience, they tend to be concentrated in areas dense with corporate offices and advertising agencies, like New York City, but historically, places like Columbus, Ohio, which give the client the feeling of reaching Middle America, have also been home to many such facilities. Over the last turn of the century, use of the method increased sharply, from 110,000 focus groups in 1990 to almost double that number in 2002 (about 218,000 sessions).[10] Though this book centers on the United States, the motherland of the focus group, it is a global phenomenon: there were, in 2002, an estimated 245,000 focus groups conducted throughout Europe, Latin America, and Asia-Pacific. Today, almost all Fortune 500 companies use focus groups, especially for branding, public image, or marketing.[11] Globally, according to ESOMAR, a global market research association, spending on focus groups in 2012 totaled about $4.6 billion.[12] Focus groups were developed first in academia, then in advertising agencies. While agencies certainly still conduct focus groups, today much of the work is done by firms dedicated to market research. Some of these have as few as one employee, while others are big business. The largest of the latter is Nielsen (most famous for tracking what you watch on TV), with over $6 billion in global revenues in 2014.

This book tells the story of the focus group as a story of the relationship between elites and the masses. In part, it is a story of elite degeneration. While in the middle of the twentieth century, elites listened in part to figure out how best to make social democracy work better and to fight fascism (as well as to sell things that might make our lives easier, like cake mix or kitchen appliances), as the century wore on, the purpose of elite listening changed. Increasingly, elites listened in order to figure out how to sell us products we didn't need, and, in the political realm, policies we didn't want, that were starkly at odds with our material interests.

This book also tells a story of the degeneration of democracy. The current culture of consultation has flourished and become more necessary in a period in which the actual power of ordinary people relative to the rich—whether in the workplace or the political arena—has greatly diminished. Listening is not the same as sharing power. At the same time, as our society has become more unequal, and gaps in everyday experience much wider, the need for listening has only grown more obvious.

Ordinary people—especially working class women—don't have much political or economic power. In addition to telegraphing some of the desires of such people to cultural, political, and corporate elites, the focus group is a ritual allowing those elites to send the message that they are listening (and sometimes even responding). Elites do this in a variety of ways: by communicating to focus group respondents themselves through the rituals of recruitment and participation, to the general public through advertising that—often inventively—references focus groups, through televised performances like those staged by Fox or CNN after a presidential debate, as well as through rumors and controversies over famously "bad" focus group decisions (to change the flavor of Coke in the nineteen eighties, for example), and finally, to fellow elites, through the persistent use of focus group data to argue that a particular perspective, position, or campaign is supported by "the people."

Over the past decade and a half, whenever protesters have gathered to defend the values of the left—values of equality, inclusion—they have chanted, "This is what democracy looks like." A focus group, whether convened in an office park in Columbus, Ohio, or in a brightly lit conference room near Madison Avenue, is not at all what democracy looks like. But a focus group is, in some ways, what democratic participation feels like, given our current low standards. It is one of the ways we crack the egg and feel we are doing something.

As part of my work on this book, I have participated in many focus groups myself, on topics including corporate tax breaks, paper plates, Juicy Juice, train travel, and personal finance. I did not tell the recruiters or the clients that I was writing about this subject. I'm sure many would take a dim view of the ethics of this approach, especially since when recruiters asked if I was employed in the "media" industry, I would always say no (if I had told the truth, I would have been disqualified from most groups). But the market researchers I interviewed seemed unperturbed by my deceptions, which are, as we will later see, typical of focus group participants. Indeed, during an interview for this book, when I told veteran focus group leader Andy Tuck, founder of Applied Research and Consulting, what I'd been up to, he had only one question: "Are you a good respondent?"[13] And indeed I am. I love conversation and I like to think I am pretty good at it.

The appeal of conversation helps explain why the focus group is such an enduring method. Most of us like participating because we like talking to other people, and we like having an impact on our world. But the conversation can extend beyond the one-way mirror. Nathaniel Wice, who worked in advertising for five years, and later at media giant Time Inc., recalls, laughing, that at Time, the focus groups were the bane of our existence. One person in a focus group would say, "I don't understand the mission of the magazine," and that would send the whole company scrambling to define its mission![14]

Sounds absurd, right? Even more absurd given the situation. Wice was working on a launch for a magazine for the rich and tech-savvy, which would, oddly, be distributed free to new AOL subscibers. "The focus group was funny because it revealed this confusion about audience. These people were just getting an AOL address in 2001." The participants were, to put it bluntly, marginal people. "We kept asking," Wice remembers, "What rock did these people crawl out from?" But, Wice admits, the funny thing was that "we started asking ourselves, 'Wait, what *is* our mission? And these people aren't our audience, but who is?' Listening to people talk [in the focus groups], we'd think, maybe we should have these conversations with each other." And they did.[15] In most corporate workplaces, real conversation is in short supply. One of the subversive—and sometimes powerful—aspects of the focus group is that it *is* a conversation. It forces people to slow down, talk, and above all, listen.

In this book I will argue that we could all benefit from doing the same. We should indeed listen to what people say around those conference tables, but also to what the focus group has meant to our culture. It has been part of the evolution of our expressive democracy—that is, a society in which the expression of opinion has been dramatically democratized, while the distribution of everything else that matters (political power, money) has only grown more starkly unequal.

Participating in a focus group makes you feel as if people—powerful people who make decisions—are listening to you. Many moderators bring to the process a great respect for participants, and a genuine interest in their opinions and feelings. Donna Fullerton, who has been moderating focus groups for major brands since the nineteen eighties, takes such an approach. Reflecting on her nurturing style in an interview, she says:

> I feel like I've always been able to get people to open up very quickly, even if they're talking about incontinence or erectile

dysfunction, because I come from a place where I honor that you're here and am interested in what you have to say. The best thing I can hear at the end of every group is when people say, "God, I really felt like you were listening to what I was saying."[16]

The focus group offers us the experience of having a voice and the possibility of influence in a world that offers most people little control over their lives, and little opportunity to influence anything.

"Perhaps they will use my idea!" one hopes. Maybe the movie ending I voted on will prevail, saving viewers around the world from sadness or banality. Or perhaps I'll see my own language in this antacid commercial. Participation is pleasurable because the focus group is an avenue for influence, and when people lack such avenues, we cherish our crumbs of significance. A focus group—with brand managers, campaign managers, all kinds of important people behind the mirror hanging anxiously on every labored word of these ordinary working-class Americans' discussion—can feel like a populist triumph. It takes quite a ritual to produce that feeling.

For ordinary people, focus groups perform influence. *I'm going to tell them what to do.* For elites, focus groups perform the act of listening. It's important that corporations and politicians appear to listen to the people—the legitimacy, and even functioning, of market democracy depend upon it.

Traditionally people advance their own interests by organizing and confronting the powerful. They do this by working together in groups. The focus group harnesses this cooperative impulse, to serve the interests of the powerful rather than the participants themselves. Groups have often been a means—for those without money, the only means—of building power, but the focus group, like the isolated individual, can only influence. This is why the focus group is a quintessential ritual of, to borrow historian Lizabeth Cohen's phrase, "a consumer's republic."[17]

Within organizations, and even in public discussions, focus groups are often venerated as a populist tool, a way to invite those outside the airless conference rooms of power inside to have a snack, and offer their ideas. Those who don't want to listen to them may be slammed as elitist, sometimes with good reason. Debate over focus groups often pits the dumb, regular people against the geniuses—the film directors, the Don Drapers, the Steve Jobses—who know better.

Does wisdom reside primarily with experts, or with the folks? The focus group dramatizes, yet sometimes also implodes, such questions, often parodying the very idea of the average—and of the expert. But of course, as historians of populism have noted, one of the reasons this tension between elite experts and average people has long dogged American society is that American political culture has never come close to delivering on its democratic promises: most people don't have much genuine political influence, or even control over their own lives.

The major purpose that focus groups serve—whether the topic is Social Security or soft drinks—is to bridge the divide between the feelings and experiences of the masses, and those of elites.

Most people in the corporate or political elite have no idea what the majority of people—whose votes or consumer dollars they badly need to win—are like. They don't know people who are not like themselves. Elites live in different neighborhoods, and even in different cities,[18] and have different values and habits from most people in America.

Speaking of the clients on the other side of the mirror, former moderator Kara Gilmour says,

> A lot of those people are really out of touch. They think they have all the answers because they're the professionals. But when was the last time that they went shopping in a mid-range mall? They never shop in a mid-range mall. They get all their clothes at the sample sales...[19]

This vast gulf in mind-set and everyday experience between ordinary Americans and elites is the reason the focus group needs to exist at all. Conceived by elite social democrats whose politics were shaped by Red Vienna in the nineteen twenties and by the New Deal in the nineteen thirties—a story told in the first chapter of this book—the focus group took on special importance as American society began to take its own class hierarchies for granted. Americans became more reconciled to having elites, but for consumer capitalism and democracy to flourish, those elites would need ways to measure the thoughts and feelings of the rest of the public. The ruling classes—and even the professional managerial classes that make decisions for those rulers—might be increasingly disconnected with ordinary America, but they had to know what it wanted, in order to sell things and win votes.

The divides between the elites and the masses are real, and focus groups can help, particularly when reaching demographic groups that aren't well-represented among the corporate elite. Upper management, being predominantly white and male, for example, undoubtedly has trouble imagining the perspectives of women of color. Revlon, in the nineteen nineties, found this out when it tested an ad campaign for Creme of Nature, a hair relaxer, in focus groups of African-American women,[20] led by a black female moderator. As Richard Kirshenbaum and Jon Bond, the founders of the Kirshenbaum, Bond and Partners (KB&P)[21] agency, which rebranded the product, write in their book *Under the Radar*, the focus groups were a revelation to the cosmetics giant. The researchers found that rather than being happy that big-name company like a Revlon had a product for black women, the focus group participants found the Revlon name off-putting. In Kirshenbaum and Bond's words, the women saw it as "a big white company." Revlon had been featuring black models in its "The World's Most Beautiful Women Wear Revlon" campaign, but the black women in the focus groups did not feel represented by them. They felt alienated by the implied colorism[22] of the images: supermodels like Beverly Johnson were light skinned and wore hair extensions, and the consumers in the groups felt they were "white-looking." Kirshenbaum and Bond recall, "What we found was so surprising because no one had ever asked the right questions before, and the answers we got were so incredibly different from what we or Revlon originally thought." When, in response to the focus groups, KB&P made the Revlon name far less prominent in the "Creme of Nature" campaign, and chose models with more color diversity, consumers responded happily.

In order to win and keep black customers, Revlon needed to listen, and needed to show it was listening. The listening, according to

Kirshenbaum and Bond, "demonstrated that the company respected [the black consumers] enough to try to understand their needs."

Donna Fullerton says bridging such divides is often the primary purpose of the focus group research. Divides between elites and nonelites can be racial or gendered; they can also be geographic. Many advertising campaigns originate in New York City, and the New York City sensibility may well offend people elsewhere in the country. So the client may want to do some research to ensure that the campaign is not off-putting—or culturally irrelevant—to mainstream Americans. Fullerton once worked on an ad campaign for margarine products, and, she recalls, "it was based in opera metaphors. So yeah, you're in New York and you go to the opera . . . you would get that point of view. It wasn't until we went to Kansas or other Midwestern cities and when people were like, 'We don't understand this.'" Fullerton speaks regretfully of this campaign, which the creative people at the ad agency were so excited about: "There was a lot of heart for that one. It was so clever . . . but once you heard what people were saying . . ." She trails off and shrugs.[23]

The focus group frequently reveals what lies outside the elite bubble, which is not only bounded by privileged experience or cultural reference, but also by certain political assumptions. Julia Strohm, who has worked with Tuck at ARC, recalls a project for an apparel company, testing an ecologically sensitive clothing line:

> And we did groups in St. Louis, Westchester, and San Francisco. And it was pretty startling, the difference in people's consciousness about the ecology and the environment. St. Louis: nice people, and they could not care less. In fact, they were kind of offended about the hoopla about the environment . . . They weren't offensive about it but they weren't well educated about the topic . . . Their idea about being environmentally conscious was maybe to recycle.[24]

The focus group came to be—and became as important as it is today—precisely because of such jarring points of disconnection between elites and the rest. While both democracy and consumerism depend on the participation of ordinary people, and indeed, are supposed to be powered by their desires, it became clear over the course of the last century that American-style capitalism would ensure the economic, political, and cultural domination of a small elite. The focus group became one of many—highly imperfect—ways of managing that contradiction in both practical and rhetorical terms.

The story of the focus group, then, is the story of the interdependent relationship between the elites and the masses in a market democracy, offering one small but telling window on how both have sought to manage that relationship.

This book will also show why listening to the people sometimes works so well for elites, and why the focus group is—even apart from its propagandistic value of providing the appearance of inclusion—an important way to gather knowledge. It's long been fashionable to bemoan the outsized influence of the focus group, but it's worth asking, are there elements of this method that deserve celebration? Can the culture of consultation perhaps be used to change the world for the better? At the very least, are there elements of its long reign that offer hope for the project of more genuine political engagement?

An examination of the focus group is more relevant today than ever, because that culture of consultation has taken over our lives. By logging on to Facebook, posting on our blogs, or simply listening to music on our phones, we may be participating in market research at almost any minute of the day. We no longer need travel to a depressing office park to be part of the culture of consultation; we can experience the rush and the pleasure of expressing our opinions and being heard, constantly, from our own homes and cars, through our phones and iPads and computers. (Indeed, we get to do this so often that sometimes the open invitation to express our opinions all the time can feel like a burden.) And the corporate and political elites no longer need pay us to be experts on ourselves; through Facebook, Twitter, and Instagram, we give the Mark Zuckerbergs of the world minute-by-minute insight into our everyday desires and feelings both small ("need coffee!!") and large ("bummed out about climate change"). The focus group, far from receding in importance, as some in the marketing industry have suggested, has taken over our lives.

We should value much of the focus group's spirit of listening and engagement, but we should not be content with the culture of consultation. This book will consider how we might learn from it and use it in our quest to demand real power for the majority. Around the globe, this past decade, ordinary people have been organizing against plutocracy and demanding more democratic and inclusive institutions, whether in the so-called "Arab Spring," Occupy Wall Street, or Black Lives Matter. Insurgent political movements have been backing Bernie Sanders in the United States, Jeremy Corbyn in the United Kingdom, or calling for women's strikes worldwide. These contain the seeds of a movement that just might, from the babble and din of consultation and influence, ask, What if powerful institutions did more for us than simply listen?

It's another way of asking, What if we had no elites? What if our political and creative classes didn't have to devise such artificial ways to hear from us, because they lived and worked among us every day? The focus group has helped to contain our desires for such an egalitarian world, yet the impulses it harnesses—to share, to discuss, to work together—could be the seeds for creating it.

New York, 2011

The first ad shows simply a view from a train: "Go your own way."

We find it lonely. There are no people in it.

We are middle aged lesbian and bisexual women, and otherwise a diverse group. Amtrak has convened a group to test its efforts to advertise to the LGBT market.

The moderator is a straight man. He thoughtfully wonders aloud if this is a problem for the group. We assure him that we don't mind. The presentation is low tech: he shows us posters for possible print ads. All have little rainbow flag icons in the corner so that the point won't be missed.

We see another ad with a pretty Asian woman, smiling to herself with anticipation, and looking out the window: "The only view that matters is your own."

I am the only one who likes this ad.

I think she is excited about a project she is working on, enjoying the solitude of the train to write and think. Or perhaps she is on her way to meet a lover.

Everyone else hates that she is alone. They goodnaturedly dismiss my opinion: "Of course you want to be alone on the train! You're a mother." Fair enough. I concede, like an outvoted juror. The instant camaraderie of the group makes it easy to let it go.

Another features two young women: "Travel like you love. Without limits." We find the women young, but we like that they are a couple, and like the message.

The fourth one we all love. A cute gay male couple with kids are looking out the train window together. One woman feels weepy, moved: "These guys look just like my best friends who just got married and want to adopt a couple kids!"

The facilitator asks, "What about this term 'in your face'? Isn't a gay male couple with kids 'in your face'?" No, we say, this is just one of many normal families in the world. On the internet, his comment would spark ire and outrage; people would denounce him for his blinkered question. But here we understand he is doing his job.

The ad is not in our face. We like that the couple seems a little flirty with one another.

We are a little puzzled by Amtrak's exhortation to click on its "diversity" web page: what would we find there?

We tell him that we don't want to be patronized.

Chapter One: The Birth of the Focus Group

The story of the focus group does not begin in a political campaign war room, nor over boozy *Mad Men*–era lunch on Madison Avenue. It begins in a far more staid—but perhaps even more socially complex—context: an academic dinner party.

Sociologist Robert K. Merton arrived with his wife, Suzanne, at the Manhattan home of Paul F. Lazarsfeld and his wife, Herta Herzog (significant in focus group history in her own right, but here, like many women of mid-century, relegated to the domestic sphere). It was November 1941 and both Merton and Lazarsfeld were the two newly hired sociologists at Columbia. The men hadn't socialized with one another before this evening, and it's likely that both couples anticipated the dinner with some tredipation; after all, the men had very different sociological approaches and had, as Lazarsfeld would summarize it years later, been "appointed to perpetuate the feud"[25] between statisticians and theoreticians in the department.

Lazarsfeld was a specialist in quantitative social research, and the department needed to have such a person in order to compete with other sociology departments; quantitative sociology was still young, and its methodologies were gradually taking shape. But data and statistics had their skeptics in the department among the social theorists, so Robert K. Merton, a celebrated big-ideas man, was hired as well. Years later, Merton would be hailed in the *New Yorker* magazine[26] as the world's most famous sociologist, particularly well-known for his studies on how people influence one another. He popularized concepts that are still widely understood, such as "unintended consequences," "role model," and "self-fulfilling prophecy."

The two men's social backgrounds were even more distant than their academic orientations. While Lazarsfeld had been raised by middle-class socialists in Vienna, Merton, born Meyer Robert Schkolnick, was a child of immigrants raised in a Philadelphia slum. His adolescence had included a brief career as a party magician—hence his invented name, adopted because it sounded a little like "Merlin"—as well as periodic gang membership.

Merton and Lazarsfeld regarded one another somewhat warily at first. After all, like birds shipped in for a cockfight, it was not their job to become the best of friends.

Lazarsfeld, the older of the two—and by nature a political operator—thought it would be gentlemanly to invite Merton to dinner. But when the appointed evening rolled around, an awkward conflict arose. Lazarsfeld's Bureau of Applied Social Research had a contract to test propaganda for the Office of War Information (then called the Office of Facts and Figures), using technology Lazarsfeld had developed with his colleague Frank Stanton when testing radio programs for CBS. Although it was a Saturday, his government bosses called letting him know they needed him, on very short notice, to test a new program that night—when the Mertons were due to come to dinner. "It was extremely embarassing," Lazarsfeld would recall years later, "because the whole situation was rigged for Merton and me not to get along anyhow."[27] Canceling seemed out of the question.

Instead, when the Mertons arrived, Lazarsfeld told Robert Merton not to take off his coat,[28] that he had something to show him at his studio that would interest him. "We left the ladies here," Lazarsfeld remembered. "What they did with the dinner, I don't know."[29]

The two rival sociologists hurried downtown to the Office of Radio Research, a run-down old building on 59th Street—where a test audience was watching *This Is War*.[30]

Conceived by the U.S. Office of Facts and Figures—the year before it became the Office of War Information—this series, broadcast on all four commercial networks, was America's first attempt to counter Nazi propaganda by explaining the war to Americans. The broadcast (as it ultimately aired) reads as an earnest meditation on reason, facts, and the role of media—even state-funded media—in a democracy. Archibald MacLeish, prominent poet, Librarian of Congress and director of the War Department of Facts and Figures—read a sober letter from President Roosevelt. "The difficulty the American people have in following and understanding this war has been constantly on my mind of late," the president mused in his letter. "This challenge to understanding, like the war itself, is a challenge we can meet successfully." Though framed with childish simplicity, the series was nonetheless explicitly cast as rational, to distinguish it from Nazi-style appeals to primitive urges, as MacLeish emphasized that *This Is War* would "meet the Axis strategies of lies with the United People's strategy of truth."[31] In the premiere, which was broadcast on February 14, 1942,[32] a voice-over promised to counter fascist "lies with facts." There was an implicit message here: the Allies can beat fascism because of, not despite, democracy's appeals to the mind. As historian James Spiller has pointed out, the series was indeed propaganda, a sharp departure from radio networks' previous neutrality on the war, slandering any dissenters as Axis stooges. Still, the Allies side was framed as intelligent, intended for thinking citizens. This was in keeping with the program's portrayal of Axis masculinity as defined by depraved sex and violence, in contrast with the "manly self-control" of American men, who were domesticated for the greater good, defending the "house of civilization."[33] Narrator Robert Montgomery taunted Axis leaders with a measured confidence, no sneer or tough-guy bluster, only quiet contempt: "Hear that, Adolf? Hear that, Benito?"[34] The rhetoric used in this program would serve as a model for U.S. government radio rhetoric throughout World War II,[35] and it was shaped in crucial ways by the tests conducted by Lazarsfeld and his team at Columbia.

Americans during this period were not eager to go to war, either to engage in bloody conflict or to make the necessary sacrifices. In fact, though FDR is now remembered as a popular president, during the war he faced considerable opposition to his policies and began putting particular emphasis on public opinion research.[36] Lazarsfeld's project was one of many examples of how FDR's administration used social science methods to figure out how to communicate with the public.

Though Spiller is correct that these efforts were propagandistic, they also offer a window on an elite rather different from the one that would rule the nation in later decades. Roosevelt and MacLeish seem confident that the American people are rational and capable of democracy; they see themselves as helping to inform and lead a body politic that could rise to the challenges of political engagement. It's difficult to disagree with the central persuasive project of this political class: urging the masses to fight fascism and make democracy work. The focus group was created as a tool in this elite's arsenal. (As we will later see, as this elite degenerated, the focus group's purpose grew considerably less inspiring.)

In the shabby studio on 59th Street, there was no one-way mirror enabling observers to watch the discussion unseen, as there would be in a focus group situation today, so Merton and Lazarsfeld had to find spots at the edge of the room to watch the action as unobtrusively as possible.[37]

A group of listeners—a little over a dozen—pressed buttons to indicate its "likes" and "dislikes," which were then recorded by an early version of a computer. This was a contraption called the Lazarsfeld-Stanton Program Analyzer, an early precursor of the programs that now allow us to see the feelings of Frank Luntz's focus groups graphed live on national television—or that greet us if we are part of a test audience for a Hollywood movie.

Such technologies are commonplace in political and entertainment research today, but Lazarsfeld and his colleagues had only just developed them, so the sight was startling to the uninitiated. Merton, in a talk years later, would recall it as a "strange spectacle," asking his 1987 audience to "try to see it through my then naïve eyes and remember that your present sophistication is the legacy of almost half a century of evolving inquiry."[38] Poor Merton was not only confronting the unfamiliar, he was also hungry and restless; this wasn't how he would have chosen to spend a Saturday night. According to the 1961 *New Yorker* profile of the eminent professor, he "found the whole thing a bore, and thought regretfully of the *gulasch* and *patlatschinken* that he was missing."[39]

Then a young colleague of Lazarsfeld's interviewed the audience, trying to probe why they pressed the buttons they pressed—not just "did they like it," but *why*. Merton got interested. He began to observe the interview keenly, and to send Lazarsfeld notes—why doesn't the interviewer pick up on what the interviewee is saying? Why hasn't he followed up on this point?[40] (Notes from meddling observers—usually clients—are now an omnipresent feature of the focus group.) Why is the interviewer guiding the respondents' answers?

Lazarsfeld asked Merton, if he thought he could do so much better, why not try it himself?[41] "As I was to learn over the years, this was altogether typical of [Lazarsfeld]," Merton would later explain, "he promptly co-opts me . . . That was not a defensive-aggressive question, as you might mistakenly suppose it was."[42] Merton did take a turn interviewing, and the older man was thrilled with his approach. The two men telephoned their wives at the Lazarsfelds' place, to let them know they were still working, then "unchivalrously"—as the New Yorker writer editorialized—retired to the Russian Bear, ate caviar, drank champagne, and talked into the morning.[43]

A lifelong collaboration between the two social scientists was born that night, one that significantly shaped the field of sociology. More importantly to contemporary culture, politics, and everyday life, their friendship and partnership gave us the method that we now call the "focus group."

Merton—who would, remember, later become famous for coining the term "role model"—jumped into Lazarsfeld's project wholeheartedly, embracing the older man's obsession with methodology. Merton explained, six months later, in a letter to his friend Kingsley Davis, another prominent sociologist, that he was spending six to eight hours a day on the *This Is War* research, and was happy to do so, partly out of patriotism, but also because the evolving methodology was exciting, allowing the researchers to test listeners' reactions to material "on the spot" and, even more significantly, to be able to test "preliminary analysis and hunches . . . by direct observation of human beings in action."[44]

He sometimes chafed at some of the government's rigid requirements. He wrote letters to his War Department supervisor complaining that the Army was pressuring his research team to deliver quantity over quality:

> Now it is true that with some inarticulate groups twelve or fifteen minutes is quite enough because there is little to be gotten in any case. But with groups who really open up, thirty minutes for the interview itself is a dead minimum. Working on our present schedule I found it necessary time and again to cut off interviews long before they were fully exploited in order to race back to the preview room to instruct the next victim on the technique of pushing buttons. It seems a shame to devote so much loving care and attention to the entire set up and then have it go awry simply because we think ourselves compelled to operate on a group-per-hour basis.[45]

Merton felt the research would be stronger if they interviewed half as many groups and spent more time with them. But he was resigned to the fact that he wouldn't be heard, writing, "But then you've heard all this before and I suppose we'll have to bow to the dictates of the U.S. Army . . ."

Because of this work, and the effort he made to explain it to other researchers, Merton would be widely hailed as the "father of the focus group."[46] (Although he would also distance himself from the method, coyly remarking in 1987 that "there can't be many people in the field of social science and certainly none in the related field of marketing research who know less about focus groups than I," he would also acknowledge the many continuities between his own work and the modern focus group.) He would later clarify the principles he developed while working on these OWI projects in an article—later a booklet—called "The Focused Interview," the article from which the "focus group"—a term not used until much later—would derive its name. The idea, as Merton outlined it, was that the interview would find out out what people thought by focusing on a particular thing—a written text, a broadcast, a product they had just tried, an experience they have had—rather than conducting a wider-ranging exploration of their views.

Hence, rather than asking people how they felt about Nazis, ask them to listen to a specific radio program about Nazis and answer specific questions about the program.

The focused interview made Lazarsfeld's war propaganda research so much more revealing, because it allowed the team not only to collate and analyze yeses and nos, but to ask why people reacted as they did. Lazarsfeld and Merton went on to do many more studies for the government on war propaganda and listeners' reactions. And what they found out about listeners' reactions to the war propaganda was often surprising, and could never have been revealed by button-pushing alone.[47]

At times the propaganda had the opposite effect on the audience than its creators intended. For instance, the programs, to convince Americans of the importance of fighting the Nazis, initially presented the Nazis as unusually bloodthirsty and brutal, inclined to treat civilians with cruelty and sadism. But this did not make Americans want to go to war with the Nazis—quite the contrary. If the audience had simply been pushing buttons, this would have been a mystifying finding—why not try to stop these horrible monsters? But the focused interview allowed the researchers to discover something no one had considered: portraying the Nazis in very scary terms was a mistake, because then the American audience wanted nothing to do with fighting them, and was actually too frightened to support the war effort.[48] Instead, American propaganda would emphasize our superior values: democracy and rationality.

To defend democracy, then, the Roosevelt administration had to first figure out what was going on with that mysterious *demos*. And that was the challenge out of which the focused interview—and later the focus group—emerged. Focus groups grew out of a unique moment in world history, in which democracy seemed threatened by enemies, yet full of potential. It was one in which leaders were beginning to grasp the gap between themselves and the masses, yet these same elites had great faith in the power of persuasion. They knew the people did not always agree with them, but were confident they could be convinced.

The World War II liberals didn't see themselves as sinister propagandists in the mold of Leni Riefenstahl, but neither did they want their actual policies to be shaped by public opinion. They drew a sharp distinction between themselves—the experts—and the general public. These technocrats wanted to convince the public that their ideas and values were the correct ones. The focus group was a fitting listening strategy for such an elite, allowing the researchers to focus on specific approaches, rather than discuss issues open-endedly, as in a town meeting. FDR's propagandists saw Nazi propaganda as emotional and manipulative, but saw their own as a form of rational persuasion.[49] The massive propaganda effort conducted by the Roosevelt administration during this period signaled a mistrust of the people on the one hand—the sense that they wouldn't come to the right conclusions just by reading the news—but on the other hand, a faith in their rationality. (This faith in objectivity, even as they developed methodologies to explore people's highly subjective and emotional reactions to everything from radio jingles to racism, was critical to mid-century liberals.) This administration was confident in the idea that soft persuasion was better than force: no one was forced to save or buy bonds, and there was no labor draft. The public was convinced—rather than forced or manipulated—to cooperate in the war effort.[50]

Today focus groups embody the status quo—what is a more contemptuous political dismissal than to describe a position as having emerged "from a focus group"? But at its birth, the focus group emerged from left-leaning thought, from a liberal intelligentsia and elected leadership class, both of which sought to gain the masses' consent for bold, ambitious plans. While Lazarsfeld and Merton invented the focus group in the New Deal context, Lazarsfeld, and his approaches to research, were shaped equally by an earlier and more radical political moment.

Paul Lazarsfeld came of age in Vienna during World War I, one of the most promising moments in world history for both democracy and socialism.[51] It was also an intellectually and artistically engaged culture. Democratic socialists had won electoral victory, and the city was deeply engaged in experimenting with municipal socialism (socialism in one city, not easy to achieve with a hostile right-wing national government). The idea of democratic self-governance was as new as that of socialism, since Austria had previously been ruled by a monarch. The Viennese socialists also firmly opposed forcing socialist revolution upon a society through violence, as the Bolsheviks had done in Russia. Their slogan was "against the idea of force, the force of ideas"[52]—a parallel to the FDR Democrats' strategy of persuasion over coercion. But with democracy so new, and a leadership so full of ideals and plans, it became particularly important for the party to hone persuasive strategies by finding out what the people were thinking.

Adding to the urgency, the Viennese socialists' backgrounds, cultural capital, and values were quite distant from those of working-class Viennese. Historian Helmut Gruber has described Vienna of this period as an "experiment in working-class culture,"[53] as socialist leaders, despite their own often-bourgeois origins, tried hard to create citizens who were suited for both socialism and democracy. Party leader Otto Bauer called this "a revolution of souls"[54]—it was not just society's economic and governmental structures that had to change, but the people themselves.

The Viennese socialists did not exalt or idealize existing working-class culture as the American Communist Party and some other left parties worldwide did during the same period. Rather, they wished to convince the working class to develop "better" taste and habits. The Viennese socialists tried, through classical music concerts, sports teams, and chess clubs, as well as propaganda against smoking and drinking and in favor of physical fitness,[55] to democratize bourgeois culture, a Leninist effort that could be seen as elitist.

It helped that the city was already a world capital of high culture. It was home to an art and music scene out of which Gustav Klimt, Egon Schiele, Johannes Brahms, and Gustav Mahler had emerged, as well as the intellectual greenhouse for exciting developments like psychoanalysis and radical politics. But the Vienna of Lazarsfeld's youth was brimming with all this and more. Lazarsfeld later described it this way:

> So what you had in Vienna of this time was a fabulous intellectual peak, you see, which is a mixture of politics, psychoanalysis, Marxism. During the day, you distribute anti-war pamphlets, ineffectively, when you are fifteen, and then you go every evening to a concert standing. It's quite an amazing world.[56]

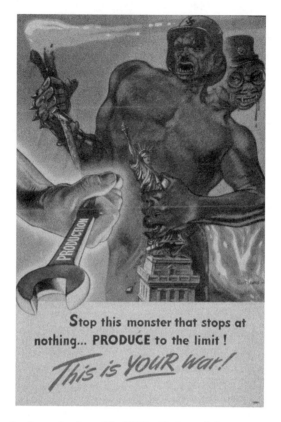

Stop this monster that stops at nothing... **PRODUCE** to the limit !

This is YOUR War!

U. S. propaganda poster from World War II. One of the reasons Americans had to be persuaded to cooperate in the war effort was that enormous extra productivity was required of workers. Focus groups discovered that propaganda like this, which depicted Nazis in particularly terrifying and demonizing ways, was less effective than a reasoned appeal to defend the American way of life. And indeed, who would want to take this guy on? He has two heads. "STOP THIS MONSTER THAT STOPS AT NOTHING. PRODUCE TO THE LIMIT. THIS IS YOUR WAR, 1941 – 1945." Creator: Office for Emergency Management. Office of War Information. Domestic Operations Branch. Bureau of Special Services. (03/09/1943 – 08/31/1945). Propaganda.

Lazarsfeld's mother, Sofie Lazarsfeld, a psychoanalyst herself, was the center of an influential intellectual and political circle. She was sexy and charismatic. Several prominent socialist men were in love with her. Furthermore, she had a beautiful garden, so her home became a popular meeting spot for the left.[57] Young Paul was active in organizing youth camps—the socialist equivalent of Boy Scout troops—to mobilize but also ideologize young people. A leader of a major socialist youth group, he was a rising star in the party but could only climb so far, because he was Jewish. There was considerable anti-Semitism even on the left in Austria during this time.[58]

During and after the First World War, Vienna endured intense and widespread immiseration, partly because the Entente powers—France, Britain, and Russia—imposed a blockade on Austria, which meant that there was a drastic shortage of food and clothing. Even after the embargo was over, the costs of the war wrought crippling inflation that obliterated the savings of many middle-class Viennese. Despite his bourgeois home, Lazarsfeld remembers, toward the end of the war, "I was continually hungry." Others were even worse off.

All this imbued young Lazarsfeld's politics with a particular intensity. He remembered looking out the window of a room in his parents' house, as a teenager, with a friend, and seeing a woman begging on the street. He turned to his friend and said, "If it would help to bring socialism so there wouldn't be such beggars, I would gladly jump out of the window and be dead."

Interviewing Lazarsfeld, Daniel Bell, in 1962, ventured that Austrian socialism in this period had a "religious" quality. Lazarsfeld strongly dissented, arguing that the intensity of the Viennese commitment to socialism was a rational one:

> There was . . . a feeling that this world is unbearable. Then we are told that Socialism will help. The feeling is not pathological in the sense—religion is not right. It was absolutely visible how horrible things were.[59]

At an early age, Lazarsfeld became infatuated, not just with socialism but also with democracy. German Social Democratic Party leader Rudolf

Hilferding, a friend of Lazarsfeld's mother—and then a leading socialist economic thinker—liked to take young Paul hiking with him. He gave the boy books to read describing elections, "how the first returns come in . . . this I found terribly exciting," Lazarsfeld recalled. "I found out what an election was, and then I wanted to find out, what was a Social Democrat." Hilferding gave him more books, young Paul kept reading, and by the fall of 1916, he was a committed Social Democrat.[60]

The Viennese Social Democrats represented a dramatic break from both monarchy and capitalism, but were also committed to keeping the city's working class from getting too radical. As some workers rioted in the streets and joined communist parties who wanted to foment Bolshevik-style revolution, the Social Democrats, many of whose leaders came from the middle class, aggressively sought to crack down on both.[61] They wanted to keep order and preserve democracy, but they didn't trust the working class to govern itself.

In seeking to create a new kind of working class culture, they again displayed that lack of faith, as they discouraged existing working class forms of fun, from beer to sex outside of marriage. The Social Democrats were particularly concerned that ordinary women were always in imminent danger of prostitution.[62] In all these ways they resembled the American Progressive-era reformers, many of whom became New Dealers. In Vienna, as in the Roosevelt administration, technocracy prevailed; the idea was not to take leadership from or share power with ordinary people, but to find ways to reshape them, to make them into the kinds of citizens that a better society would require.

Lazarsfeld's interest in sociological methods grew out of his social democratic commitments. While a socialist youth leader in Austria, he was also getting his start in academia, and made his name by doing a landmark study on unemployment in Marienthal, a town in which nearly everyone was unemployed. The study became well known for offering insight into the psychological experience of joblessness.

Socialist Vienna would also shape Lazarsfeld's interest in how media can help create better citizens, questions he would later explore for the Roosevelt administration. In 1931, the Viennese socialists tried to figure out what kind of radio programming the city's working-class people wanted, and hired young social scientist Lazarsfeld to do the research. The socialists had favored programming that the leadership felt would help democratize high culture and uplift the working class—chamber music, choir music, literary readings, symphony concerts, and lectures about music—but Lazarsfeld's research found these to be the least popular types of radio shows. Rather, the working class preferred "light and cheerful" music, and lectures on "sensational" subjects.[63]

The project underscored the challenges of shaping a new citizenry. Conservative national government in Austria quickly and gleefully praised this survey, concluding that it showed that the socialists were out of touch with the people, and used it to diminish the radio programming that the socialists had favored.[64] The conservatives were not wrong: the reason the research was necessary was because of the huge cultural gap between the elites and the working class.

These initial efforts were idealistic, based as they were on a desire for democracy or socialism—both, in the case of the Viennese—but they were also paternalistic, revealing a limited vision of democracy in which elites would still exist, and remain at a distance from the rest. The idea was to bridge the gap, but social democratic leaders still saw themselves and their culture as superior. As Lazarsfeld would explain years later about his introduction to research in the Socialist Party, "we were concerned with why our propaganda was unsuccessful."[65] The Austrian socialists may have failed to revolutionize souls, but this did not stop the New Dealers—and Lazarsfeld—from trying to reform them, nor from developing the research methodologies that could help leaders better understand them.

Because he was Jewish, Lazarsfeld's future in the Austrian university was limited, and he looked to the United States for opportunities. Lazarsfeld's passage from Vienna to New York in 1933, at the age of thirty-two, was, along with many other developments in the social sciences during this period sponsored by the Rockefeller Foundation, which was active in pushing, through its funding, the social sciences away from the purely theoretical and academic into directions more directly practical for government and industry. Lazarsfeld did not come with formal refugee status—despite being a Jewish socialist—but as the political situation in his own country deteriorated (first a right-wing government defeated the socialists, then the Nazis came in), staying in the United States and becoming a citizen seemed like the only possible choice.[66] His talents—founding and running research institutions and working innovatively with research methodologies—were well suited to the American academy's growing need to serve industry and government demand for data on the opinions and feelings of the public.

Asked years later about the connection between his socialism and his sociology, Lazarsfeld—unusually for him—struggled to articulate a reply. He talked about how objective structures shape subjective experience, as well as in class stratification.[67] But methods like the focus group seem also intertwined with Lazarsfeld's early technocratic approaches to democracy. The focused interview followed closely upon a nineteen forties exploration, by social scientists—supported by media industry dollars and led by Lazarsfeld's Bureau—of what sort of media would help democracy work. It was part of a broader effort prevalent among technocrats of the era, to use media to produce the kind of citizens fit for democracy—citizens who would see things as they, the elites, saw them. In the case of World War II–era Americans, the Office of War Information hoped they would understand the importance of defending democracy and making collective sacrifices for the good of all.

As the historian Fred Turner has argued,[68] during World War II, research was animated by an extraordinary sense of common purpose, which fueled unusual collaboration between social scientists, military personnel, and government administrators, and gave rise to more robust research institutions (like Merton and Lazarsfeld's Bureau). The focus group was a product of that idealistic and inquisitive time.

Lazarsfeld's politics were shaped both by late nineteen thirties United States and by Red Vienna. These were societies whose emerging social democratic leaders sought much greater economic equality but did not trust the people. Without extensive study and persuasion, they feared, people could easily turn to fascism or communism (and, the Viennese social democrats also worried, bad music and silly soap operas). There's a distinct continuity between Red Vienna and FDR's Washington, D.C.—in both contexts, the focus group and other qualitative research methods were needed because there was so much distance in experience and worldview between the elites and the masses.

Focus groups—the ancestors of our contemporary culture of consultation—emerge, then, from the ambivalence in the hearts of twentieth-century democratic reformers, even at their most zealous. Despite the populism with which focus groups are often promoted, they exist because even well-meaning elites don't know much about the public and regard its taste and judgment warily.

In the United States, the national elite project shifted after World War II from fighting fascism to building a consumer society and fighting communism, aims that turned out to be complicatedly intertwined. The focus group's rapid adaptation by Madison Avenue, as I will discuss in the next chapter, reflected that shift.

Back in Morningside Heights, after the war, Lazarsfeld and many of his students increasingly used their talents to serve private industry. Academic social science, like many other U.S. industries, had become dependent on the war effort for funding. When the war was over, the Bureau lost its biggest client, and was eager to keep the funding coming in.

Social science, like private industry, needed a government bailout. The government had kept food manufacturers in business, providing Spam to our nation's soldiers, for instance; without that market, the makers of such prepackaged food products would need to find other ways to sell it.[69] The purveyors of social science found themselves in the same position as the makers of Spam. And they were also poised to be part of the cure for all that ailed the postwar economy.

Corporate America, losing the huge customer that was the wartime U.S. government, needed to replace it with ordinary American shoppers. To do that, corporate America's advertisers needed immediately to convince a nation that had been sold on sacrifice to start buying again, more than ever. To convince them, Madison Avenue had to listen. The focus group had found a new home.

We are in the waiting room, and soon some of us will be chosen for a Juicy Juice moms focus group. Even though I don't actually let my kid drink much juice, I am being considered, the recruiter says, because my "demographic" is hard to find. I am not sure what she means.

The room is silent except for the woman on my right, who is on her phone. "I just wish I could see my husband's face," she gloats, "when they serve him the papers."

An attractive woman of about forty-five looks at the sodas on offer and jokes, "They ought to have have vodka, for the moms."

"Seriously," murmurs of assent sweep the room.

She goes on, "I swear I never drank before I had kids." Another laughs sympathetically, "And you haven't stopped."

Chapter Two: "The Snowball Interview": The Focus Group Comes to Madison Avenue

The women are discussing cornmeal. Mrs. Johnson weighs in:

> Sometimes I use the yellow to give the bread a color. A *healthy* lookin' color, especially when you got a lot of dark green vegetables, something you want to make appetizing.

Mrs. Smith jumps in, agreeing with her, "Yellow cornmeal is *healthier* than white: more vitamins, I say."

The researcher, later writing about this 1951 focus group discussion, is delighted: "What the tape shows, that the printed word does not, is the emphasis placed on the word 'healthier' where it was used. It was the highlight of the exchange of comments."[70]

The focus group emerged at mid-century as part of a new way of understanding citizenship: Americans were newly imagined to be powerful specifically *as consumers*. Industry placed great emphasis on hearing their voices in this role rather than any other. It was a notion of empowerment meant to substitute for other kinds of equality. After all, the idea of consumer sovereignty (a term drawn from economics) became a rhetorical tool against communism, as consumer power was increasingly understood to be the reason that the American system was better than any other. Consumer power could even stand in for political power: the black women in the cornbread focus group described above, for example, could tell the copywriters what they thought, but in much of the country they lacked the right to vote.

In the early days of the focus group, as we saw in the previous chapter, ideals of social democracy and liberalism fueled elites' desire to listen to—and propagandize—the people. After World War II, it was the industrialists who were particularly intent on bridging the gap between elites and ordinary people—even the most disenfranchised, like African-Americans. Armed with new methodological insights from social science and psychoanalysis, the pioneers of the focus group were quickly pressed into service by capitalists who needed to figure out how to persuade Americans to resist communism—and, even more urgently, to invigorate the economy by buying things, after years of austerity and sacrifice. As historian Lizabeth Cohen has documented, citizenship was increasingly defined as consumerism; postwar Americans were told that consuming was not selfish, but a social good, as it would help the economy to grow. *Life* magazine, in copy accompanying a spread showcasing a family with stylish clothes and shiny appliances, urged people to buy more for themselves to "better the living of others." The magazine's writers explained that buying more would lead to "full employment and improved living standards for the rest of the nation."[71] In the nineteen fifties, a handbook distributed by *Brides* magazine made similar claims to the civic virtues of materialism: by buying "the dozens of things you never bought or even thought of before," the writers exhorted, "you are helping to build greater security for the industries of this country." Consumption, in this story, was "vital . . . to our whole American way of living."[72]

As the nation prospered and quickly embraced consumerism, industry had to adapt to new competitive pressures. There, too, market researchers' talents—and social science's new methods—were badly needed.

Both in its structure—people working together in a group—and in its premise of consumer empowerment, the focus group was a fitting tool for elites at mid-century, a time when anti-communism, consumerism, and tensions over the needs of individuals versus those of "the group" were defining themes in public discourse. It also coincided with—and was shaped by—the importance in American intellectual and popular culture assumed by psychoanalysis. Even as psychoanalysis, led by Jewish refugees from Europe, was shaping American culture, the field was in turn being remade by that same culture, newly exploring group conformity and group dynamics, beginning to willingly provide subjects for a consumerist and capitalist order.[73]

The U.S. was clearly going to continue to have a class system, and the trade-off was that it would also have democracy and shiny, desirable consumer goods. To make all of that work, despite vast social inequalities, the ruling class would need tools to find out what the masses, including the most disenfranchised, wanted. How else to win their votes and sell them stuff? The focus group—along with a host of other market research methods—emerged, on the eve of the long American war on communism, just in time to help solve this problem.

Although the purpose was always top-down—to find out how best to persuade or manipulate the masses—the focus group could also be explained in terms that celebrated and invited the ideas of the people. As the focus group moved from the academy—and from primarily serving the liberal state—to Madison Avenue and corporate America, it became more widespread, and assumed an increasingly important role in the culture.

The massive propaganda campaign to turn Americans into consumers yielded explosive growth for the advertising industry. But to convince people to buy, admen had to find out what they wanted and what they were thinking. Thus in these postwar years, the demand for market research and other forms of opinion research grew, and the industry began to organize itself into trade associations: the American Association for Public Opinion Research was founded in 1947, and the Market Research Association was founded a decade later. The industry's growth was not limited to the United States: the World Association for Public Opinion Research was founded in 1947, and the European Society for Opinion and Market Research was established the following year.

The Bureau was ready for this moment, because its researchers were already extensively involved in commercial work by this time. Market research was not an abrupt departure for Lazarsfeld or for his colleagues. Even in his Socialist Party days back in Vienna, he had set up a research institute, the *Wirtschaftspsychologische Forschungsstelle* (Research Institute of Market Psychology). Lazarsfeld had become interested in the application of psychology to marketing problems when the owners of a local laundry asked him to help figure out how they could increase business. It turned out that women felt guilty sending out their laundry—as if by shirking this chore they were inadequate wives and mothers. (If you're beginning to think that the history of market research is in large part a cartography of feminine guilt—remember Dichter's egg—you're not wrong.) But if there was an emergency—say, a death in the family—they felt justified in trying it. They would then love the convenience of sending out their wash so much that they would continue to use the service. Lazarsfeld thus recommended that the laundry owners send promotional letters to any households in which someone had recently died. They did—and it worked.[74]

One of Lazarsfeld's students at the Forschungsstelle, Herta Herzog, became a groundbreaking focus group researcher (as well as, from 1934 to 1945, Lazarsfeld's second wife). She credited him not only with inspiring her interest in market research, but also with its very inception:

> . . . it was his concept that one could interview ordinary people and by use of proper questioning techniques learn about their attitudes and motivations in their handling of everyday matters.[75]

Herzog described their work at the *Forschungsstelle* as the dawn of many qualitative research methods that are still used today. Since the research was usually sponsored by a business, she noted, the academics also learned there how to translate research findings into commercially useful recommendations.[76] The commercial work helped to fund other work that the institute did, exploring the social-psychological dimensions of economic problems, as Lazarsfeld had done in *Marienthal*, his famous study of unemployment. At Columbia, the Bureau followed the same model as the *Forschungsstelle*.

The focussed interview technique quickly gave Bureau researchers access to commercial contracts as the method caught fire among market researchers. Clients included Pfizer, Ford Motor Company, Betty Crocker, *Time* magazine and Phillip Morris. They tested commercials for Ex-Lax and liniment. Research questions included: Should Bloomingdale's have a restaurant? What kind of daytime musical radio program would reach middle-aged, middle-class women? What do greeting cards mean to people—and why do some resist them? Why do some people not read *Life* magazine? And even more compellingly, "Do people have more subtle desires to which we could link the use of a refrigerator?"[77]

Columbia did not value the Bureau or provide it with significant resources. One veteran, sociologist Jonathan Cole, recalled years later that their work was "almost invariably carried out on a shoestring."[78] The first offices of the Bureau were shabby and dingy, smelling like mildew.[79] They were located not in Morningside Heights like the rest of the university, but nearly sixty blocks from campus, on 59th Street, a long commute that emphasized their marginality to the institution (until 1949, when the Bureau moved to 117th Street, right by Columbia's main campus).

The scholars working at the Bureau felt pressure to produce work that was academically serious, yet the commercial contracts kept the operation alive and funded much of the non-commercial research, on voting, racial attitudes, and other matters of social importance. One researcher recalls:

> We all looked down our noses at the bread and butter. Lazarsfeld would say, "Make something of this." We tried to put our market research into an academic context. The university questioned the commercialization of the Bureau, yet forced us into it.[80]

Patricia Kendall, a graduate student and researcher at the Bureau who co-authored *The Focused Interview* with Merton, played a major role in developing the focus group (and would become Lazarsfeld's third wife in 1949, a development that the couple kept secret from Bureau colleagues— even Merton, a close collaborator of both scholars—for some time).[81] She would later reflect on the ambivalence that she and others at the Bureau felt about the commercial work:

Some of us disapproved, no, not disapproved, felt reluctant about some of the studies that were taken on. The first study I ever did on my own was for Sloan's Liniment. I felt it was a pity ... it was a good experience for me. I did everything from beginning to end. I felt it was a pity, it was a good study. A pity that it had to be on something so trivial as that. But I knew if I was to stay at the Bureau my salary had to be paid.[82]

Lazarsfeld was especially skilled at acquiring this kind of work for his institutes. But it is also true that industry deliberately and strategically recruited academics for market research in this period. First, businesspeople needed to learn more about the inner lives of these consumers, who had been saving and sacrificing for years, and needed to now be convinced to spend. Like the Red Viennese leaders, they needed to create new kinds of people. And once the newly prosperous and materialistic nation was ready to shop, research was needed even more—how else to figure out how to persuade them to choose one brand or product over another? In 1956, W.B. "Pete" Potter, director of advertising for Kodak, addressed Kodak advertising managers in London, emphasizing the need for scholarly expertise to assist admen in this daunting task.

... [W]e have got to do a deeper type of market research through studies of cultural anthropology, social psychology, and psychoanalysis. We have got to know what people want, why they want it, and what makes them buy. And we can't always take their rationalized answers. We have got to know the deep-down reasons why people want Kodak goods instead of competitors' goods.[83]

Kodak was a major client of J. Walter Thompson in this period, and Howard Henderson, a J. Walter Thompson executive, found Potter's remarks so important that he circulated them to his colleagues in the firm's international offices as well as at headquarters. A few months later, Herb Fisher, a PhD on the Thompson research staff, sent the same colleagues a note making a similar case for market research as an intellectual endeavor demanding academic expertise:

With their fingers attuned to the consumer pulse, the researchers are in a focal position for producing profitable insights. And, like the writers and artists, they should be allowed the widest latitude . . . Demanding our marketing attention today are the enormous surges of development in such fields as psychology, sociology, mathematics, statistics and economics—fields producing ideas and techniques that can be applied for profit in marketing . . . there is hardly an area of academic endeavor which cannot be mined for pure gold in marketing by the application of its tested principles within our business framework.[84]

The use of academia in market research appears to have been discussed extensively within the J. Walter Thompson company. The following year, Howard Henderson wrote a summary of the firm's market research efforts—also for his colleagues—explaining that "how human beings think, feel and act has long been a primary concern of the Thompson Company." Even in the early twenties, Henderson noted, the company's staff had included three former full professors from Harvard, Yale, and Johns Hopkins.[85] (Famous behavioral psychologist John B. Watson had worked for Thompson in that period, pioneering the discovery that despite strong brand loyalty among smokers, they often could not identify their favorite brands in blind tests.)[86] "Today," Henderson exulted, "the Thompson Company is even more a 'university...'"[87]

Thompson's flirtations with academia and intellectuals were typical of nineteen fifties ad agencies. Their use was covered extensively in trade journals of the period, and featured prominently at advertising industry conferences.[88] In 1953, a *Printers' Ink* survey of leading advertising agencies and executives found they "overwhelmingly" favored the use of social science and social scientists in campaign planning.[89]

Not everyone viewed this as a positive development. "Seduced by the advertising industry, an increasing number of social scientists are turning into super-hucksters," lamented Ralph Goodman, a writer for *The Nation* magazine, in 1953, noting that most of these social scientists were politically left-wing, yet were putting their talents to the service of consumer capitalism. (Goodman did not single out anyone by name, though he did discuss the McCann Erickson research department and thus, by implication, Herta Herzog, who was by then leading that department.) "If the social scientist becomes the hireling of advertising and business, how can he study objectively their social implications?"[90] He was concerned, too, with the misuse of social science to manipulate people, and worried about the potential of advertising to contribute to a growing malaise. Goodman felt the social scientists ought to know better:

> The entrance of bona fide social scientists into the field of marketing is all the more shocking in view of the known damaging effects on personality of advertising which stimulates desires but offers no real means of satisfying them.[91]

These relationships had their critics within academia, too, including many of Lazarsfeld's Columbia colleagues. The most eloquent of these was C. Wright Mills, one of the most important sociologists of the mid-twentieth century, who felt that the use of sociology for market research on commercial products debased his field. Mills, author of *The Power Elite*, a landmark (and best-selling) analysis of the ruling class, criticized the Bureau's work, not least because to him many of the subjects they investigated— the consumption of soap operas, tea drinking habits—were so trivial. Mills thought sociologists should be concerned with weightier matters of power in our society—such as who has it, and how it works—and called out Lazarsfeld and other BSR social scientists for becoming "specialists in the technique of research into almost anything," a "fetishism of method," or "method for its own sake." Mills coined the term "abstracted empiricism" to describe this sort of social science, and in 1959 criticized its practitioners for selling out to commercial and government interests, and for research that seemed dubious as "science":

> ... because of the expensiveness of the method, the practitioners have often become involved in the commercial and bureaucratic uses of their work and this has indeed affected their style ... it is usual to say that what they produce is true even if it is unimportant; more and more I wonder how true it is ... If you have ever seriously studied, for a year or two, some thousand

hour-long interviews, carefully coded and punched, you will have begun to see how very malleable the realm of "fact" may really be.[92]

Lazarsfeld, who remained a socialist, wryly remarking in a 1961 interview, "I can still sing any damn workers' song,"[93] could be defensive when critics like Mills implied that he had sold out, but enjoyed trying to sell the Bureau's research to corporate America, often describing this side of his work as "a good game."[94]

What also comes across in Lazarsfeld's own explanations is the technocracy that so enveloped the social democratic politics of his particular historical moment, whether in Vienna or in the Roosevelt administration. Mills was correct that research methods and elite expertise were fetishized in these circles, sometimes over any particular political ideal or even content.

In a skit performed by Lazarsfeld's graduate students, "Lazarsfeld" has a baby and is congratulated heartily. Asked if the baby is a boy or girl, the fictional Lazarsfeld explains, "I don't know, I'm only interested in the method."[95] Explaining this story to an interviewer, Lazarsfield said:

> I know it is hard for you to believe. This interest of mine in the process of research, or any kind of research as a question of procedure, has since my student days been so dominant. It has always overshadowed any substantive part of what I did, see.[96]

This logic—and the technocratic political culture from which it emerged—explains how people who aimed to make democracy and socialism work better ended up happily using the same methods on behalf of capitalism, and paving the way for a culture of consultation that would later nourish that system in some of its most undemocratic forms. Technocracy had a political basis: social democrats were more interested in smoothly functioning societies than in popular power, and they were comfortable with a democracy in which professionals ran things, and the people were merely consulted. Technocrats, whether their project was the New Deal, Austrian social democracy or the British Labour Party, were more concerned with finding ways to hear people's voices, understand their opinions, and mold them into better citizens, than with redistributing power. In fact, each of these political formations either opposed popular power—including more dramatic forms of economic redistribution such as communism—or placed important limits upon it. They thought they knew what democracy should look like, and sought to nudge people into becoming the sorts of citizens who could handle it.

The social changes that Lazarsfeld and many of his contemporaries anticipated or hoped for—whether democratic socialism, greater democratic participation, or, in Lazarsfeld's case, both—never materialized. In Vienna, the socialists lost power when the country fell to dictatorship, first to a right-wing coalition that opposed socialists and fascists alike, and then to the Nazis, who eventually took over for the duration of the war. In the United States, though Lazarsfeld believed that FDR's election signalled the advent of social democracy in the United States[97]—and certainly some in the business community agreed[98]—this turned out not to be the case, as we have seen.

In Britain, too, focus groups—and the impulse to use research for both commercial and political purposes—came from the left. British cultural historian Joe Moran argues that while both critics and defenders of focus groups in the nineteen nineties tended to assume that they—and their use in politics—were a new innovation, market research in England had been intertwined with political culture since the late nineteen thirties, generally initiated by the political left, which was motivated by the problem of apathy among the Labour Party's core supporters.[99] Like the New Dealers, Britain's sociological technicians were motivated by problems of social democracy and trying to make it work by decoding popular consciousness. Moran traces, in Britain, a strikingly similar pattern to the history of U.S. focus groups, in which qualitative research methods are initiated in part out of a progressive impulse to understand how people feel about important issues, and to help democracy function better, but "came to be directed at the narrow question of deciphering consumer choice—whether in the marketplace or the polling booth."[100]

The focus group continued to grow in popularity on Madison Avenue, thanks in part to skilled and innovative Lazarsfeld students, many of whom left the Bureau to work in industry. The most significant of these were Herta Herzog and Ernest Dichter.

Herzog studied with Lazarsfeld in Vienna, long before he came to the United States. Born in Vienna, Herzog had endured hunger growing up during World War I. Food was rationed severely and people mostly ate turnips. She would recall, decades later, that she and her sister only survived because the American military distributed food in public schools: "Mostly beans, but on Friday we had some kind of cake and cocoa," she remembered. "We looked forward to this day."[101]

Herzog's mother ate less than her share of the rationed food. When she caught a bronchial infection on a train, she was in a weakened state from malnourishment, and thus unable to recover from it and became terribly sick with tuberculosis. Herzog recalled that her mother took "seven years to die." Eager to bring her ailing mother good news from the school day, Herzog adopted a lifetime habit of hard work and high achievement. Despite the family's hardships, Herzog had an excellent education, studying violin, Latin, and Greek.

At the university, Herzog was drawn to the relatively new field of social psychology, where Paul Lazarsfeld was her dissertation advisor on the first large-scale radio study ever conducted in Austria. She studied listeners' responses to different voices reading the same text.[102]

When Lazarsfeld left for the United States, she took over his teaching duties briefly. But the two scholars had fallen in love, and in 1935, she left for New York to join him, and they were married that year. Herzog first became an assistant to Robert Lynd, a Columbia colleague of Lazarsfeld's (who would become famous for his landmark study *Middletown*, exploring the attitudes and values of people in Muncie, Indiana, written with his wife, Helen Lynd), but soon joined Lazarsfeld at the Princeton Radio Project. There she continued the work on radio listening, building on what she had learned in Vienna. She became one of the authors of the famous "Invasion from Mars" study, which explored why listeners had believed Orson Welles' famous 1938 parody news report of an alien invasion. One of Herzog's best-known studies explored women's pleasure in daytime radio soap operas, and how the stories related to their own lives.

Herzog moved to Columbia in 1939 with Lazarsfeld and his institute, which became the Bureau of Applied Social Research. There she took to the group method, perhaps more than anyone else at the bureau.[103] (Alhough Lazarsfeld and Merton are rightly credited with inventing the focus group, many of their "focused" interviews were conducted with individuals.) Herzog can be considered one of the first sustained practitioners of the modern art of focus group moderation.

Herzog not only worked with Merton and Lazarsfeld on *This Is War*, the project that birthed the focus group, she developed the method further, running focus groups for the Bureau testing Office of War Information propaganda, including a pamphlet called *The Negro and the War* and a Frank Capra movie series, "Why We Fight."[104] Herzog also ran many commercial studies using focus groups while at the Bureau. She tested responses to new synthetic fibers for DuPont.[105] She studied consumers' feelings about tooth powder and indigestion relief.[106] On the latter, her psychoanalytic training was evident in the questions she posed:

> For what should Bisodol be advertised? Do people mind the implications of over-indulgence? Has jittery stomach acquired a new meaning in these times? Should one emphasize how badly a person might suffer from stomach distress? Do people dislike to hear about sickness . . .?[107]

In 1943, Herzog was offered a job heading qualitative, motivational research for McCann Erickson, a large advertising firm. She recalled years later:

> I was tempted. It seemed intriguing to put the methodologies developed in an Ivory Tower setting to the tough test of performance in the competitive marketplace.[108]

She left the Bureau for the ad agency, and found that she did indeed enjoy the challenges of the "competitive marketplace."

> I never regretted the move although it meant a radical change from academic life. I was on my own now.[109]

She brought the focus group—and other methods—to McCann Erickson, where she became director of research for over two decades. Her research helped to sell Coca-Cola, Swift bacon, and Gillette razor blades. Herzog distinguished herself in the field, combining group depth interviews with other motivational research methods—including Rorschach tests. She essentially invented image research: getting subjects to describe, and sometimes even to draw, the pictures of products in their minds. She would also have consumers draw themselves using products.[110] (Image research is used to this day, often in a focus group setting.) She recorded the dilation of consumers' pupils. She also used more conventional quantitative methods like surveys. Herzog was particularly famous for work she did in this period on matching personality types to cigarette brands: she found that aggressive types were partial to Lucky Strikes, while hypochondriacs preferred Phillip Morris.[111] These sorts of applications of psychoanalysis to marketing problems were often referred to as "motivational research." Asked years later how new it was in the United States at that time to use these particular psychological techniques in marketing research, Herzog answered simply, "Nobody had done it before."[112]

Herzog is most likely the real-life inspiration for the fictional Dr. Gutmann character on *Mad Men*.[113] A psychologist with a thick Austrian accent, Gutmann gets a cold reception in Draper's office when she comes to offer her research just before his presentation to Lucky Strike. "Freud—what agency is he from?" sneers Draper, puffing on a cigarette with great emphasis as Dr. Gutmann peddles her finding that people like smoking because it appeals to their "death drive."[114]

In 2010, at the age of ninety, discussing her career with British filmmaker Adam Curtis, Herzog reflected that her aim had always been to adapt psychology to problems of marketing. Herzog, who died later that year, reflected in the interview that she had gone beyond other qualitative researchers of her time in her interest in the consumer's psychology. "People don't analyze themselves. You have to help them to express what is on their mind."[115] She explained that she was always interested in "asking people not just what they did but why they did."

Her clients included many car companies. "I was beginning to see what people really see in a car, what a car means to them," she said, then describing how market research participants could be drawn out by being asked to draw pictures. "It would never be something they would just tell you, because it might be a little ridiculous sometimes. You know, for example, the way the tire is set in the body. No one would talk about that, that this is important . . ." But these preoccupations became apparent in people's drawings.[116] What emerged from her research were ad campaigns depicting cars in extremely sexy ways. (As Herzog had told an interviewer back in the nineteen sixties, "Right after the war, the car was supposed to be this dream thing for the young man, like a mistress, that would really make him happy.")[117]

Continuing, in the Viennese accent that almost comically evokes the psychoanalyst for the English-speaking listener, she explained, "It was fun . . . I didn't know that people had such funny ideas. About products. I had them myself . . ." She told the interviewer, with a sly smile, "You have them, too."[118]

Like Lazarsfeld, Herzog had emerged from a Viennese intellectual world much influenced by psychoanalyst Alfred Adler. The Viennese social democrats were attracted to Adler's emphasis on community, and on fulfilling the individual through social relationships. But as Russell Jacoby has pointed out, Adlerian psychology, though it emerged from this socialist context, was fundamentally about self-improvement and adaptation.[119] Adlerianism marked a break from Freud, who assumed that society was deeply flawed and that human beings couldn't adapt to it. To Freud, the best psychoanalysis could offer the patient was to recover from his neuroses and endure "ordinary unhappiness." The Adlerian variation on psychoanalysis, with its emphasis on striving, was ultimately much more influential in the United States. As Jacoby argues, Adlerian psychology in the United States helped guide the field toward an emphasis on easing patients' conformity to capitalist society. It was much better suited than Freudianism to creating the kinds of subjects that American consumer capitalism needed.[120] Though the type of society the Viennese socialists envisioned was quite different than that of mid-century consumerist America, some of the aims of its elites for the citizenry were similar: that they should beome adaptive, resilient, socially competent subjects, able to think for themselves yet also respect authority. In the nineteen fifties, such optimistic strivers would be well-suited to newly energized consumer capitalism as productive workers and—especially, more than ever—eager consumers.

Not only did mid-century psychologists acclimate patients to consumer capitalism, many actually profited from it by working in market research, shaping the focus group in the process. The Adlerian emphasis on striving and self-improvement was particularly applicable to advertising, since it was undoubtedly true that a desire to improve one's status and live up to one's potential would inform consumer behavior.

Herzog was an Adlerian Viennese, and her work at McCann Erickson reflected this, as Lawrence Samuel has explained in his 2010 book, *Freud on Madison Avenue*. Her small department—only five researchers—emphasized "the will drives"—the individual's drive to become more powerful and achieve goals, as well as the equally Adlerian belief that individuals could change.[121]

Another Adlerian student of Lazarsfeld's from the Vienna days, Ernest Dichter, is said to have coined the actual term "focus group."[122] Dichter was made infamous by Vance Packard's exposé *The Hidden Persuaders* (discussed in the next chapter). Though probably not as innovative as Herzog, he was a brilliant self-promoter and is probably to this day the most famous market researcher in history.

While Dichter came out of the Viennese socialist milieu just as Lazarsfeld did, he did not continue to sing workers' songs in the New World, nor is there any evidence that he fretted about the politics of selling out. Not only did Dichter make millions from hawking his motivational research on Madison Avenue, like many mid-century elites, he also saw these psychoanalytically informed persuasive projects as part of a larger social good. Dichter believed that what he called a "strategy of desire"—that is, unleashing human urges into consumerism and allowing individuals to realize them through products—would lead to a more stable society.[123] He imagined that consumerism would encourage this Adlerian striving, and this would help people to be happier. His widow,

Hedy Dichter, explained that her husband had believed that the person fulfilling her consumer desires would be better-adjusted, better "able to go out in the world and and do what [she] want[s] successfully."[124]

The Adlerian emphasis on ego and striving, and its relative indifference to the unconscious, then, was particularly well-suited to postwar, anti-communist American culture. Jacoby observes, "One helps oneself because collective help is inadmissable . . . while business dominates mind and body, one is admonished to mind one's own business."[125] And while the relationship between socialism and early European psychoanalysis was an intimate one, the analysts themselves, arriving as refugees from the Nazis in postwar America, suddenly found themselves in a society in which people could lose their jobs for expressing Marxist or socialist ideas.[126]

Jacoby points out the seamless relationship between Adlerian-influenced American psychology and consumer society at mid-century:

> The drive for security is accepted as such, and not traced to an insecure existence within the insecure collectivity . . ."personality," "identity," "becoming," and "authenticity" move to the fore as unadvertised specials of the affluent society which is already a bargain hunter's delight. "When material needs are largely satisfied," writes Carl Rogers, "as they tend to be for many people in this affluent society, individuals are turning to the psychological world, groping for a greater degree of authenticity and fulfllment." This clear distinction between material and psychic needs is already the mystification; it capitulates to the ideology of the affluent society which affirms the material structure is sound, conceding only that some psychic and spirtual values might be lacking. Exactly this distinction sets up "authenticity" and "fulfillment" as so many more commodities for the shopper.[127]

Dichter, in this vein, was able to help consumers work through complex feelings about products we now take for granted, as well as about the social changes that these products both signaled and enabled. In one of his late-nineteen fifties focus groups, a group of pretty, young housewives are smoking profusely while discussing salad dressing. This was a new product: at that time, most women would not have bought dressing in a store, but would have made their own at home. One of the women says cautiously, with a timid smile, "I like this . . .very much, I wouldn't hesitate to use it for company." Another woman goes deeper: "You know what this is? It's a compromise for a woman feeling creative." But the discussion takes an even more profound turn when a housewife addresses the unease they all feel about ready-made food, trying to reassure herself and the group: "It has a place in our American way of life."[128]

Today, we take for granted that advertising tries to stoke our aspirations for self-improvement, our drive to become more sophisticated, and especially sexier, versions of ourselves. But Dichter and his fellow Adlerians pioneered that. He conducted groups for Mattel on the Barbie doll, interviewing 191 girls and 45 mothers. Mothers hated Barbie, especially her large breasts, but the girls themselves were hooked, and that was what mattered. Dichter's wife told writer Robin Gerber, "He interviewed girls about what they wanted in a doll. It turned out what they wanted was someone sexy looking, someone they wanted to grow up to be like. Long legs. Big breasts. Glamorous." (Some girls thought Barbie seemed "snobbish" or "too glamorous," but that was a minority view.) Dichter's groups confirmed Mattel president Ruth Handler's view that Barbie would be part of a girl's rich fantasy life. The Viennese analyst suggested enlarging Barbie's breasts to make her even more compelling to girls. He also suggested a way that marketers could appease squeamish moms: position Barbie as "educational" for girls—she could teach them how to become ladies and accessorize. This would mute her distressing hint of sexual precocity just enough.[129]

Of course, Dichter and Herzog were influenced by Freudian assumptions about the importance of unconscious feelings about sex and death. The attempts of nineteen fifties advertisers to exploit these would make sensational copy for decades to come. But their emphasis on the more Adlerian—and more American—themes of aspiration, self-transformation, and ambition may have played an even more significant role in their success. And the Adlerian interest in groups and sociability may have been most influential of all.

Group therapy had existed since the early twentieth century, informed in part by insights from industrial psychology on the effects of group dynamics on workers' productivity, but it became much more widespread after World War II because of psychology's Adlerian interest in conforming to social norms and the way that this coincided with the pressure individuals felt under consumer capitalism. In the mid-nineteen forties, Irving Yalom, Carl Rogers, and some of the other psychotherapists most influential in the field began to practice and write about group therapy, exactly at the same time that the focus group began to move into market research. By 1956, group therapy was, according to historian Jonathan Engel, a "somewhat marginal but accepted" approach to psychological counseling, with about a thousand practitioners, and many social work schools beginning to teach the concepts.[130]

Many of these social psychologists, armed with group expertise and steeped in a version of Freudianism that was not critical of consumerism, found employment leading focus groups for Madison Avenue.

Ernest Dichter, according to Fritz Gehagan, a psychologist and market researcher who worked closely with him, asked, "Why can't we have a group session therapy about products?" Dichter had a room built above his garage in bucolic Westchester County, New York, in which he did just that. "This became the focus group," explained Gehagen.[131] Of course, as we have seen, Dichter did not invent the focus group. But he was one of several early practitioners, and notably brought a therapeutic approach to the method.

As with the use of academic research to sell products, the use of psychoanalysis for commercial purposes was not universally admired. Indeed, analysts were criticized just as academics were for dallying in the realm of advertising.

Herbert Marcuse, the Frankfurt School philosopher who greatly influenced many on the New Left, deplored his colleagues' involvement in focus groups and other forms of motivational research, feeling that it was a debasement of psychoanalysis to use its insight into the human spirit for capitalist marketing.[132] He called it a "childish application of psychoanalysis, which does not take into account the very real political, systematic waste of resources" caused by consumerism, "planned obsolescence, for example, the production of innumerable brands and gadgets which are in the last analysis always the same." But it was not simply the corruption of psychoanalysis that bothered Marcuse. He also objected to the analysts' participation in a system—consumer capitalism—that he felt was psychologically destructive, producing a kind of "schizophrenia"[133] in Americans, as they constantly found that even prosperity was not satisfying.

The Bureau had placed most importance on the "focused" piece of the method, conducting some interviews in groups and some not. Merton and Kendall's manual, *The Focused Interview* (written for fellow researchers in 1946 and published by the Free Press in 1956), is primarily about how to get participants to focus on one thing, in depth.[134] Yet Merton and Kendall, from the beginning, identify specific advantages to group interviewing over one-on-one, never viewing the group as a mere efficiency. They observed that many people feel less inhibited in a group, and that a group discussion may yield more varied responses than one-on-one interviews. They also offered tips on getting the most out of the groups, by regulating the group dynamics (emphasizing the importance of curbing the particularly loquacious members, drawing out the quieter ones, and making strategic use of silences to encourage more people to jump in).[135] Yet for many early practitioners, the "group" aspect of the focused group interview was more critical than it was for Merton and Kendall, and this emphasis grew more pronounced in the nineteen sixties.

In 1949, a market researcher published an article describing his foray into the method this previous year, the first sentence of which was "This is an account of an experiment."[136] Things changed rapidly. By the early nineteen fifties, focus groups had become widespread in market research. Throughout that decade, they were used to study consumers' feeling about baby food, low-sudsing detergent, whiskey, and the merits of squirting shaving cream from an aerosol can, to name a few.[137] Early focus groups ranged in size, from five to eleven. (The range is now about eight to twelve; though smaller groups exist, many researchers find that they aren't varied enough to stimulate good discussion.) Free merchandise was the most common incentive; cash payment wouldn't be common in the industry for another couple decades. A moderator would sometimes start the discussion with a questionnaire to get the participants thinking—this also happens today. Questions were often projective: "What kind of family do you imagine would drive this car? What sort of woman would drink this tea?" Recruitment was haphazard in the early days; when arrangements fell through, investigators simply invited passersby to participate. They used community centers, youth clubs, and other organizations to find respondents. The key principles were that the groups be homogeneous enough for participants to relate to one another and especially that everyone in the groups have a strong relationship to the product under discussion (they should all be beer drinkers, suffer from intestinal distress, or listen to radio soap operas). "On the whole," Abrams shrugs, "finding groups of people who could act as informants was easier than we had originally thought."[138] Then, as now, people liked to be heard.

Initially, group interviews in the marketing industry were viewed mainly as a cost savings—talking to a group was cheaper than conducting individual interviews because of the savings on the interviewer's time. It was also a good way to get more input—hear from more consumers—under deadline pressure. In fact, several researchers first tried the group interview because time constraints required an alternative to the traditional door-to-door survey.[139]

While Lazarsfeld and his students played key roles in developing the group interview and bringing it to Madison Avenue, some market researchers also discovered it on their own, in some cases almost by accident. In one case in 1957, a psychologist with the Opinion Research corporation, conducting a study using individual interviews, found that one day several participants showed up at the same time—some were early and some were late. He decided to make the best of the situation and experiment with a group interview—and ended up sold on the technique.[140]

Yet the group method was also attractive to social psychologists and marketers who felt that the group itself was productive. Psychology had new insights about how to manage relationships between people in groups, as well as how to probe people's unconscious feelings without shaping or influencing them; all this helped shape the focus group. Many researchers drew upon their clinical experience as group psychotherapists in their market research focus groups.

Alfred Goldman was one of those. For example, he had found the concept of "false termination" helpful in group therapy: the most important material might emerge in the last few minutes of the session, because as patients feel that time is almost up, they feel freer to speak. "In this way,"

Goldman explained, "the person who would like to contribute something that may be embarrassing or threatening to him has only a few minutes during which he must endure the discomfort." Thanking everyone for coming and creating a sense that the session was ending could yield fruitful material.

The same was true in focus groups. Goldman gave an example from a focus group discussion of drinking in taverns rather than drinking at home. After the "false termination," one member of the group told another, laughing, that he didn't like to drink in a bar because he held his liquor poorly and was afraid of making a fool of himself. This off-hand comment, made after people felt the "real" discussion was over, led to a rich conversation about the different kind of intense feelings and impulses that can be expressed in taverns yet are otherwise socially unacceptable, revealing much more, both about the appeal of the bar, and people's anxieties concerning it.[141]

Some researchers drew on group therapy literature and, usually, their own experience, showing that when individuals come together as a group, they can—with the right moderator helping them to get beyond the social desire to make small talk—tap into a collective unconscious, which can be larger and sometimes more thoughtful than the sum of its individuals.[142] In 1951, one market researcher explained that at his firm, they dubbed the focus group the "snowball interview" because of the way respondents' answers and ideas build cumulatively into something much larger.[143] This idea that people could be more productive in a group than as individuals as a way of gathering knowledge, is a crucial one (and intriguing in light of the pervasive anti-communism in this period).

In one of Goldman's groups, discussing which supermarkets shoppers preferred in a particular neighborhood, consumers were adamant that they avoided one in particular. They implied that there was something unclean about it, but they were unable to be specific. They admitted that the shelves were stacked and the floors were clean. They even agreed that it was cleaner than the stores they actually patronized. Finally one woman made an offhand reference to a bad smell. After that, everyone else felt more comfortable discussing the real problem, and the group reached a consensus that it was a "bloody, meaty" odor. This happened spontaneously in several groups in the same study, and led the supermarket to fix the clogged drainage system in the meat room.[144]

A group discussion could, sometimes awkwardly, reveal social dynamics surrounding consumption that a one-on-one interview would not.

> In one group, the timid admission by one housewife that she hated washing floors and did so only when forced by fear of social rejection brought immediate and firm support from other group members. They then verbally "turned on" the two group members who washed floors more frequently and meticulously. Here the attitudes of women toward washing floors was reflected in the way they behaved toward each other *in the group*.[145]

In another of Goldman's focus groups, housewives, ranging in age from twenty-five to forty-five, discussed how they felt about their weight, and the effect of such concerns on their diets. The youngest, skinniest woman in the group noted that she wasn't much concerned with her weight, but assumed that some of the older women in the group would be. Realizing she had offended the others, she dug herself in deeper: "Well, as you get older, you get fatter." The young woman didn't win any friends with her tactless comments, but what ensued was a discussion of feelings about weight, body image, and growing older, which a moderator or interviewer would never have been able to deliberately provoke.[146]

As Goldman pointed out, not only were new ideas much more likely to emerge in a group interview setting than any other, the group allowed researchers to see, too, how consumers react to each others' ideas:

> The idea can be readily and enthusiastically taken up by the group and ultimately accepted or rejected. The idea can be discussed without a decision being reached, with considerable confusion expressed in the process. The idea can be discussed briefly and then dropped not to be mentioned again. Sometimes, and most significant of all, it can be studiously ignored and avoided, despite the moderator's reiteration of the idea. This

behavior, when accompanied by indications of anxiety, such as lighting cigarettes, shuffling uneasily in seats, clearing throats, and so on, suggests that a particular idea has provoked sufficient psychic discomfort and threat as to require its rigorous avoidance in open discussion.[147]

Goldman also observed that the group, better than a survey or a one-on-one interview, could illuminate how likely consumers might be to change their minds. That was because the group discussion exposed them to other points of view, just as the real world did. People might state an opinion with great conviction at the beginning of a discussion and say something else altogether at the end, in response to what others said. Others might dig in even more vehemently, or become less confident in their opinion. It was revealing to see what swayed them—and what didn't.

Goldman and other researchers in his cohort were finding that the group setting would often inspire more honesty. As market researcher Mark Abrams had written in 1949,

> The group climate can be used by informants to express views and feelings which, if voiced in a person-to-person interview, might sound selfish or intolerant, and would therefore be repressed.[148]

This might sound counter-intuitive—isn't it easier to bare your soul to one person than to a group? Actually, no (as any twenty-first-century denizen knows, after seeing a close friend confess to hundreds of "friends" on Facebook secrets entirely obscured from her). Journalist Vance Packard, describing group depth interviewing in the nineteen fifties, observed that many people "tend to become less inhibited in a group . . . in the same way that some people can only warm up at a party." As one psychologist and market researcher told Packard, describing his focus groups, people might be reluctant to discuss personal matters with a stranger, but a group can spark more honesty:

> What happens is that one member makes a daring, selfish or even intolerant statement. This encourages someone else to

speak in the same vein. Others tend to sense that the atmosphere has become more permissive and proceed accordingly. Thus we have been able to get highly personalized discussions of laxatives, cold tablets, deodorants, weight reducers, athlete's foot remedies, alcohol, and sanitary napkins.[149]

The method was valued most of all for its ability to give professionals more access to the thoughts and feelings of ordinary people, from whom their privileges might estrange them. Madison Avenue needed to find ways to listen, even across some of society's most dramatic divides. Because of its subtle ability to illuminate the consumer's feelings, the focus group could invite advertising and corporate elites into the intimate lives of regular people. Because the consumers were in a more "natural" situation—talking with people like themselves, instead of being interrogated one-on-one by an interviewer of higher social class—the industry assumed they were using more ordinary language and being more authentically their ordinary selves. In a 1951 *Printers' Ink* article, a chief copywriter is quoted lamenting the elitist social isolation of his profession:

> Copy and the creative end of advertising stands accused of coldness and superficiality. It is accused of talking to itself instead of to the public; it is said that copy today lacks warmth and humanity.
>
> . . . copy writers once rubbed shoulders, clinked glasses with different kinds of people—and now too often only talk to other copy writers.[150]

Cy Mullen, the copywriter, went on, ". . . copy writers must be kept close to the common expressions of common people."[151]

He continued:

> . . . how people talk and the general feeling or spirit that surrounds their words, must be known and felt by copy writers . . . the technique used in our interviews is invaluable in keeping our writers close to the interests and expressions of average men and women.[152]

Mullen didn't mention race or gender, but clearly class was not the only important divide that Madison Avenue needed to bridge. In 1940, a leader of the Los Angeles Urban League wrote an article for *Businessweek* offering tips on wooing black customers. Market research began, throughout that decade, for the first time, to study black consumers. In the late forties, Pepsi, Lucky Strike, and Beech-Nut gum all launched ad campaigns targeting African-Americans.[153]

Conscious of such differences—whether in race, gender, class, or cultural capital—between interviewers and ordinary consumers, these mid-century researchers discovered that respondents would often be more candid when in the company of others who were more like themselves. These researchers saw the focus group as a way around the discomfort of the typical interview, in which the interviewer's higher social status could be alienating and inhibiting to the interviewee, as Abrams put it, "where the informant comes to feel that he is being cross-examined by the representative of authority." By contrast, in the focus group, he "feels that he and his gang are doing the talking."[154]

Writing in *Printers' Ink* in 1951, Perham Nahl, associate research director at Needham, Louis & Brorby, agreed. The focus group, Nahl noted, allows the consumer to hang out with her peers and speak freely, "in a relaxed informal frame of mind. She chats about products as she would over the bridge table or the back fence."[155]

In such a setting, participants could be emboldened by each other's confessions. The women who hated to wash the floor could confidently join with others who also despised the task, knowing that they wouldn't be branded lazy deviants. In another example Goldman described, consumers who were members of a racial minority at first denied that they preferred to buy from a salesperson of their race, then after an intense discussion about racism, admitted that they did indeed feel that way. The group setting could also bring to the surface shameful behavior: small businessmen would, in the company of fellow scalawags, admit to cheating customers.[156]

Like group therapy, market research focus groups became prevalent in the United States at a time when ideas about groups in general were explored with increasing anxiety and eagerness. Sociologist David Reisman's study *The Lonely Crowd*, published in 1950, worried about the rise of the "other-directed" personality, and a society that increasingly prized conformity over autonomy. Movies like *Rebel Without a Cause* (1955)—as well as just about every film by Douglas Sirk—documented the repressive nature of this conformity and its toll on the restless, passionate individual. Such anxieties reflected Cold War worries about communism and its threat to individual freedom, but even more, concerns (perhaps unconscious) that mid-century consumer capitalism was waging its own assaults on human autonomy.

Yet people were also exploring the pleasures and potentially productive aspects of life lived in groups—and perhaps more to the point, industry was aggressively promoting these productive pleasures. Like the Viennese socialists who nurtured Paul Lazarsfeld and Adlerian psychology—and promoted chess, swimming, handball, boxing, "hammer throwing" and many other types of recreational clubs[157]—postwar corporate America encouraged citizens to play together in groups. Workplace-sponsored sports had been common in blue-collar industries earlier in the century, but by the early nineteen fifties, white-collar companies embraced them, too. Many businesses sponsored bowling clubs. In addition to its 120 bowling teams, the Lockheed Corporation offered workers softball, basketball, and tennis leagues.[158] The Red Viennese leadership and the nineteen fifties American captains of industry shared the assumption that people who could play well with others would also work well with others.

New technology also played a role in the spread of the focus group, allowing for a more nuanced exploration of the rich terrain of group dynamics and—like social media today—seeming to give professionals a more intimate view of the ordinary consumers' psyche. In very early focus groups a stenographer recorded the discussion;[159] this alone gave the focus group an advantage over the one-on-one interview because the transcription would be more complete and detailed than the interviewer herself could manage. Yet the stenographer added to the labor cost of a project and, also, her presence could be intrusive. For example, researchers running all-male groups wouldn't use them, because the stenographer was inevitably female and her presence would be distracting, perhaps inhibiting them from a candid response.[160]

The emergence of the tape recorder—available to consumers in 1946 and coming into widespread professional use in the early nineteen fifties—was a great boon to the focus group. Its advantages went beyond questions of tact or gender; what it could record was sometimes more valuable than a mere transcript. A visible microphone would be connected to a tape recorder in the other room; this to Nahl was particularly important because rather than simply writing down or tabulating answers, the device would capture the consumers' "own words." Nahl delighted in explaining how the "exact verbal flavor of these answers could be passed along to advertising copy writers so product ads will more than ever talk the language of the buyer." This way, the admen would get "a direct, uncolored word picture of consumer thinking." The tape recorder, unlike a stenographer, would capture the "emphasis given by the speaker" and thus the "nuances of meaning," as in the woman's emphasis on the word "healthier" in the cornmeal group.[161]

By 1958, market research, including focus groups, was bigger business than ever before. That year, *Printers' Ink* estimated that some $10 million was spent on market research annually.[162] Other sources suggest that it was even higher—as in a 1955 trade journal estimating $12 million on motivational research alone.[163] There were plenty of other methods besides focus groups, from surveys to individual interviews to asking consumers to draw pictures or keep a daily record of their purchases. Some approaches were psychoanalytic, probing consumers' unconscious feelings, while some were more straightforward. But focus groups used the period's knowledge of—and commitment to—group dynamics and depth interviewing to solve a very mid-century problem: building a democracy of consumers.

People were, in fact, buying more things than ever before. Between 1945 and 1949, Americans bought 20 million refrigerators, 21.4 million cars, and 5.5 million stoves. In the nineteen fifties, these trends intensified, with sales of cars dramatically increasing. Additionally, about 5 million televisions were sold every year of that decade, to families across the class spectrum.[164]

Yet elite Cold Warriors also touted the new consumer society as a sign that the American system was better than its communist alternatives. In 1959, when Nixon and Khrushchev met at the American trade exhibition in Moscow, the two men toured a model American kitchen. Nixon gloatingly showed off the washing machines, toasters, and juicers. The Russian leader was unimpressed ("You Americans expect that the Soviet people will be amazed. It is not so. We have all these things in our new flats") but he was not the intended audience. Rather, the exhibition was part of a propaganda war to remind America and the Third World that capitalism would deliver a more comfortable life to the masses.[165]

Yet consumerism was a source of great anxiety in this period. Social critics and ordinary people alike worried about growing materialism and alienation. Market research itself would become a target of such concerns. Furthermore, both critics and defenders of market research were deeply embedded in the rhetorical war over communism versus capitalism.

Market research elevated the voices of ordinary people and helped to organize mid-century class relations so that the new consumer society could function. But for its critics, its prevalence—whether the focus group or any other method—was disturbing. As market research of all kinds moved more visibly into the public sphere during the nineteen fifties, it attracted criticism from those disturbed by the rise of big business and of advertising, by the spread of acquisitive materialism and consumerism after years of high-minded sacrifice, and by the ascendance of psychology as a modern way of knowing. As we'll see in the next chapter, one of the most outspoken of these critics was the journalist Vance Packard. Industry, in defending market research from critics like Packard, did so on both populist and anti-communist grounds.

Midtown Manhattan, 2011

We are all women over thirty-five. We are welcomed by a man who has a PhD in anthropology, who explains that Yahoo! wants to know how we feel about aging.

We do have some feelings.

One woman is optimistic. Her kids have grown up. She has at last met a wonderful man and is fulfilling her lifelong dream of becoming a truck driver. He is a driver, too: they will be on the road together, taking turns driving while the other sleeps.

We are all happy for her and we say so.

To quote Anna Deavere Smith, "And that's when we had our AA meeting."[166]

A woman talks about how invisible she feels. Men never look at her anymore, she says, now that she is in her forties. She cries.

Most people in the room nod sympathetically. But an actress, about the same age as the crying lady, has no patience for this pity party. She routinely turns down men in their twenties who ask her out. It's almost annoying to her how often this happens. She has never been more sexually enticing. *It's your attitude that is the problem,* she tells the crying lady.

No one is sure what to do now.

But Yahoo! has already learned a lot about us.[167]

Chapter Three: "King Consumer": Market Research is Attacked—and Industry Responds

The writer's imagery was dramatic and sexual—just like nineteen fifties advertising itself. He accused market researchers and their advertising industry clients of "depth probing on little girls to discover their vulnerability." The writer was Vance Packard, and the picture he painted of Dichter and his colleagues in his 1957 exposé of motivational research, *The Hidden Persuaders*, was a scary one. To a nation immersed in, yet still wary of, both psychology and advertising, motivational researchers like Ernest Dichter could easily come across as sinister predators—and in Packard's account, they did. He saw motivational researchers as the able agents of a corporate America that had discovered the means to manipulate consumers beyond reason: to buy new cars they did not need, to eat sweets despite tooth decay and even, against their better judgment, to allow their little girls to get home permanents.[168]

As market research methods became more prominent, they attracted intense public criticism, and not only from the academy or the pages of *The Nation* magazine. No one was more responsible for popularizing the critique of the use of psychoanalysis in market research than Vance Packard. A Pennsylvania farm boy raised by strict, hard-working,

Methodist parents, Packard was a journalist who became the one of the most widely read social critics of his time,[169] questioning consumer culture from a populist and left-wing moralist perspective. This meant that his writing combined a left-leaning anti-corporate bent with a decidedly conservative prudishness and provincialism, an orientation that continues to inform left-leaning writing on the advertising industry and market research to this day.

Vance Packard's book became a smash best-seller. Packard accused Madison Avenue of sinister psychological manipulations. To Packard, market research was an intrusive, creepy enterprise, in which advertisers probed consumers' needs, desires, and drives—psychological material that Packard, and many readers, thought was nobody's business but their own—in order to sell stuff. The political world was also beginning to use some of the tools of market research, and Packard viewed this development as a serious threat to democracy. Packard missed the overwhelming Adlerian emphasis of shrinks like Dichter and the implications of that emphasis, so distracted was he by the pornography of Freud. Packard's book is densely populated with Freudian analysts, with their much lampooned sexual obsessions. Vibrating with anxiety and outrage—which both reflected and stoked the mood of the public—the book portrayed the methods of Madison Avenue shrinks as simultaneously absurd and sinister.

Packard seemed to find Freudian ideas shocking and exotic. Ernest Dichter's theories—men want convertibles yet buy sedans, because they want mistresses but are loyal to their wives, for example—loom large in Packard's book, and are always presented as flatly ludicrous. Packard couldn't seem to believe that people would really be so driven by sex.

This was a common attitude at the time. Although American psychotherapy had, as Jacoby argued, left Freud far behind in this period, his ideas pervaded mid-century American pop culture, which constantly referenced unconscious drives. The analytic process and its concepts, along with the European-accented stock figure of the analyst, surfaced constantly in movies, and Freud himself was featured on the cover of *Time* magazine in 1956, the centennial of his birth. Yet the mid-century

American fascination with Freud was tinged with anxiety and disavowal, often expressed as skeptical mockery. For example, the expression "sometimes a cigar is just a cigar," always attributed to Freud—and intended to convey that not *all* our impulses were sexual ones—seems to have originated around 1950, long after Freud's death. It was wishful thinking on the part of mid-century Americans who disliked the idea that they had drives and desires of which they were unaware, and desperately wanted a cigar just to be a cigar. There is no evidence that the father of psychoanalysis—a heavy cigar smoker—ever said it, but the misattributed quotation reveals the postwar longing to make his ideas go away.[170]

Packard was of this moment. He doubted that humans were really all that obsessed with sex, but even more, he was alternately incredulous or alarmed by the equally Freudian idea that adults might still be driven by infantile needs. Reporting on the industry's depth interviews about soup, he wrote:

> An astounding theory made by a psychiatrically-oriented ad man from one of the largest agencies was advanced in *Advertising Agency* magazine. "Consider what the psychologist has to say about the symbolism of soup," he said. ". . . soup is unconsciously associated with man's deepest need for nourishment and reasurance. It takes us back to our earliest sensations of warmth, protection, and feeding. Its deepest roots may lie in prenatal sensations of being surrounded by the amniotic fluid in our mother's womb."[171]

There is a nineteen fifties sci-fi atmosphere to *The Hidden Persuaders*. Packard explores motivational researchers' supposed use of hypnosis and subliminal messaging. He discusses, for example, James Vicary's study of eye-blinking housewives in the supermarket. Counting the number of blinks per minute, by hidden camera, Vicary found that women, once in the supermarket, entered a "trance." They passed friends and neighbors without recognizing them. They walked around with a "sort of a glassy stare . . . plucking things off shelves at random."[172] They were assisted in doing this, Packard noted, by the massive body of psychological research on color, packaging, and even location of items in the store. Women, researchers found, respond eagerly to a product packaged in red.[173]

Packard's language was often sensational and verged on the puritanical; he called marketing to kids, for example, the "psycho-seduction of children."[174] Like many intellectuals of his time, he saw the threat of totalitarianism everywhere: motivational research evoked "the chilling world of George Orwell and his Big Brother."[175]

Packard mentions focus groups, but does not distinguish closely, in his examples, between group and individual depth interviewing. It's clear that he views all motivational research as part of the same malevolent project.

The public was intrigued by Packard's argument that motivational research was intrusive and that advertising was manipulative. The book spent six weeks as the nation's number one best-seller and a year on the nonfiction best-seller list. A 1968 study funded by the American Association of Advertising Agencies reported "a new peak in concern over advertising's social malfeasance" after the publication of *The Hidden Persuaders*.[176] And even before the book's publication, people had already been worrying. As novelist Philip Quarles noted in a short 2012 essay on Packard, the social critic had an "uncanny ability to anticipate the concerns of the reading public."[177] And that public was fretting about the pervasiveness of advertising and about unchecked corporate power.

The response to Packard from the advertising industry was fast and well-coordinated, in some cases part of a deliberate public relations campaign.[178] Advertisers took to public forums, took out ads, and wrote their own articles and books to refute Packard's view of the industry as sinister and manipulative, and of market research as a new intrusive Big Brother. Industry argued that it wasn't about manipulating consumers into buying stuff they don't need; rather, market research allowed the buying public to run the show!

Many admen framed their defense of the profession as a defense of American-style capitalism itself—as opposed to fascism or communism. In a public debate with Packard in the fall of 1957, one agency executive called Packard's account "malicious," and argued that hidden persuasion was better than "the concentration camps, or banishment to Siberia."[179]

Others easily debunked some of the book's sketchier sources, like James Vicary, the subliminal messaging guru, who was later discredited after he claimed to have greatly increased popcorn sales in a New Jersey movie theater by flashing the word "popcorn" across the screen so quickly that the customers didn't even realize they'd seen it. This never happened.[180] Packard had not actually claimed that subliminal messaging worked, and indeed, took a skeptical view of it. But the book had used Vicary as a source, and had fueled alarmism about such methods.

Many in the industry argued that consumers were are too smart to be as easily manipulated as Packard had assumed. Under this line of reasoning all methods were justified: the poor admen needed to do everything they could to figure those fickle housewives out.

Some in the industry took Packard on in the ads themselves. Leo Burnett, a leading agency of the period, ran an ad in a trade journal headlined "The Un-hidden Persuaders." The text read:

If you draw your conclusions from the self-styled experts in the field these days, advertising and selling are pretty sneaky stuff.

To hear these boys talk, you'd think advertising was one part psychiatry to two parts brainwashing, with a couple dashes of henbane and dragonwort thrown in.

We happen to think most people buy things because they need, want or can use them . . . regardless of their libidos or ids . . ."[181]

Industry's response to Packard included highlighting the more rationally oriented market research methods, which often included focus groups. Though a group interview could consist of Dichter-style groups tapping into sexual fantasies, it just as often might consist of consumers having a calm and reasonable conversation about their choices. But more important than the different methods were industry's efforts to reframe the focus group and market research. In this narrative, market research was necessary, because the consumer, far from being a victim, was so powerful. Indeed, the consumer was the most powerful person in the American economy.

A 1958 article in *Nation's Business* by Pierre Martineau, a motivational researcher who appears in Packard's book, hailed a "new generation" of consumers, demanding novelty and up-to-the-minute sophistication: "[T] he consumer is king. He will continue to reign with greater power."[182] Thus the need to listen to him, a project that could not be achieved by simple polling:

> Success in today's—and tomorrow's—highly competitive market will depend on how well business can harmonize its own thinking with that of this new consumer.

> First step toward such understanding is to put this consumer in focus as a human being, because he is acting less and less like an economic statistic and more like a creature activated by social and psychological currents.[183]

Indeed, given the consumer's power and the force and complexity of his desires, Martineau contended, companies were, *contra* Packard, not doing nearly enough motivational research:

> Again and again consumer research turns up situations wherein consumers complain that business does not understand the way they live and how they want to shop. For instance, the young family today feels uncomfortable and not accepted in the atmosphere of traditional conservatism and austere dignity offered by most banks . . .

> The new shopper . . . is looking for versatility, moderation, and casual styling in her clothes. She says she prefers shopping in the new suburban plazas because "they understand me," which implies she feels that many stores are not sensitive to her changing way of life.[184]

Despite the "king" language, Martineau equated shopping with democratic participation, arguing that the consumer

> votes weekly on a host of products for herself, her family and her home. And she votes on a highly personal basis. She buys

gasoline at the station with friendly, helpful attendants and she shops at the stores she feels are for her.[185]

Entire books were written to counter Packard, all of them by admen. One of these was Steuart Henderson Britt, a psychologist and professor of marketing and an executive at McCann Erickson, Herta Herzog's agency, which was, as discussed in the last chapter, most influential in the development of market research. In his book *The Spenders*, published in 1960, Britt, a longtime editor of the *Journal of Marketing*, argued that market research was badly needed if companies were possibly to survive, because the customer was "unpredictable," and breathtakingly powerful:

> The modern Goliaths of industry are being challenged by 20 million Davids: over 180 million American consumers.[186]

For Britt, the reign of the consumer represented a new and more benign stage of capitalism, one in which the ordinary people ruled: "Not the adventurer . . . not the exploiter . . . not the 'robber baron' but the consumer is king today."[187]

Like Martineau, Britt moved seamlessly from the undemocratic image of the "king" to the metaphor of shopping as democratic participation:

> Because of his dollar ballots the consumer will continue to be king . . . Business has no choice but to serve his wishes, even his whims.

In other words, Britt fumed, *contra* Packard, that the consumer is not "a poor manipulated thing whose supposed wants are synthesized by New York's Madison Avenue or Chicago's Michigan Avenue."[188]

This "king" imagery pervaded the business press. "[T]he ruler of American industry is no industrialist," intoned the *Wall Street Journal* in a 1957 book review of several books defending the consumer economy, including Britt's, "he is King Customer, commanding what shall be produced and who shall produce it."[189] The *Journal* review didn't mention Packard by name but nonetheless went out of its way to refute his arguments. There was a recession that year and that, too, was widely understood as a sign of the sovereignty of the consumer:[190] through his fickle decisions to buy or not to buy, he could make or break even an economic superpower.

For groups without political power—like women, poor people, and racial minorities—this idea of consumer power seemed an intriguing proposition. An African-American newspaper in Pittsburgh gleefully proclaimed in 1960 (caps in the original text), "NOT the emperors, kings, commissars nor dictators are the RULERS of the universe today, but the fellow with a dollar to spend." The editorialist continued, "In our FREE economy, the consumer is king, because he can make or BREAK the greatest business on earth," and ended by proclaiming the consumer the "BOSS."[191] This last contention might have been even more provocative, considering that "boss" has always been a far less fanciful concept in American discourse than "king."

It probably seemed like a fresh debate; after all, before Packard, no one had ever written critically about market research in such a popular book. But the understanding of market research propagated by its industry defenders in the nineteen fifties, that it was a democratic and populist endeavor, was actually older than either the focus group or motivational research and had been carefully cultivated.

In a 2011 paper, Stefan Schwarzkopf, a British business historian at the Copenhagen Business School, points to an ad agency's 1939 ad for its services, making this political argument. Market research was a tool of democracy:

> The final arbiter of advertising is the common man. That is why advertising can fairly claim to represent the best methods of democracy . . . That is why advertising is never tired of studying the needs, desires and fears of the . . . consumers . . .[192]

Schwarzkopf observes that Lazarsfeld himself contributed to this narrative:

> As a young socialist in Vienna, Paul Lazarsfeld had been drawn to new modes of social research investigations because he noticed the "methodological equivalence of socialist voting and the buying of soap" . . . Lazarsfeld and other market researchers

made a political, not scientific, decision to equate consumer choices and political choices as equivalent or even identical . . . At the heart of this engineered transformation of voting . . . into mere "choice" was the consumer/voter panel . . .[193]

Schwarzkopf also points to the emergence of the phrase "consumer jury," tracing the repeated invocation of imagery that suggested that the research mimicked or mirrored the democratic mechanisms of the judicial system—ads, for instance, set in a courtroom and suggesting consumers would deliver a "verdict." He notes that this metaphor became politically important as advertising faced more criticism from the public: "rather than manipulating consumers, advertisers and their scientifically-trained market research personnel allowed the democratic voice of the real sovereign of America—the hard-working housewife, the honest shopper—to be heard as loud and as clear as possible."[194]

This is why such claims emerge so forcefully in the nineteen fifties. With the industry under fire from Packard, the founder of one market reseach company even went so far as to claim that his field enabled "the new consumer democracy."[195]

Indeed, looking at the history of advertising in the last century, focus groups do emerge with particular visibility and are more enthusiastically touted as part of the vox populi at moments when the public is especially skeptical of corporations and their marketing. By publicly making much of the focus groups, companies assure consumers that they are listening. They're saying, in effect: *We're giving you what you asked for. You're really the boss.* Focus groups not only helped the the mid-century advertising industry to understand the consumer better, they also, in light of Packard's criticisms and the broader public's discomfort with advertising, helped the industry to redefine market research as consumer empowerment rather than consumer manipulation.

Right at this time, two developments helped industry and the business press hammer home their message that market research was a tool of populism and consumer empowerment. The first was the Ford Motor Company's promotion of a curious new car called the Edsel, and the second was the company's spin on the Edsel's abrupt demise.

Introduced by Ford Motor Company in 1957, the same year that *The Hidden Persuaders* was published, the mid-priced car—with a grille design widely derided as resembling a vagina (perhaps especially jarring in a commodity normally phallicized)—was preceded by more market research than any previous product. When the Edsel then performed disappointingly on the market, the dominant narrative of the episode ended up just where industry wanted it. Market research was cast as the villainous buffoon—yet the story affirmed what Cold Warriors and Madison Avenue admen most wanted Americans to believe: that the consumer was the boss.

Rather than being shadowy and secretive about their market research, as some of Packard's hidden persuaders were, Ford boasted about the market research they had done on the new car, as a way of assuring the public that it been consulted, and implicitly, not manipulated. Ford touted the research in Edsel newspaper ads by Foote, Cone & Belding, a prominent agency: "YOU are the reason behind Edsel. Every new idea started with our opinion of your opinion." These suggested (misleadingly, as we will soon see) that all the new features—the push-button transmission, the car that unlocks from a key at the dashboard—came from customer research[196]. TV ads, too—in a singsong jingle—proclaimed the Edsel "a new idea—a YOU idea . . . It's a car designed around YOU."[197]

There had been research. Social scientists from Lazarsfeld's Bureau of Applied Social Research (BASR) asked hundreds of consumers how they felt about the personalities of various cars. What social class did they associate with different car makes? What was the relationship between speed and masculinity? What kinds of cars would women drive?[198] They found, *The New Yorker* reported, that Ford was seen as a

> fast, strongly masculine car, of no particular social pretensions, that might be driven by a rancher or an automobile mechanic. In contrast, Chevrolet emerged as older, wiser, slower, a bit less rampantly masculine and slightly more *distingué*—a clergyman's car. Buick jelled into a middle-aged lady—or at least, more of a lady than Ford . . . with the devil still in her . . .[199]

The Columbia team explored such issues as social influences on car buying, associations of different auto makes with class, occupation, and gender, and had intriguing psychologically minded titles like "Who Passes You on the Road—the Car or the Driver?"[200]

The "You Car" was hyped to dizzying heights. A 1957 commercial called it "the most elegant car of your lifetime."[201] A print advertisement proclaimed, "There has never been a car like the Edsel."[202] One Ford official traversed the nation making inspirational speeches on the upcoming car, declaring, "Never again will we be associated with anything as gigantic and full of meaning."[203] The Edsel's launch, which was more costly than that of any pre-1960 consumer product,[204] was accompanied by an hourlong CBS TV special—pre-empting the *Ed Sullivan Show*. Electrified by the star power of Frank Sinatra, Rosemary Clooney, Bing Crosby, and Louis Armstrong, it was one of the year's most popular programs. By the weekend, nearly 84 million Americans over the age of twelve could identify an Edsel.[205] The expectations for the car were immense: Ford had anticipated selling at least 200,000 Edsels the first year. [206]

"There may be an aborigine somewhere in a remote rainforest," John Brooks wrote in *The New Yorker* in 1960, "who hasn't yet heard that things failed to turn out that way."[207] The Edsel sold not even close to 200,000 after two years, and was widely regarded as a spectacular failure in the marketplace. Three days after "Edsel Day"—September 4, 1957, the day of the car's unveiling—an Edsel was stolen in Philadelphia. Brooks quipped that the crime was "the high-water mark of public acceptance of the Edsel; only a few months later, any but the least fastidious of car thieves might not have bothered."[208]

Conventional wisdom gleefully blamed the Edsel's blowout on its much-publicized market research, which, thanks in part to Vance Packard's just-published book, the public and the media loved to hate. In a sneering analysis headlined "The $250 Million Flop," *Time* magazine blamed the failure of the Edsel on the market research "with its 'in-depth interviews' and 'motivational' mumbo-jumbo."[209] S.I. Hayakawa, who later became a conservative U.S. Senator—and in California, a crusader against bilingualism—wrote a widely quoted article called "Why the

Edsel Laid an Egg," in which he blamed Ford for "listening too long to the motivation-research people." Like Packard, Hayakawa derided corporate America for trying too hard to satisfy sexual fantasies, alleging that in creating a vehicle with a vagina-like grille, Ford had failed to provide a working car, overlooking the "reality principle."[210] Hayakawa had great fun with the silliness of the idea that men would buy cars as sex toys—after all, he pointed out, with what reads today as almost deliberate obliviousness—cars are expensive, while Playboy only costs fifty cents![211]

This interpretation of the Edsel's failure is cherished by conventional wisdom around the world to this day. A 2003 *Telegraph* editorial titled "Trust Intuition, Not a Focus Group"[212] joins today's blogosphere in detailing the Edsel drama as one of failed market research. It is now a cliché in the marketing, product development, and automotive worlds: rely too heavily on focus groups and you may end up with an Edsel. Angus Mackenzie, editor in chief of *Motor Trend* magazine interviewed about the Edsel in 2007, told the *Washington Post*, "Market research has never created a great car."[213] A typical lesson drawn from the episode is summed up by Leslie Wexner, founder and CEO of the Limited: "You can't use focus groups to create an idea . . . a focus group would create an Edsel."[214]

The story that focus groups caused the Edsel's failure remains popular. It also appears to be a total myth. Groups, as well as one-on-one "focused" interviews, were indeed used in the market research for the car. But no major decisions about the Edsel were based on focus groups or any other type of market research.[215]

Take, for instance, the name of the car, which is often blamed for its failure, and was indeed widely hated by the public. In the focus groups, consumers did object to the name, feeling that "Edsel" sounded too much like "weasel."[216] But executives went with it anyway.

Perhaps most strikingly of all, while many, then and now, have blamed focus groups for the car's jarring appearance, the car was designed entirely without any research.[217] The professorial, pipe-smoking,[218] cosmopolitan David Wallace, the company's director of planning for market research, who worked closely with the Columbia team, felt that research was useless in the design field "and that the Ford boys know this intuitively."[219]

The design of the Edsel struck many Americans as just plain weird. Senator Hayakawa was not alone in feeling that its most striking feature, the front grille, looked like ladyparts. The grille loomed massively large in most of the commercials, sometimes coming onto the screen before the rest of the car even appeared. America in the sexist and sexually repressed nineteen fifties probably wasn't the best environment in which to ask people to drive something so conspicuously peculiar. But the Georgia O'Keeffe–like imagery can't be blamed on focus groups, as the design was completed well before any motivational research began.[220]

There were other factors in the Edsel's demise, and all of them were unrelated to market research. The economy was terrible that year. Edsel grew out of the company's observation that the market for medium-priced cars was fertile, but by the time the Edsel was launched, the country was in a recession and the demand for the mid-priced car was hit hardest of all. While Detroit sold 3.5 million mid-priced cars in 1955, by 1958 that number had dropped 60 percent, to 1.2 million.[221] So the Edsel was, through no fault of the company's, badly timed.

It seems clear that the market positioning of the Edsel was way off.[222] Originally, Ford's idea was that the Edsel would be just a bit more upscale and expensive than the Mercury, Ford's existing mid-priced car, but more affordable than the Lincoln. But as automotive historian Thomas Bonsall has detailed, this tidy plan went horribly wrong and the pricing of the Edsel and the Mercury ended up much too close, in competition. Later, Ford lowered the price, and advertised it accordingly, as a "king-sized value in the low-priced field."[223] At that point, however, changing the positioning probably looked desperate; it was too late.

In an equally grave development—and equally unrelated to the market research—the car didn't work. Being one of the most hyped consumer products in history, the Edsel was especially vulnerable to mockery when it failed to deliver even basic functionality. A former executive of the Edsel Division told the New Yorker's John Brooks that about half of the early Edsels were mechanically defective.[224] Unfortunately for the car's public image, many of the lemons were given to the press. On a test

The Ford Motor Company's Edsel was released in 1957 to great fanfare, and was widely regarded as a market flop. Immediately a mythology emerged blaming the focus groups for its woes, a narrative which persists to this day yet has little basis in fact. Public Domain.

drive granted to reporters, one car lost its oil pan and the motor seized; another crashed through a tollgate when the brakes failed.[225] In a piece of particular bad luck for Ford, the influential *Consumer Reports*—which at that point had 800,000 subscribers—bought a car in which the axle ratio was wrong, an expansion plug in the cooling system blew out, the power-steering pump leaked and the heater blasted hot air when turned off. *Consumer Reports* hated the car, declaring the "amount of shake . . . well beyond any acceptable limit . . ." The watchdog magazine called the Edsel "more uselessly overpowered, more gadget-bedecked, more hung with accessories than any car in its price class," and rated it dead last in its roundup of new cars from that year.[226] No amount of motivational research could have sold people a car they couldn't drive.

Some argue that the company's biggest mistake was giving up on the Edsel too quickly. Bonsall points out that the Edsel was only a spectacular failure if measured against management's spectacular expectations. But the market for the medium-priced car shrunk dramatically, and even after all the fiascos, 5 percent of the mid-priced cars sold in 1958 were Edsels—exactly the same market share as the Mercury in its first year.[227] But management expected the car to be such a sensation that when it was not, it was judged a flop. Instead of building on the Edsel's modest success, Ford just gave up. In 1958, the Edsel sales department was reduced by 90 percent—from 1,200 people to 120.[228]

The word "Edsel," then, has become synonymous, in the business world and beyond, with failure. But another historian, Tom Dicke, writing in 2010, shares Bonsall's more forgiving view of the car, calling it "at most an ambiguous failure." Dicke argues that the Edsel failed because the company didn't want it to succeed. Ford gave up quickly on the Edsel because the company was going through a change in leadership, and a shakeup of its corporate organization. The Edsel, Dicke writes, simply didn't fit into the new regime's long-term plans. The restructuring—within which a new mid-priced car with its own division no longer made much sense—was under way before Edsel Day. Once it became clear just how unpopular the Edsel really was, it was easy for Ford to give up on it. The company began planning for the phase-out just seven months after "Edsel Day."[229] In 1959, even before the mid-priced car market revived, Ford announced the Edsel's death.

Market research was supposed to guide the branding and advertising, but in the end, as the company went into panic mode, much of that work was ignored.[230] Motivational research was embraced by some at

Ford as a sign that the company was cutting-edge, and there were people on the Edsel team who advanced their own careers—before the actual launch of the car—by going on speaking tours and touting it.[231]

But for those within the company who hated research, it made an excellent scapegoat. And many of these voices were powerful.

Within Ford, there was a persistent hostility to any kind of outside expertise[232]—and especially that coming from either psychoanalysts or universities. (It's instructive to see that anti-intellectualism has, at times, so pervaded American life that many will defy their own profit interests just for the pure populist fun of deriding and ignoring scholarly theory and academic research.) Research was viewed with special suspicion. Wallace—an intellectual type who refused to live in Detroit, preferring the more scholarly Ann Arbor,[233] home of the University of Michigan— disdained the "decimal point minds" of many his colleagues, and was ever-conscious of his Ford colleagues' hostility to "long-haired academic stuff."[234] He complained to Lazarsfeld that the Edsel sales department had "expressed itself openly against 'any of that 'motivation' stuff."[235]

Clearly people were ready to criticize and undermine the Edsel research even from within. But there's no evidence that research contrib- uted to the car's failure. In fact, it's possible that Ford didn't do enough market research. The Edsel might have done better if Ford and the BASR had conducted focus groups while the car was still being designed and conceived—as suggested in a thoughtful and quirky history by the Edsel Owners Club. [236] Focus groups might have shared the embarrassing asso- ciations, and talked about whether they wanted to drive a car whose front looked like a vagina, and if not, why not? (Why not indeed?) But there's no doubt that the company's other mistakes, conflicting corporate plans, and the economy mattered more.

Today the Edsel, looking gorgeous at fifty plus, is one of the most popular cars for collectors worldwide.[237] But it's most famous in business and popular culture as a notorious failure.

The myth that market research killed the Edsel was thoroughly debunked by a two-part *New Yorker* story by John Brooks, one of the period's foremost business writers. That story was published in 1960, immediately after the whole debacle. More than four decades later, Thomas Bonsall's book, *Disaster in Dearborn: The Story of the Edsel*, also discussed the popular myth blaming the market research, and pointed out that "it is a simple fact that there were no critically important decisions made regarding the development of the Edsel that were significantly influenced by motivational research."[238] Historian Thomas Dicke, in an equally thorough 2010 exploration, concurred.[239]

After fifty years of thorough thrashing by serious journalists and historians, it might seem strange that this myth still thrives. But it does so in part because the coincidence of the release of the Edsel and of Packard's *Hidden Persuaders* in the same year was so culturally powerful. Having been easily whipped into a frenzy over the evils of market research, the public and the media found it reassuring—and fun—to now declare that it didn't even work.

For its part, corporate America loved and nurtured the myth that market research killed the Edsel. It was perpetuated at least in part by the Edsel team itself, along with other Ford insiders, some of whom were looking for a scapegoat, and others in the company who opposed market research. There were also plenty on Madison Avenue eager to deride the Edsel research because of its Columbia connection: those toiling for commercial firms downtown resented that the academics could undercut their prices.[240] They also resented the personal prestige that the Columbia name conferred upon Ford's David Wallace.[241] And within the media, the corporate elite and the general public, many wanted to hate market research, and the Edsel provided the perfect excuse.

Even better, this dominant version of the Edsel story—that Ford was burned by market research—countered the charge that corporate America was manipulating consumers. On the contrary, industry argued: we listen to consumers to our own detriment—they have too much power.

The idea that the market research had failed the Ford Motor Company bolstered the increasingly dominant story of the powerful consumer. An editorial in the *Wall Street Journal* suggested all this Packardian hysteria about advertisers "manipulating" the public was overblown. Indeed, the Ford Motor Company's Edsel woes, the *Journal* editorialists argued, showed that this notion was flat wrong. The *Journal* writers took the dominant metaphor of consumer as "king" a step further:

> We have such a big concern as Ford dropping a multi-million dollar project, for all the market research and engineering skill that were invested . . . And the reason, simply, is that there is no accounting for tastes . . . When it comes to dictating, the consumer is the dictator without peer.[242]

"Dictator" may seem an odd choice of word, but Cold War readers were so bombarded with propaganda about communist—and recently fascist—dictatorship that the playful notion that the ordinary Joe was a dictator would have amused them.

Other newspapers echoed the comforting message that the Edsel failed because the consumer was in charge, and Dicke suggests that the appeal of this idea may be one reason that the Edsel "failure" has been so grossly exaggerated.[243]

While there were Don Drapers within the corporate establishment who would have loved to see market research die out altogether, many more embraced the Edsel "failure" as an ideological defense of their practices. The power of the consumer was celebrated as a triumph of capitalism and democracy even while the very language ("dictator") suggested that consumer power might be excessive, somehow even beyond democratic.

Even more sober commentators joined the chorus celebrating the consumer's power. The Hungarian-born economic psychologist George Katona argued, in a book called *The Powerful Consumer*, published in 1960, that the U.S. economy was imperiled and that recovery depended on corporate America learning to better understand the consumer. He felt that the consumer's power was ultimately a good thing because

> . . . consumer thinking is inherently conservative and sane, and not inclined toward sudden and excessive fluctuations. While far from fully rational, consumers are not puppets in the hands of unscrupulous manipulators.[244]

He argued, too, that the power of consumers could safeguard against human error. Consumer capitalism would be more stable than any other economic arrangement because there were more—indeed, millions of—decision makers, as opposed to a few government bureaucrats. This, to Katona, was why the United States didn't need European socialism.[245] He wasn't the only mid-century thinker making such arguments; Austrian economist and philosopher Friedrich Hayek was advancing a similar faith in the collective wisdom of consumers, which, often more abstractly called "markets," would become central to the economic libertarianism of today.

This new order, of which the consumer was wholly in charge, was already promoted with particular force as part of industry's defense against Vance Packard and the rising public mistrust of market research, and the Edsel affair occurred at just the same time to help it along.

The notion of consumer as king, or dictator, or boss, was propaganda, emphasizing what a great system consumer capitalism was for average Americans. Such rhetoric was part of a larger Cold War story that business elites were spinning about how consumer capitalism would beat the Soviets "at their own game" by creating a classless society, as historian Lizabeth Cohen has argued.[246] Home and car ownership were particularly celebrated. *House Beautiful* magazine exulted, "Our houses are all on one level, like our class structure."[247] A series of industry-funded documentaries hammered home this idea, arguing that American consumerism was proof of our freedom: Americans are "far better off than the rest of the world . . . freely buy and sell . . . right down to the brand of cigarettes they do or don't smoke."[248]

Talk about "King Consumer" constituted an eye-rolling joke about how whipped corporate America was by the shoppers. Like jokes in the same period about wives being the ones who really "wore the pants" in a household, it reflected a concern that the powerless might get too much power. Market research allowed consumers a very limited voice—recall from the last chapter that a group of black women from the South could and did tell corporate America how to make cornbread, but lacked voting rights. But the emergence of the focus group in the nineteen fifties did also coincide with genuine challenges to such power structures. As this happened, the focus group began to be sold to consumers in a different way, less as a sign of their ultimate dominance, or as a triumph of capitalist democracy, and more as a way of being heard, of having influence.

Women were one group in particular that was getting more power—and not just in the marketplace. Just as focus groups help elites manage mass communication in an unequal society, they also helped predominantly male industries reach the women who were left out of their boardrooms, but made most of the purchasing decisions for their households. As women's roles—and desires—were changing, from mid-century on, the focus group became an ever more vital tool for bridging this gap.

Columbus, Ohio, 2013

"It's hard but it's worth it, I think," she says, reassuring herself, but not sounding entirely sure. "It is." Michelle, a soft-spoken young mother of two, is speaking about balancing childcare, housework, and a full-time job outside the home.

Sharon, a stay-at-home mom, says her interests are "trying to figure out how to be stress-free, being at home with the kids."

Teresa calls herself as a stay-at-home mom, too, although she actually works part-time as a waitress. She heartily seconds Sharon's emphasis on stress: "I just can't wait till bedtime."

The women, all mothers of young children, are introducing themselves to one another, and describing the difficulties of balancing work and parenthood, time pressures, and many other shared problems. The aim of this focus group is to explore consumer reaction to a new product. These women are the target market.[249]

The mothers describe time pressure, and the burden of "husbands who don't really want to do stuff." Not a single woman fails to be animated by the conversation or the product; everyone is engaged. "How would you imagine that?" the moderator asks constantly, inviting the women to think creatively

about how the product might best transform their lives.

One woman bring one word of hope to the discussion of how the product might make her feel: "Relief."

The conversation gets into intimate child-rearing detail. The women's graphic descriptions of poop "blowouts" at the shopping mall, or on an airplane, would resonate with any parent. Others describe less-dramatic crises. "She goes like this after every meal," one mom imitates her toddler, putting her hands in her hair. "I need to give her a bath but there's not always time for that."

"What do you do now in these situations?" asks the moderator, a warm and deeply attentive listener. She never assumes she knows what they're thinking.

No bath, was the consensus.

If the baby doesn't get a bath: "Then you feel really guilty," one mom explains, to murmurs of agreement. "Because you're a terrible mother."

"When would you see using something like this?" the moderator asks them, about the product. Not surprisingly, given the magic powers they've already bestowed upon it, one woman says quickly, "As soon as possible."

When they test the product, however, the moms don't love it as much as they loved the idea. They complain about the texture. It's not obvious how best to use it. The room quiets down.

Chapter Four: Viper, Fool, or Expert?
The Consumer as a Woman

In one early nineteen fifties focus group, conducted by George Horsley Smith, one of the first motivational researchers to write about the method for the advertising industry, the women were intently discussing dish soap.

Dr. S: One thing struck me as you reported on how you wash dishes and what you use for them. You seemed to stress getting the job done quickly and efficiently. Is that right? Maybe you didn't mean to put it just that way.

Mrs. J: Yes, that's right—it's three-times-a-day process.

Mrs. H: More than that, with coffee, snacks, somebody dropping in—

Mrs. J: That's true.

Dr. S: Maybe this is a leading question, but it has to come in sometime. I have been under the impression that women are anxious to keep their hands beautiful—yet nobody has stressed that in this discussion!

Mrs. R: A housewife doesn't worry about her hands.

Mrs. T: I will say one thing. [BRAND NAME REDACTED FROM TRANSCRIPT] really hurt my hands—some people are sensitive to certain things. It's not a question of gorgeous, delightful hands, but some people are more sensitive to chemicals; when it gets to the point where your hands hurt, you stop.

Dr. S: I don't want to seem contrary, but I am not altogether convinced, because I thought women's hands were very important.

Mrs. T: Look at all of us—I bet none of us have had manicures!

Mrs. J: Oh, here's one over here!

Dr. S: But don't you pay any attention to the claim, "Protect your hands"?

Mrs. T: Advertising is overplayed. I don't think any of us pay attention to any of those things.

Dr. S: I don't believe that. I am very stubborn.

Mrs. R: I do use a hand cream after washing dishes; I don't want my hands to get rough. I don't think my hands are beautiful—they never were—but to keep them from getting rough I use a hand cream.

Mrs. T: All of us do that.

Mrs. B: In the cold weather every woman does.

Dr. S: Mrs. H, do you do that?

Mrs. H: Yes. I don't always think about it—that's why I don't believe in claims too much. When you are in a rush, everything has to be done, and all of a sudden the baby cries; you don't worry about your hands, you just stop, that's all.

Dr. S: *You're certain about this?*

Mrs. H: Yes. Many times when I go out I say, "I should have been more careful about my hands," but when Monday morning starts out—

Mrs. T: You have the telephone to answer and a thousand things to do. All of us would like to sit in the shade, but let's face it.

Mrs. J: I don't think washing dishes is much worse than a lot of other things we do with our hands.

Dr. S: For example?

Mrs. J: When the children are in the house, things get on the floor; you pick up a glass . . . that's how I spent last week . . . you are constantly putting your hands in water and cleaning crayon off the floor with [BRAND NAME REDACTED] . . . Those things hurt your hands. We won't go into that—[BRAND NAME REDACTED]

Mrs. T: Let's face it! If we were really unhappy about our hands we would use rubber gloves to be perfectly practical.

Mrs. H: You just don't have time to worry about hands.[250]

The conversation about dish soap had quickly turned to the housewives' feelings about their hands, the drudgery of housework—and their annoyance with the male moderator. The distance between the everyday lives of these women and that of Dr. S. was apparent at every conversational turn. The gulf in understanding and experience between the group and its moderator offered a window onto the entire purpose of the focus group in this period—and onto its limitations.

The focus group of the nineteen fifties not only gave professionals access to working-class consumers, it also allowed the men in advertising and industry access to the thoughts and feelings of another powerless group: women. Despite phrases like "the consumer is king," the consumer was usually seen as a woman. The focus group was revered as a way of divining the mysteries of feminine desire, but also at times held in contempt because it gave voice to women, and women were seen as stupid or trivial. Yet defenders of market research often defended the female consumer against such detractors, arguing that their field was necessary mainly because women were too smart to be fooled by advertising.

Indeed, women were viewed, increasingly, as experts in the realm of consumerism—and focus groups offered an opportune way for corporate America to capitalize on that expertise. Positioning the female consumer as an expert could rhetorically elide the imbalance in power between the men in the boardrooms and the women standing in line at the supermarket, even though that structural inequality would remain in place for a long time.

Contrary to the stereotypical view of nineteen fifties women as bored Stepford Wives,[251] the role of women during this period was undergoing a major transformation. Increasingly, they worked outside the home.[252] Though many middle-class women did keep house and raise their children full-time, the widely promoted image of the nineteen fifties housewife was at odds with many families' reality, reflecting society's ambivalence about where a woman in fact belonged.

But the image served many purposes. Most saliently, it encouraged consumption, an ideological and marketing feat nailed by Betty Friedan in *The Feminine Mystique*, her 1963 denunciation of the prison that was domesticity for many white, middle-class women:

> Why is it never said that the really crucial function, the really important role that women serve as housewives is to *buy more things for the house?* (Italics hers.)[253]

The image of the housewife in advertising, imbued as it was with maternal and wifely caring, also helped to cast consumerism in a virtuous light, at a time when mass consumption and mass marketing was brand-new and still viewed with suspicion. Thus both criticism and defense of consumerism and market research in this period often took a gendered turn, with critics and defenders of consumer society quarreling about the nature of women. Were they crazy or reasonable? Helpless or powerful?

While class snobbery has often anchored elite ambivalence to consumer research, sexism has been part of the picture as well. Male elites—in advertising and in any other area in which focus groups have played a role—have regarded the female consumer as mysterious and unknowable, and sometimes contemptible and stupid. These attitudes persist to this day and extend into politics (recall the obsession of political consultants and pundits, first with the Soccer Moms, then the Walmart Moms, which will be discussed in a later chapter). Sometimes market research was attacked on paternalistic grounds—it would manipulate poor, silly women into buying things they didn't need. Commentators picking up on Packard's fears about advertiser manipulation often took this sexist tack.

At times, the focus group's defenders—whether gallant, feminist, or self-serving—insisted that women were not stupid. Rather, as consumers they were savvy, powerful decision-makers, and their experience as consumers constituted a kind of expertise. The focus group was empowering to women, some on Madison Avenue argued, because it gave female consumers a voice.

Generally, the idea that there would be elites, and that they would be male, went unquestioned. Market research in this period focuses particularly on women, because like all "ordinary" consumers, women were socially distant from the admen themselves. Of course, some especially so—black women, for example. It is almost certain that the male copywriters or account executives in New York City had never cooked a classic southern meal of cornbread and dark greens of the sort that Mrs. Johnson described, and that these admen's lives were vastly different from those of the black women in the cornbread focus group. But even the everyday experience of most white, middle class women diverged from that of their nineteen fifties male counterparts. The dish soap focus group makes a striking illustration: the moderator struggles to overcome his assumption that women are obsessed with their youthful appearance, when the women in the focus group are simply trying to get through the day and accomplish all the necessary labor of the household.

Awareness of the role of market research in helping admen to understand women long predates the focus group, going back even to the days of Frances Maule at J. Walter Thompson, which, in the nineteen twenties, had an entire department for female advertisers and copywriters. Advertising this to clients, the agency trumpeted women's special access to the female consumer, pointing out that 85 percent of retail purchases were made by women, and ". . . this staff has illustrated that women, thoroughly trained in advertising, working with men . . . can establish facts which cannot be approximated by men working alone."[254] As Maule herself wrote, the company recognized the "special utility that women have in appealing to women as the chief purchasers of goods."[255] J. Walter Thompson invested heavily in the women's department: its billings for copy in 1918 were over $2 million out of a total copy budget of nearly $4 million.[256]

Market research's relationship with feminism may be even older than its relationship with the social democratic left. Museum curator and scholar Kate Forde has observed, for example, that at J. Walter Thompson, many of the women researchers and copywriters came from socially progressive or feminist backgrounds.

Maule, who worked for the company's Women's Editorial Department in 1921, posing as a sales assistant demonstrating Cutex manicure products at Brooklyn's Abraham & Straus Department Store, had been an organizer and speaker for the leading women's suffrage organizations. Maule brought to her work a sense of the rationality of the female consumer, emphasizing to her bosses the importance of "substantial reasons" and "practical considerations" rather than just selling fantasy about products. Maule and her colleagues were, as Kate Forde has written, invested in trying to counter the idea that female consumers were irrational.

Indeed, the industry often vacillated between understandings of the female consumer as rational on the one hand, and as subject to crazy temptations, voracious greed, and dark desires on the other.[257] At the dawn of the twentieth century, new kinds of retail unleashed anxiety about women's ability to manage such an abundance of consumer choices. Keep in mind that in this period, there was widespread panic that respectable bourgeois women would be lured into white slavery. Department stores were widely feared, both as new kind of public spaces that could expose women to countless urban dangers and as sites of consumer temptation that would morally corrupt women and lead them to make unwise decisions—either way, the specter of prostitution loomed large.[258]

Scholars like Erika Rappaport have shown that this discussion was widespread, but few writers have captured it better than Theodore Dreiser in his 1900 novel *Sister Carrie*, about a small-town girl who comes to Chicago and must endure horrible working conditions and dull, unfriendly relatives. Succumbing to the city's lurid consumer temptations, Carrie ends up selling her body to unsavory men who buy her things. Here is Carrie's inner state, in a department store, just on the brink of accepting such an arrangement:

There is nothing in this world more delightful than that middle state in which we mentally balance at times, possessed of the means, lured by desire, and yet deterred by conscience or want of decision. When Carrie began wandering around the store amid the fine displays she was in this mood. Her original experience in this same place had given her a high opinion of its merits. Now she paused at each individual bit of finery, where before she had hurried on. Her woman's heart was warm with desire for them. How would she look in this, how charming that would make her! She came upon the corset counter and paused in rich reverie as she noted the dainty concoctions of color and lace there displayed. If she would only make up her mind, she could have one of those now. She lingered in the jewelry department. She saw the earrings, the bracelets, the pins, the chains. What would she not have given if she could have had them all! She would look fine too, if only she had some of these things.[259]

Dreiser assumed that women lusted with a feverish irrationality for consumer goods, and that they could easily be seduced into wanting more.

Maule and her colleagues took an opposing view of female consumers, assuming that women were rational and just wanted more facts about the products. This led them to a view of advertising itself as informative rather than seductive. Rather than manipulating consumers, Forde writes, they "viewed advertising as a form of social service."[260] This entailed extensive outreach, and Maule ventured deeply into the city's residential neighborhoods to talk to women who lived far from Madison Avenue. By getting out into Brooklyn where the real people lived, she felt, advertising, and the beauty industry, could better inform—and therefore better serve—the people. (Contemporary readers, for whom "Brooklyn" has quite a different valence, should keep in mind that this was nearly a century before the borough became better known as a mecca for those seeking artisanal honey and multi-million-dollar homes. Indeed, for Manhattan elites of Maule's time, "Brooklyn" signified the unknown world of working-class; Walter Lippmann wrote in 1920, "I live in New York, and have not the vaguest idea what Brooklyn is interested in."[261])

Debate over whether female consumers were stupid, crazy, feverishly desiring, or sensible had thus been raging for decades before the nineteen fifties. But in this decade, it took on new prominence as women's roles were contested; consumerism became more dominant and market research itself more visible. The discussion that Packard helped ignite, about whether advertising manipulated people, and whether consumers were rational, took an acutely gendered turn at times. Discussions about the female consumer were revealing not just about male attitudes toward women, but elite attitudes about the public, which, consciously or unconsciously, they tended to imagine as female. Sometimes the female consumer was seen as capable and thus offering hope for self-governance, while in other contexts, she might be seen as deeply irrational, or just plain dumb. Many anxieties about consumer society—some of which I've discussed in the last two chapters—were projected onto women.

"Women as an idle class, a spending class, a candy-craving class, never existed before,"[262] wrote Philip Wylie in *Generation of Vipers*, a 1943 book that became much more popular in the nineteen fifties. By 1954, it was in its twentieth printing. Having sold more than 180,000 copies, *Generation of Vipers* was much discussed and clearly resonated with the dominant culture. It was controversial; as critic Jonathan Yardley wrote in 2005, "If there was a single group that Wylie failed to offend, its name is not recorded."[263] This may be true, but women would have been the largest and most aggrieved group. Wylie, who wrote the book after a stint in the Office of War Information, is like Theodore Dreiser on hallucinogenic mushrooms. In his brilliantly original and demented prose, Wylie, a prolific author of science fiction as well as nonfiction, articulated one of the period's preoccupations: the greedy, voracious female consumer and her corrupting effect on society as a whole. In a rant that shows how intertwined anti-consumerism and misogyny could be in this period, he fumed:

> The main waft of the current, gathering inertia from itself, pours over us all the mighty river, butterscotch on top, and underneath, sewage. Boating about on it all is the child wife, the infantile personality, the woman who cannot reason logically, the bridge fiend, the golf fiend, the mother of all the atrocities

we call "spoiled children," the middle-aged, hair-faced club-woman who destroys everything she touches, the murderess, the habitual divorcee, the weeper, the weak sister, the rubbery sex experimentist, the quarreler, the woman forever displeased, the nagger, the female miser, and so on and so on and so on, to the outermost lengths of the puerile, rusting, raging creature we know as mom and sis—unrealists, all—flops in the impossible attempt to become Cinderellas, shrill ones, pushing for more yardage in the material world, demanding only that the men, obviously no Princes, at least make up in some small way by acting like Santa Claus who has become, also, an Americanized archetype.[264]

As over-the-top sexist as this is, Wylie's rantings weren't that far removed from the way Betty Friedan herself, who is often viewed as the fore-mother of second-wave feminism, described housewives in this period, as manipulated by advertising that had made them childlike, "mindless," and "thing-hungry."[265]

Quoting liberally from *Generation of Vipers,* Henrik de Leeuw in his 1957 book, *Woman: The Dominant Sex,* joined this condemnation of the nineteen fifties woman as greedy, materialistic, and largely to blame for the excesses of consumer society. Women demand tribute, he wrote, and "American men work themselves to death in order that they may give their wives and offspring every type of luxury and comfort."[266]

The female consumer was not admirable in this view, but she was powerful. Indeed, de Leeuw argued that she

controls the economy of the USA . . . Women spend 85 percent of every dollar, and the *poor* American male may be permitted to spend the remainder. No wonder, then that American industry gears its merchandise mainly to please women buyers, not men. She is, therefore, greatly courted by industry and money-men alike.[267]

The "hidden persuaders" so maligned by Packard often justified their market research work by evoking a less malevolent—but still flaky—image of the irrational lady consumer, so fickle that her whims could challenge scientific prediction. A *Chicago Tribune* writer summarized the views of one motivational researcher, Packard nemesis Louis Cheskin, a psychologist and the founder of the Color Research Institute, a motivational research firm, who authored a book called "How to Predict What People Will Buy," in this way:

> . . . he warily makes allowances for that feminine prerogative so often invoked—the privilege of changing her mind. Sometimes he even loses bets with his office force on the results of consumer polls of new packaging.[268]

Most importantly, industry and its business media mouthpieces viewed female consumers as mysterious. "Does any woman really know why, in a super-market or a shop, she will reach for one product while leaving another equally good, standing unsold upon the shelf?" the same *Chicago Tribune* writer demanded.[269] If she is opaque even to herself, this line of thinking went, was it any wonder the industry needed help figuring her out?

Watching *Mad Men* could easily lead the contemporary viewer to believe that mid-century admen viewed the female consumer as a fool, and thus regarded the focus group as a waste of important men's time. One of the partners says, just before a lipstick focus group, "I don't speak moron. Do you speak moron?" With a shrug, he gets ready to hear from the consumers. When the group assembles, Joan, the head secretary, gives the women their instructions. "Brainstorming," worries one lady. "That sounds intimidating." "There are no wrong answers," Joan assures her. "Just be your pretty little selves." Back behind the mirror, the ad men are, with libidinal relish, enjoying the view of the women trying on lipstick. "They're *brainstorming*," says one fellow derisively. "I wouldn't expect more than a few sprinkles."

This sort of condescension, in the context of the show, may have been intended as a commentary on the sexism of admen of the nineteen fifties and nineteen sixties, but it more likely reflects our own time. In the nineteen fifties, by contrast, admen were more likely to assert loudly that they respected women's intelligence, while critics outside the industry advanced the view that female consumers were dopes.

In the debates over subliminal messaging in advertising (discussed in the previous chapter), for example, it was clear that some of these critics viewed women, like children, as helpless, in need of protection from this kind of sneaky advertising. In Texas, for example, Representative Jim Wright proposed a bill imposing fines of $5,000 or thirty days' jail time for subliminal messaging. "Try to imagine what would happen to the old bank account," he explained, "if during your wife's favorite television show some advertiser started sneaking in flashes to 'buy a mink stole today.'"[270]

Those defending the market research industry tended to advance a more progressive—and, to contemporary ears, more accurate—view of female intelligence. Researchers argued women were too smart to be fooled easily by admen, and thus, that admen had their work cut for them trying to understand the canny creatures and convince them to buy anything. Though of course self-serving, this view was also rooted in the advertising industry's experience, while many critics were simply opining out of prejudice and hysteria. Hidden persuader Ernest Dichter, the leading villain of Packard's book, insisted that women were harder to fool than men. "Women are more practical," he explained, "and they usually know what they want. Men are suckers . . ."[271]

Advertisers were eager to demonstrate that they were listening to women, and that they respected the female consumer's intelligence. Indeed, one enormous focus group—a meeting of one hundred housewives gathered for *McCall's* Third Congress for Better Living to give feedback to advertisers—generated exactly the media coverage Madison Avenue desired, showing advertising as helpless in the face of the canny female consumer. "Madison Avenue's 'Hidden Persuaders' bounce off the brains of most of America's housewives," reported the *Washington Post*. The women had "no innate desire to look like Gina Lollobrigida[272] and resent the 'extravagant' cosmetic ads which claim their products can change them into leopard rug ornaments." (And far from feeling guilty about using a cake mix, these particular women thought it was "one of the greatest boons since baby food."[273])

Steuart Henderson Britt, who in *The Spenders* (discussed earlier) attacked Vance Packard and celebrated market research as a sign of consumer sovereignty, did so in specifically feminist terms, declaring, "Women are Here to Stay."[274] Women of the nineteen fifties were, he noted, equal partners in marriage, and better educated than in any time in history. Some were working outside the home. Women were the primary consumers for the household (which he noted was "natural" since they were keepers of the home, a point that wouldn't today be associated with advanced gender politics). Britt argued that women's mental capacities were equal to those of men. He viewed their ascendance into new roles, even outside the home, as a positive development. He argued that being better-educated consumers than ever before, more savvy about money and with better taste and higher standards, women presented a challenge to advertisers—hence the need for market research. Though writing as an interested party, defending the market research industry that paid his salary, he clearly had a more progressive view of women's capabilities than many of the industry's critics did. It was women's new roles and new capacities, Britt argued, that made market research so necessary; otherwise, how would advertisers know how to reach them?

Indeed, market researchers often viewed female consumers not as silly or gullible, but as experts. This idea of Mrs. Consumer as expert on the home had emerged earlier; during the New Deal, the government even organized housewives, as consumers, to enforce price controls through protests, boycotts, and "consumer councils."[275]

But in the nineteen fifties, with companies so eager to encourage Americans to buy, women's knowledge as consumers was more valued. Industry also recognized a political advantage to asserting its own respect for women: unlike its critics, market research saw women as experts rather than flaky dupes of advertising or slaves to their own fickle impulses.

Focus groups emerged as one way to make use of this expertise, but there were other, similar efforts at the time. Tupperware parties, for example, conceived by Brownie Wise in the late nineteen forties, became widespread in the nineteen fifties, when Earl Tupper, creator of

Tupperware, hired Wise to lead the company's marketing efforts through the house party model. Rather than traditional salespeople, the company relied on ordinary housewives who opened their own homes and invited their friends and acquaintances to come socialize and check out the merchandise. Like the focus group, the Tupperware house parties relied on the chemistry of the group. The motto of Wise's enterprise was, "It isn't you or I, or even Tupperware as a whole, but the perpetual togetherness of every single soul that makes Tupperware Home Parties the kind of organization it is!"[276] It was equally important that the Tupperware Party model drew on the housewife's expertise as a housewife and consumer. The company emphasized that hosting Tupperware parties and being part of the Tupperware House Party "community" was a job that required only skills the housewife already had: social and domestic.[277] In company literature, Tupperware House Party participants were presented as experts on both the kitchen and the products:

> Why has Nellie been so successful? "I just demonstrate the products," she says. She loves to cook and shares her years of experience with party guests. "I make a red velvet and pumpkin spice cake that are wonderful in twelve minutes in the TupperWave Stack Cooker system . . ."[278]

While female consumers were seen as expert consumers, within the market research industry, female researchers were viewed as experts on those same female consumers. This was true even in the earliest beginnings of market research, in the late twenties and early thirties, which is why J. Walter Thompson hired so many women during that time.[279] In the nineteen fifties, however, with interest in the female consumer reaching a frenzy, women came into their own as market researchers. Many women were hired in research departments, and some even began their own research consultancies. They were seen as having more access to—and insight about—female consumers than male researchers would have, and perhaps unencumbered by the kind of awkwardness evinced by poor Dr. S in the dish soap discussion that opened this chapter. These women played a critical role in shaping the early focus group.

Paul Lazarsfeld deserves credit for engaging the intellectual contributions of the women who helped to shape early focus group research. He seems to have been years ahead of his time in creating institutions—both in Vienna and in the United States—that could nurture emerging female scholars. Many women researchers worked at the Bureau and co-authored articles with Lazarsfeld, at a time when few women were tenured professors.[280] Robert Merton, too, repeatedly collaborated on articles with women, especially Patricia Kendall, Lazarsfeld's third wife.

In addition to his professional support for women, Lazarsfeld seems also to have been drawn romantically to intellectual women. All three of Lazarsfeld's wives were accomplished scholars who shared his intellectual obsessions: Marie Jahoda, Herta Herzog, and Patricia Kendall. Marie Jahoda collaborated with him in Vienna on the Marienthal study (which did not use focus groups but in its qualitative methods is often seen as a precursor to the focus group work done at the Bureau). Both Kendall and Herzog made significant contributions to the focus group, Kendall as co-author, with Merton, of *The Focused Interview*, and Herzog as a pioneering market researcher in her own right.

Herta Herzog, Paul Lazarsfeld's second wife, had been a leading researcher at Columbia's Bureau of Applied Social Research (BASR). There she used group discussions extensively, as discussed in chapter two, and her "woman's perspective"[281] was highly valued by Lazarsfeld and her other colleagues.

Herzog also did groundbreaking work for the Bureau on women who watched soap operas, finding a feminine fascination with love and romance that was seemingly at odds with American individualism.[282] Herzog continued to pioneer the focus group—and make use of her interest in the psychology of women—when she moved on to the McCann Erickson agency. After McCann Erickson, Herzog would go on to become a partner in an experimental "think tank" started by McCann, called Jack Tinker and Partners, founded to work on creative problems in the ad industry that couldn't be easily addressed by agencies. In the nineteen sixties *Mad Men* era, Tinker would be widely regarded as the most exciting place to work.[283] At McCann, and in her later endeavors, she also hired and continued to train

In the nineteen fifties, in addition to focus groups, companies devised other ways to profit from the consumer's expertise on the product. Tupperware parties like the one pictured (in Sarasota, Florida, 1958) made the customer into a salesperson. **State Library and Archives of Florida. Flickr and Wikimedia Commons.**

Rena Bartos, a former graduate student from the Bureau who had gone into market research. Bartos would, in the early nineteen eighties, become a pioneer in using feminist insights to help marketers sell to women.

Herzog did not appreciate having her career viewed through a feminist lens, however. In a letter to researcher Elizabeth Perse, a communications professor at the University of Delaware, answering several of the scholar's questions about her life and career, she bristled at a question about gender and objected to the possibly gendered emphasis of Perse's project:

> . . . I did not really get what you are after . . . Why the question about female . . . researchers? Gender has never played

a role in my professional life. I am not a feminist but I understand if others are. If the emphasis of the book is Women in capital letters, I'd rather not be included.[284] I'd understand the omission.[285]

Another woman who substantially influenced the focus group in the nineteen fifties was Mimi Lieber at the agency Tatham-Laird, beginning in 1955. Her first interviews were on the American housewife and on the changing role of women. Significantly, Lieber was also one of the first women to branch out on their own as freelance focus group moderators. By the end of the century, these independent contractors, the vast majority of whom were women, would account for a significant proportion of focus group moderators. (Plenty would also be employed by advertising companies or in market research departments of large corporations.)

Of course, the femaleness of the researcher was a double-edged sword. Men in advertising were often disinclined to respect female coworkers in this period. Since the researcher was a working woman, admen would (perhaps reasonably) question how much she really understood the drives of the "ordinary" housewife. Her own "averageness" was questioned. Though her career depended on the assumption that she understood the female consumer by virtue of sharing the same sex, male advertising colleagues sometimes derided her for her distance from real housewives' lives.

Marian Schott was one of those early self-employed focus group moderators, the niche pioneered by women like Mimi Lieber. A client's response to one of Schott's reports offers some insight into the paradox inhabited by such professionals.

The 1967 report for the J. Walter Thompson company described a research project Schott had done testing the Uracell Wiper, a disposable product intended to be similar—yet superior to—the sponge or the paper towel. The focus group participants—all women, some in Louisville and some in Miami—used the product at home, on their own, and watched five possible commercials. In the groups, they discussed the commercials and their experiences using the product. They were paid $5 for participating in the focus groups. They mostly liked using the Wiper, and their comments on that experience were detailed: ". . . it stands up under cleansers which paper towels wouldn't . . . My husband washed the car and I washed [the Wiper] out after he finished and it came out clean. A rag or sponge would never do that." They liked the possibility that the product could allow them time for pursuits other than cleaning: "Any woman wants something that will make work a little easier or cut a little time off there."

Despite this praise, the women weren't impressed by the proposed advertisements. One participant said, "If I'd seen this commercial first, I'd never have used the product, but the product was very good and I enjoyed it—dusting with lemon oil or using it wet." One commercial showed a British Navy man wiping down a ship. The housewives were perplexed: "I don't think it showed how the product is used in connection with our daily lives. How many of us have portholes to wipe?" "It doesn't apply to a woman." "I don't enjoy any man telling me how to clean my house."

Some objected to the spots in which the housewife seemed to be exerting herself too much: "Who wants to work that hard? That poor woman was wearing herself out! Forget it!" Another woman offered a more sweeping critique of the spot: "They could improve this by not doing it at all." Others were more constructive, suggesting the motif should be more contemporary: "The modern girl—would stress it helped you save yourself."[286]

Summing up their reactions, Schott pointed out that some of the commercials showed a woman working hard at cleaning, which looked like drudgery. She also wrote:

> Any new commercial should make both the product and the housewife compatibly modern. This means that this product does a good job for her and gets her out of the house and into the world. She must be a woman who enjoys and cares for her possessions but also is freed to enjoy herself.

And

> Modern housewives . . . are looking for efficient shortcuts. Life is made up of values beyond the home as well as in the home,

and the value of products must be in making it possible for her to get out.[287]

Jerry Ohlsten, in Thompson's Marketing Research Department, which had commissioned Schott's focus groups, was appalled, finding her report "consistently horrendous."[288] Despite Schott's report's copious use of evidence from her focus groups, Ohlsten accused her of "bias" against the commercials, stemming from her hostility to the role of the housewife. He then proceeded, in the popular argot of his time and his industry, to psychoanalyze her, calling the idea that women needed to escape the drudgery of housework "one of Marian's psychological hang-ups." He added, "I think Mrs. Schott's Id is showing."[289]

Ohlsten cited his own agency's research showing that many homemakers were "not eager to run away from their tasks and in fact derive deep gratification from fulfilling their 'nesting' roles."

His certitude on this matter aside, market research was conflicted on women's attitudes toward housework. Dichter had studied it extensively, finding, a decade earlier, that the modern American woman enjoyed housework up to a point, but also got quite sick of doing it.[290] When Betty Friedan interviewed Dichter for *The Feminine Mystique*, he allowed her to look at thousands of depth interviews he had conducted on the subject. One said, "It stinks! I have to do it, so I do it. It's a necessary evil, that's all."[291] Another was more typical and conflicted, and testimony like hers offered a helpful road map for advertisers:

> I don't like housework at all. I'm a lousy houseworker. But once in a while I get pepped up and I'll really go to town . . . When I have some new kind of cleaning material—like when Glass Wax first came out or those silicone furniture polishes—I got a real kick out of it, and I went through the house shining everything. I like to see the things shine. I feel so good when I see the bathroom just glistening.[292]

Dichter recommended making directions more complicated so that the housewife would feel like the "expert" that she was, as well as exploiting her "guilt over the hidden dirt."[293]

Ohlsten was clearly not familiar with the range of research that had preceded him on women's feelings about housework. But that didn't stop him from condescending to Schott. He felt strongly that as a career woman, Schott must be neurotically repelled by housework and thus unfit to understand real women. Of course, if Schott had been a full-time housewife, she probably would have lacked the research experience and skills to write such reports. An expert was needed to explain the female consumer to the admen, but the expert's femaleness, at times sought after, could also be a curse.

In the middle of the century, just as focus groups helped elites manage mass communication in an unequal society, they also helped predominantly male industries reach the women who were left out of their boardrooms but made most of the purchasing decisions for their households. Though not as disenfranchised as the African-American women in the cornbread group, white women were far from occupying political or corporate power. The focus group became, then, an important way of reaching them. (When Madison Avenue elites aimed at reaching the "real person," that real person was often imagined as a woman, a pattern that has continued today in political discourse, with consultants rushing to probe the opinions of "soccer moms.")

The focus group could be part of a process, too, of containing women's dissatisfactions. It could provide the illusion that powerful people were listening, and even use women's insights and voices to provide some of what they wanted—whether that was permission to do less housework, a feeling of sexual desirability, or a sense of purpose.

Yet as we saw in the Uracell Wiper and dish soap discussions in this chapter, listening to women was not always the same as hearing them. In those groups, the men in charge of the research refused to believe what the women were telling them. The researcher leading the dish soap group could not believe that women had more pressing concerns than whether their hands looked pretty. The men at J. Walter Thompson felt that Marian Schott must have misunderstood her focus groups: housewives couldn't really have wanted to escape the drudgery of their homes. Sometimes the focus group could not bridge social chasms. Even given a profit motive to listen to ordinary women, male elites could not always bring themselves to do so.

In the late nineteen sixties and nineteen seventies, as female social roles—and female desires—began to change, the focus group would continue to be critical. Madison Avenue would grow much more insistent and explicit about the feminist value of the focus group, often using the language of second wave feminism itself, with its insistence on "giving voice," emphasizing the importance of being listened to, and even mimicking one of its primary organizing tools—the consciousness-raising group.

Upper West Side, Manhattan, 1970

"What do you think of men?" the group leader asked the young woman, who had been complaining about her long-distance boyfriend in a low-key way.

"Men are stupid," she said. The leader asked her to tell that to the men in the group. She made eye contact with each of them. "Men are stupid," she said to the first one. "Men are stupid," she said to the second. She began crying about her father, then repeating over and over, "I deserve love. I deserve love."

When she was done, everyone in the group hugged her, and hugged each other. Then they all went out to a cheerful and relaxed Chinese dinner together. The participants appeared unscathed by the emotional intensity of it all; only the journalist who reported on this scene for *New York* magazine was stressed out enough to order a drink.[294]

This sort of thing did not constitute an unusual evening in New York City in 1970.

Chapter Five: "We Ask Them": Focus Groups in the Age of Women's Liberation

> The hand holding the pack of cigarettes in the picture was clearly perceived to be that of a man. It was felt that a man's hand was used since men are less likely to smoke low tar than women and the ads were trying to appeal strongly to men. A man's hand, it was argued, would appeal either to a man or a woman, whereas a woman's hand might appeal only to women.[295]

The 1979 Golden Lights focus groups, held in Eastchester, New York, were comprised of smokers who smoked more than ten filtered cigarettes a day. As focus groups often do, this one was trying hard to figure out what the advertisers intended. The discussion kept returning to that hand:

> The question was again raised as to why a man's hand was used in the illustration. It was thought by the women that a woman's hand would be more appropriate since women are generally more likely to smoke light cigarettes. The one illustration . . . with the cigarette pack in the palm of the hand was thought by several of the women to be unnatural. A number of the men, however, thought that holding a cigarette pack in the palm as shown would be natural and that it was, in fact, quite manly.[296]

By 1971, close to three quarters of a billion dollars was spent annually on market research.[297] Throughout the decade, focus groups became an increasingly important part of that expenditure. While in the nineteen fifties and nineteen sixties their use had been sporadic, by 1979, almost every major advertising agency used focus groups.[298]

"'Let's do some groups' is the standard buzz word these days" in corporate America, Joseph Ruben, director of research for *Playboy* (at a time when the magazine was displaying ample pubic bushes and curvy women posing on beds of leaves) said in 1976, "as it has been for about ten years and it's getting more prevalent."[299] One survey of eighteen New York City advertising executives that year found that within the previous year, each of them had been personally involved with at least five focus group studies.

While in later years dedicated focus group facilities, with one-way mirrors and sophisticated audiovisual recording equipment, would become an important part of the industry, in the nineteen seventies, groups were often conducted in a moderator's den or living room. The tape recorder would simply be placed on a table to record the conversation. While today there are many firms specifically dedicated to the focus group recruitment, in the nineteen seventies, recruitment was still casual, with clients finding participants through churches, synagogues, and social clubs.[300]

One reason for the explosion of focus groups during the nineteen seventies was economic. They were cheaper than survey research,[301] and the nineteen seventies, from the 1973–1975 recession on, was a lean time in corporate America.[302] One anonymous market research buyer for a major corporation told *Marketing News* in 1976, "We're under tremendous pressure to make things cheap. We're cutting out people. They take my pencils away from me and say, 'Draw a picture.' It's unbelievable the kind of pressure on us."

Although most companies did endure such belt-tightening during this period, the economy fueled the growth of focus groups in yet another way: by helping to foster alienation and disillusionment, as well as real political rebellion. In the nineteen seventies, much of the social upheaval associated with the nineteen sixties continued, only with more participation by the working class.[303] Americans during this period were deeply skeptical of institutions and elites, even before the 1973 Watergate scandal. In 1970, the University of Michigan's Survey Research Center showed that trust in government was low in every sector of the population, but especially the working-class.[304] Failure in Vietnam—and organizing by the antiwar movement—fueled distrust in the military. Conventional gender roles were on the attack, too, as women demanded equal pay and equal citizenship.

In this epidemic of well-deserved opprobrium, corporations and the business-owning class were not spared. There were wildcat strikes,[305] and the 1977 country song "Take This Job and Shove It" was a number one hit for eighteen weeks.[306] William Simon, Treasury Secretary under Nixon and Ford, speaking to a 1976 Business Council meeting in Hot Springs, Virginia, worried that "private enterprise was losing . . . in many of our schools, in much of the communications media, and in a growing portion of the public consciousness."[307]

Perhaps no individual better epitomized—or did more to fuel—that skeptical consciousness that so troubled William Simon than Ralph Nader, the crusading consumer advocate who wrote *Unsafe at Any Speed*, a highly polemical 1965 exposé of the auto industry's efforts to avoid spending money to make cars safer. Nader fumed in the preface,

> For over half a century the automobile has brought death, injury, and the most inestimable sorrow and deprivation to millions of people. With Medea-like intensity, this mass trauma began rising sharply four years ago reflecting new and unexpected ravages by the motor vehicle.[308]

The Medea metaphor brings to mind Philip Wylie and other sexist midcentury male commentators; fear of consumerism was deeply intertwined with fear of women and their unpredictable passions. But of course, Nader was right that cars in the nineteen sixties were extremely unsafe, and that the automobile industry had done little to improve them. Nader crusaded on this and other consumer issues throughout the nineteen seventies with tremendous visibility.

Another target of anti-corporate sentiment in this period was advertising itself,[309] which was lambasted for promoting materialism, alienation, unnatural sexuality, and a bourgeois ideal of happiness that could only enslave humans to work harder. Herbert Marcuse, a theorist of the Frankfurt School and a kind of intellectual father-figure to New Left activists, wrote in 1964 about the "false needs" imposed upon the individual by consumer society and especially the advertising industry:

> . . . those [needs] which are superimposed on the individual by particular social interests in his repression: the needs which perpetuate toil, aggressiveness, misery, and injustice . . . The result then is euphoria in unhappiness. Most of the prevailing needs— to relax, have fun, to behave and consume in accordance with the advertisements, to love and hate what others love and hate, belong to this category of false needs.[310]

In 1978, best-selling social critic Christopher Lasch—a former Marxist who had by this time turned moralistic and socially conservative—took this line of criticism even further:

> In a simpler time, advertising merely called attention to the product and extolled its advantages. Now it manufactures a product of its own: the consumer, perpetually unsatisfied, restless, anxious, and bored. Advertising serves not so much to advertise products as to promote consumption as a way of life. It "educates" the masses into an unappeasable appetite not only for goods but for new experiences and personal fulfilment. It upholds consumption as the answer to the age-old discontents of loneliness, sickness, weariness, lack of sexual satisfaction; at the same time it creates new forms of discontent peculiar to the modern age. It plays seductively on the malaise of industrial civilisation. Is your job boring and meaningless? Does it leave you with feelings of futility and fatigue? Is your life empty? Consumption promises to fill the aching void.[311]

The New Left constantly pilloried the advertising industry in this way, for contributing to an empty, acquisitive culture of endless toil.

Throughout the decade, with the spread of second-wave feminism, advertising also came under attack for its sexist portrayal of women. Women's liberation activists in 1970, demanding an end to the "exploitive" advertising in the *Ladies' Home Journal*, occupied the office of the magazine's editor. They also helped themselves to his cigars and smoked them.[312]

The industry heard such criticisms not only from protesters but from women within its own ranks. The same year as the *Ladies' Home Journal* protest, Manhattan adwoman Franchelli Cadwell stood before a Washington Advertising Club luncheon at the Mayflower hotel, sporting what a *Washington Post* writer described as a "wispy Belle Epoque hairdo," demanding that her colleagues take the feminist critique seriously. Cadwell was, she took pains to make clear, not a proponent of bra-burning, nor an enemy of lipstick.[313]

And yet she had had it with the sexism.

"Advertising," she said, "makes women look as if they have the mentality of a 6-year-old or else they're suffering from brain damage." Cadwell complained, using the Freudian language still pervasive in the industry, that in an ad, the typical female protagonist has "infantile fantasies and cleanliness neuroses." Cadwell was incensed by the industry's attack on women's bodies and sexuality. Referring to the douche ads that were omnipresent in this period, she said at the luncheon, "Women are supposed to have all these hangups about sex, so they're washing, washing, washing all the time to purge themselves."[314]

Nine years later, feminists were still making similar criticisms of advertising. Sociologist Erving Goffman observed in 1979 that advertising always showed women as homemakers, or in childlike relationships to men.[315] In "Killing Us Softly," her lecture and documentary of the same year, a young, feather-haired Jean Kilbourne calmly skewered the industry for promoting douches—dangerous products—with such messages as, "unfortunately the trickiest deodorant problem a girl has isn't under her pretty little arms." The ads, Kilbourne said, were "designed to make women feel ashamed and inadequate about being women." Kilbourne also echoed Cadwell in taking advertisers to task for showing women either as sex objects, or as "asexual," "moronic" housewives who were "pathologically obsessed with cleanliness."

Kilbourne pointed out, too, that many ads hectored women about specific body parts, with questions like "When are you going to do something about your hips?" or "Why aren't your feet as sexy as the rest of you?"

Advertising, Kilbourne complained, taught women that they were worth no more than their looks. One ad warned, "If your hair isn't beautiful the rest of you hardly matters." In another, a woman declared, "I'd probably never be married right now if I hadn't lost 49 pounds."[316]

Accusations of sexism, and of disregard for public safety. Rampant public distrust of corporate America. What could corporate and advertising elites do to address these multiple assaults? Some responded by advertising the focus group itself, in order to seem more responsive to the public. In December 1980, the Ford Motor Company and its consultants gloated in a print ad campaign: "Ford Motor Company has a simple formula for finding what American women want in a car. We ask them."

The print ad, tested by Goldfarb Consultants,[317] a Canadian market research firm specializing in focus groups, contained far more text than it would today, which described its practice of consulting "consumer panels from all over America," emphasizing the influence these focus groups had on the products.

Pictures of the participants—all women—sat cheerfully atop text describing their contribution to the improved Ford car. The ad was a series of mini-profiles of the women: "With three school-age children and a part-time job, Judy Bloom spends a lot of time getting in and out of cars." Each has a title: "How Judy Bloom helped us build a better door handle" or "How Robin Blair helped us change a tire." (Bloom's focus group suggested that an open loop door handle would be easier and more childproof. Blair's suggested a new kind of jack that made "changing a flat easier and safer. Because it lifts the car at the side (not at the back or front), the danger of a rolling car is eliminated." (Both ideas, according to the ad, were implemented). The campaign emphasized safety—fitting, given Nader's effective and relentless attack—but above all, interest in the female consumer and her ideas.

The important question to ask about this campaign, of course, is, What did the focus groups think of this focus-group-centered ad? Because naturally, it was focus-group tested.

They loved it! The "We Ask Them" campaign was tested along with a number of other ads that addressed women directly, that referred in detail to market research. The reasons women liked these ads reflect the populist appeal of the culture of consultation. The focus groups, interestingly, hated that the ads were directed to women, finding it sexist for the company to speak to women rather than men when there was nothing gender-specific about the product (which was, after all, a car, not a tampon). But otherwise, the researchers reported, they were pleased with it, "not because it was women that were asked *per se* but because the Company was asking 'people' what they thought and valued their suggestions." Goldfarb found that the focus groups liked the ad's "responsiveness:"

> People were impressed that Ford was interested enough to ask people their opinions and to act upon suggestions forthcoming that were worthwhile.

The focus groups testing the campaign also liked the inclusiveness of the ad: panelists were featured "from all walks of life"—lawyer, schoolteacher, mom, and part-time worker. Goldfarb concluded, "This implied Ford valued every woman's opinion, no matter what she may be doing or have chosen to do with her life. This was important."

Goldfarb, a research consultancy founded in 1966 that would eventually become a global company, with twenty-six offices on three continents, concluded from its focus groups that the "We Ask Them" campaign had the "potential to give people a favorable impression of the Ford Motor Company, no matter who they might be." Goldfarb even felt that the ad managed to counteract women's impressions that "manufacturers . . . were simply trying to exploit women for their own gains."[318]

Just as the advertising industry would eventually incorporate the hippies' imagery and language of rebellion, using it to sell blue jeans and cars, as cultural critic Tom Frank argued in his 1997 book *The Conquest of Cool*,[319] it would adopt a similarly savvy approach to feminism, with a special emphasis on listening to women.

Throughout the nineteen seventies, Rena Bartos was prominent in this effort. She had studied at Columbia with Paul Lazarsfeld, and then worked at McCann Erickson, as Herta Herzog's assistant, where she learned to run the Lazarsfeld-Stanton Program Analyzer and conduct focus groups. She later worked with Herzog again, when Herzog spun off her department into a separate research company. While there, in 1966, Bartos was recruited by J. Walter Thompson. After years of listening to the consumer, she concluded that the advertising industry needed to adapt to the changing roles of women.

By the end of the nineteen seventies, nearly half of all women worked outside the home. The stock character of the "housewife" hardly represented them, yet she was the star of most commercials. As Bartos would write in 1982, her qualitative research revealed that "What we need to do is raise the consciousness of everyone in the marketing process . . . This isn't women's lib, it's marketing lib."[320]

Yet Bartos also found that to many women, the image of the careerist "superwoman" was just as unrealistic as that of the cleanliness-obsessed housewife. "What you have is a new set of cliches that are as irritating as the old stereotypes," she told the *New York Times*. After all, images of the career woman always showed her enjoying far more power and status than most working women could ever imagine attaining. Bartos had heard from women in her groups throughout the decade that this archetype was resented by working women and housewives alike. Praising Bartos's book and her contribution to the industry, John O'Toole of Foote Cone and Belding, a major ad agency, admitted she had a perspective that captains of the industry lacked: "After all, most of us are men."[321]

A growing army of (mostly) women researchers was ready to oblige this corporate zeal for listening to women. While the professional moderator began to emerge in the nineteen fifties and nineteen sixties—whether she worked in agencies like McCann Erickson or was self-employed like Miriam Schott—early in the decade, most groups at this point were not led by such specialists, but by anyone at the client company or advertising agency who happened to be available, from the account executive to the research department's secretary. By the mid-nineteen seventies, this was changing, and not everyone was happy about it.

Myril Axelrod, another female leader in the nineteen seventies focus group industry, was a vice president at Young & Rubicam. Politically, like Paul Lazarsfeld and other characters in the story of the focus group, she came out of the left; before she went into advertising, she was a writer for the left-wing paper *PM* and a researcher for legendary muckraking dissident journalist I. F. Stone. In a paper discussing ambivalence about the effectiveness of the focus group method within the industry, she noted (and in part, blamed) the rapid proliferation of new focus group entrepreneurs. (Axelrod, who died in 2014, was also the mother of David Axelrod, who would became one of President Obama's closest advisors.) She wrote in 1976,

> . . . within the past few years I have seen hundreds of new prac-titioners of the "art" of focused group interviewing spring full grown upon the scene with no more experience than that they have watched a few groups and are convinced that they can, with no difficulty, do equally well. In the course of a recent talk I had with one of my clients, we went through a list three pages long of research suppliers who had done focused group work for his company in the past year, and neither of us recognized more than five of the names as trained, experienced, proven practitioners.[322]

Feminism had yielded not only demand for the focus groups, but also a supply of practitioners, however inexpert. Women's liberation, along with lean economic times, brought more women into the workforce, and focus group moderation—with no licensing or training requirements—had few barriers to entry.[323] This state of affairs caused great anxiety to veterans like Axelrod who worried about the professional status of their field[324]— but it also brought great opportunity for many new female entrepreneurs.

Elites in this period were conscious that they needed to listen to ordi-nary people, and the focus group allowed them to do that. Listening was gradually understood to be a skill and a discipline. Myril Axelrod noted, "There is nothing more important in a [focus] group than to listen intently and fully."[325]

When corporate clients in the nineteen seventies spoke about focus groups, it was clear that what they valued most was that the method allowed them to listen to customers across class and gender divides.

Kimberly-Clark's marketing manager for feminine care products, Joseph Paul, observed in 1976 that corporate elites could be out of touch, and that focus groups could help them experience real people, especially real women:

> Watching Mrs. Consumer, who comes in all sizes, shapes and colors, they tend not to stereotype demand the way I've seen it happen frequently in advertising, where the product is shown with some pretty upper middle class gal. That's not the way it is in the real market.[326]

In the same 1976 conversation—a focus group, in fact, of market research buyers for major corporations—Kelley Clowe (a man, don't be fooled by the first name), director of market research for the First National Bank of Denver, put this idea more bluntly:

> Most of us are in a different world, have higher incomes, and are a little beyond Mrs. Average Mid-America Housewife. This is particularly true with [advertising] agencies. How many commercials are beyond the average consumer?[327]

Clowe answered his own rhetorical question: "There is no better way to find out . . . just put it in story board form and show it in groups." He went on, underscoring the importance of the method,

> I've seen ladies say, "What are they talking about?" on a commercial we were about to spend maybe $50,000 to produce and put on the air. It makes you wonder.[328]

Hanes Hosiery Marketing Research Manager Tom Carrigg concurred, describing how the company's copywriters struggled to describe a new product—one that was both panty hose and underwear:

We could not communicate correctly to women what the product was, We went around and around with it. It finally came out of the groups. If we hadn't done the groups, we all would have sat there and said, "This thing isn't worth a darn."

We found out very quickly that you just have to draw a picture—literally, to show these women what the product was.[329]

One unnamed executive in the same conversation noted that focus groups can help bridge divides between engineers and the ordinary people who don't think like engineers:

We have several different uses [for the focus group], one being debugging our package, "Can you open it?" It's amazing how many packages engineers can open by the hour but the consumer can't.[330]

Focus groups conducted by the Atari video game company that same year, to test the now-legendary game Asteroids, served just such a "debugging" function. Respondents played the game and then discussed their feelings about it in a group. As the moderator's report noted,

there was some confusion about some of the features . . . there was much confusion about the use of the thrust. Initially almost all players used the thrust and had trouble controlling the ship. After playing two games, most were trying to use thrust, but perceived it as a detriment.

Initially players who did not read the instructions were confused about the game objectives. Several thought you had to move to avoid the asteroids and only shoot the saucers.[331]

Executives in this period were entranced by the way listening to focus groups allowed copywriters to mimic the consumers' own language. A 1979 study of executive attitudes in the *Journal of Advertising Research* called focus groups "no panacea but a way to keep fluent in the consumer's language." One executive observed, "Groups provide you with the language people use to describe their experiences." This was, for the executives surveyed, the greatest strength of the method.[332]

Kimberly-Clark's Joseph Paul explained why this was so important. It made the consumer feel that companies were listening—and understanding:

> Good copywriters really hear what is going on in the groups. Frequently many phrases of consumer language are real turn-ons to the consumer. If you put down in a copy block somewhere what the gal says, then they say, "They really know how we feel. They really understand us. They really understand our problems."[333]

There were instances where such listening inspired industry to make substantive changes. In the broadcast industry, for example, the use of focus groups drove the increased use of female newscasters.[334]

Of course, a great deal of listening actually worked against the public interest. Indeed, in this skeptical period, the focus group enjoyed particular growth in industries whose products were actually dangerous. In the wake of the 1964 publication of the U.S. Surgeon General's warnings on smoking and health, and extensive evidence published in medical journals on the connection between cigarettes and cancer,[335] the tobacco industry paid increasing attention to public attitudes and feelings.[336] Extensive resources were dedicated to marketing lower tar and lighter cigarettes (although later studies have showed they are no healthier than regular cigarettes).[337] University of London sociologist Raymond Lee, in a 2010 study, searched tobacco industry documents for mention of focus groups, and found only 48 from 1965–1969. By contrast, from 1970–1974 he found a sharp uptick—to 658—and from 1975–1979, an explosion (4,008).[338]

And the Ford Motor Company, too, remained far more interested in how to sell women cars than in keeping people safe. Take a 1976 focus group study on station wagons, which, like the "We Ask Them" study, was conducted for Ford Motor Company by Goldfarb Consultants. In the focus groups, Boston-area parents—of three or four children—talked about how they loved their station wagons because of the large area in the back "suitable for pillows and blankets and/or mattresses where children could stretch out, play or sleep" while parents drove. ("The way-back," as those of us who were children in this period remember.) The report continued, "A sedan necessitated that children sit all in a row. This did not work out . . . A wagon was almost a playroom on wheels for the children because of its design." Women, Goldfarb found, "were especially positive about the feeling of driving a wagon. They said they felt safe and secure in their wagons." What's more, "The secure feeling . . . carried over to their families. They said their families were safer in a wagon than in a sedan."[339]

Goldfarb was understandably excited by the marketing implications of these women's feelings. But having children bounce around in the way-back, without car seats or even seat belts, was dangerous, and the industry knew this even at the time. Child car safety advocates, organizing through groups like Action for Child Transportation Safety, began pressing for better standards and more widespread use of reliable belts and seats as early as 1971, yet most nineteen seventies parents remained clueless about car safety. (This did not change until laws were passed, throughout the nineteen eighties, obligating parents to make use of established safety methods, like fastening young children into carseats and making older kids wear seatbelts.)[340] The year before the station wagon focus groups were conducted, pediatricians Seymour Charles and Annemarie Shelness had published an article in the journal *Pediatrics* on the importance of using child safety restraints in cars.[341] And auto safety experts advised for years against having seats in the back because, even in a proper seat with restraints, sitting so close to the back of the car made passengers far too vulnerable to collision. Yet wagons with a "way-back" area were sold—and used as "playrooms on wheels"—into the nineteen eighties. Indeed, in 1981, probably responding to market research similar to Ford's, Chevrolet even advertised its Caprice Classic Wagon with a picture of a kid lounging in the way-back and parents riding up front: "Up to 462 miles between fill-ups, up to 6 feet between you and the kids."[342]

Listening, though rarely in the public interest, not only helped elites to sell things but served an ideological and political purpose. Business leaders were self-conscious about the role of market research in making their own project, selling stuff to people, seem more responsive and even ethical, especially in the face of strident criticism.

Take, for example, persistent charges—not just from social critics but also from regulators—that the advertising industry was manipulative and deceptive. In October 1971 the Federal Trade Commission asked leaders in the industry to speak to this issue. Alvin Achenbaum, senior vice president of the J. Walter Thompson Company and head of its North American marketing division, was one of them. His speech was titled "Does Advertising Manipulate Consumer Behavior?" (Spoiler: No.) Achenbaum dismissed that the image of consumers as "brainless sheep" manipulated by advertisers as a "popular myth." Refuting Vance Packard all over again, he drew on the same argument other admen had used in the nineteen fifties: Mrs. Consumer is no dope, and what's more, who can possibly divine her whims? Just as advertising's defenders did more than a decade earlier, Achenbaum pointed to the existence and necessity of market research as evidence that the consumer was not easily manipulated, but rather "fickle butterflies whose favor must be constantly sought." It was, he argued, the consumer who was in charge. He explained, ". . . the advertiser wants to know what is salient to the consumer . . . Advertisers either consider what the consumer wants and cater to his wants, or face market failure."

Achenbaum continued,

> Advertisers and their agencies seek to satisfy consumers, not manipulate them. By their use of market research, they seek to know what the consumers want, to provide them with products which satisfy those wants and to communicate with them in an acceptable persuasive manner.[343]

Achenbaum was making the same case that the Ford Motor Company had made—successfully—in its "We Ask Them" campaign: that research showed that the industry was listening to, not manipulating, the public.

Within the advertising industry in this decade, focus groups benefitted from a disciplinary flexiblity. Focus group practitioners managed to untangle themselves from the association with psychoanalytically influenced motivational research. This was to their benefit, as there was an industry backlash against Dichter and his methods in the nineteen seventies. In its early days the focus group had been shaped by psychoanalysis,

In the nineteen sixties, after extensive evidence was published over the connection between cancer and smoking, the tobacco industry paid particular attention to public sentiment and to marketing. Credit: SAS Scandinavian Airlines. PD Sweden–1969; PD–1996.

but it did not require psychoanalytic theory to interpret.[344] The move in advertising research toward behavioral science reflected a larger late nineteen sixties and early nineteen seventies cultural backlash against Freud,[345] whose ideas in the nineteen fifties, as I've discussed in earlier chapters, had pervaded not only market research but the culture as a whole. Russell Jacoby has alluded to this cultural shift, noting that when he worked in an early nineteen seventies Boston bookstore collective, his comrades rejected Freud as a reactionary and for being "nineteenth-century," as if ideas should necessarily have an expiration date. "To point out when someone was born did not seem especially insightful," Jacoby notes drily. But, he notes, plenty of intellectuals of the period were dismissing Freud on the same silly grounds. (There were also feminist objections. Kate Millet, in 1969, denounced the deceased Viennese for "habitual masculine bias.")[346]

Psychology itself moved away from Freudian ideas in this period, while continuing to emphasize more Adlerian approaches to individual fullfillment and encourage dreams of greater happiness, helping the individual adapt to a flawed society. Gone was the Freudian idea accepting the inevitable "ordinary unhappiness" of the normal neurotic.[347] (Of course, therapy in today's era of SRIs and ungenerous health insurance is even further from its Viennese origins.) In such a moment, market research took on different emphases, as advertisers, manufacturers, and suppliers grew skeptical[348] that probing consumers' childhood experiences and sexual neuroses could inform deodorant ads. Within advertising, many began to feel that Freud's emphasis on the abnormal—and on individual neurosis and history—was unhelpful for those seeking to understand how millions of consumers were responding collectively to specific brands.[349] Instead, focus groups, while not entirely abandoning the depth approach, began to zero in on consumers' habits and ask people more directly how they felt about products. The focus group method, while it could be, and had been, used psychoanalytically, could work just as well as a way of seeking more straightforward information about consumer behavior and desires.

The focus group, then, was well positioned to weather a shift in thinking about research. Looking at tobacco industry archives from the nineteen seventies, it is striking how the focus groups are mostly discussing what the consumers think the product is going to be like, and whether they are going to enjoy it. This is a sharp contrast with the exploration of sex and death drives in nineteen fifties cigarette market research. In a discussion of Kool's possible rebranding of a low-tar filtered menthol cigarette, for example, they worry about how the filter will affect the smoking experience:

"Easy filter means less pulling in the lungs."

"It's too much on the filter and not enough on the taste. I smoke for taste, not for a filter."

". . . you wonder if the cigarette is any good."

"The filter dilutes smoke."

"It looks like you'd be drawing air."

"Filter keeps your lips from burning.[350]

The moderator neither elicits nor muses upon the women's oral fixations, or the sexy flirtation with death entailed in lighting up a cigarette. Freud is entirely absent. In one moderator's report on a 1979 cigarette focus group, for example, she notes that "a few men commented on whether the cigarettes would be crushed by the hand pushing down on the pack." Where a postwar motivational researcher might have explored the men's possible castration anxiety—why *were* they troubled by a woman's hand "crushing" a phallic object?—the 1979 moderator promptly dismissed the moment: "However, this did not seem to be a serious consideration."[351]

In the nineteen seventies, moderators—and therefore participants, because people talk about whatever they are asked about—were concerned with practicalities. In Dallas, in 1979, testing a campaign for Brown and Williamson, all the focus groups emphatically rejected the new cigarette brand. The problem was the name ("Comfort") and the package.

- "It consistently evoked associations with feminine hygiene products . . ."

- "The use of the word 'soft' probably contributed to these latter associations."

The groups conducted did not like the imagery in the ad, either, which showed a woman with a flowing dress and big hat. Women found her distracting. Men found the ad too feminine. "This is not a cigarette ad," one participant complained.[352]

Herta Herzog and Ernest Dichter would have been curious about why the focus groups were thinking about vaginas, why the men feared the feminine, and how those anxieties might relate to the product. But to the contemporary nineteen seventies moderator, it was enough to say that the ad was confusing and that people didn't like it.

The move away from Freud—in both the larger culture and the advertising industry—also represented a move away from interest in the individual psyche, toward a greater preoccupation with the group, a defining part of the nineteen seventies *zeitgeist*, but also building on the Adlerian drift that had begun in the nineteen fifties. This, like the other developments discussed in this chapter so far, grew out of the left.

Group mania was a critical part of the rise of the focus group in this decade. By the mid-nineteen seventies, by one estimate, close to 6 million Americans were participating in "encounter groups"[353]—though any such estimates were dubious, since, as *New York* writer Linda Francke noted, "any four people sitting around at night, holding hands and chanting, could be considered a group."[354] These were group discussions aimed at opening participants more fully to their own emotions, many with the hope of inspiring a movement for a freer, less repressed, and happier society. Such gatherings were sometimes run by professional therapists or well-intentioned laypeople, but also by gurus and charlatans.

Encounter groups, though they might sound wacky today, were part of a nineteen seventies enthusiasm for talking about things in groups. The decade saw an explosion in group therapy of all types—confidence therapy (with "trust falls"), Gestalt, and cults like EST. One participant remembers that at his university in 1978, group therapy was the only type of psychological counseling available. "We all sat around and worked out our hostility by punching pillows," he recalls. "I said, 'Are you fucking kidding me?' I lasted two weeks."[355]

The idea of group therapy was Adlerian—that the individual needed to find a way to exist in a social context—and some people did indeed find the group to be a useful mirror of the social, family, and romantic problems troubling them in the wider world. Though the purpose of group therapy was of course quite different from that of focus groups, some of the earliest market research focus groups, in the nineteen forties and nineteen fifties, were conducted by psychologists who had been treating patients in groups. The therapy group and the focus group evolved in tandem in the nineteen fifties, and both entered the public sphere with particular visibility in the nineteen seventies, as the culture became enamored with the potential of the group experience and with the power of conversation. The growing number of psychologists trained in group therapy and group dynamics also made more experts available to the advertising industry, which further fueled the rise of the focus group.

Central to this group moment was feminist consciousness raising (CR). In these, women gathered in small groups—which, significantly, unlike the encounter groups or focus groups, had no leader—to talk about their lives. Conversations about specific husbands, boyfriends, bosses, and families were also discussions about women's collective lack of social and political power. These gave way to the insight, popular at the time, that the "personal is political." It was intricately interwined with group therapy. Feminist scholar Kara Jesella argues that although feminists wanted to stress that CR was "not therapy," its process (i.e., talk) was the same.[356] So were its assumptions: "We assume," Kathie Sarachild, the activist credited with coining the term "consciousness raising," wrote, "our feelings are telling us something from which we can learn."[357]

It was not only, then, a cultural moment that demanded that elites listen. It was also one in which the people were eager to be heard.

Historian Fred Turner has observed how deeply the counterculture and the New Left—with its emphasis on small groups, from the New Communalist interest in communes to encounter groups—shaped corporate culture.[358] With so many people curious about groups and what they could reveal, the focus group was one of many ways that countercultural exploration entered the office park and the boardroom. Wearing beads over a black turtleneck during a 1976 interview with *Marketing News*, Joseph J. Paul, manager of marketing research for "feminine care products" at Kimberly-Clark, explained that in a focus group, when it's done well, "the dynamics of the group draw out the people, their comments and their feelings about whatever the subject happens to be."[359]

Of course, these feminist and New Left efforts were not intended to end up enabling consumerism and cubicles. It's easy to make fun of the decade's shenanigans, but many who participated in encounter groups did so out of a sincere desire to change the world by helping to break down the sexually and emotionally repressive strictures of bourgeois society. More succesfully, early feminist consciousness-raising sometimes led to women, as Sarachild put it, "doing something politically about aspects of our lives as women that we never thought could be dealt with politically, that we thought we would just have to work out as best we could alone."[360] These included issues like personal appearance: women realized they were valued for the way they looked rather than for other qualities, and the famous 1968 Miss America protest was born, in which women threw girdles, curlers, bras, and other accoutrements of oppression into a big "Freedom Trashcan."[361] Some of the major feminist thinking and writing—including Shulamith Firestone's book *The Dialectic of Sex*, and Anne Koedt's essay "The Myth of the Vaginal Orgasm"—emerged in part from the writers' participation in CR sessions. Consciousness raising was, Sarachild wrote, "part of a very inclusive commitment to winning and guaranteeing radical changes for women in society."[362]

Explicitly, as Sarachild makes clear,[363] consciousness raising was not about letting everyone be heard for its own sake. It was not about self-expression, but rooted in the idea that talk could lead to better analysis of a political problem, better theories about power, and better ideas about how to take action and make change.

Yet the act of giving voice is the part of the nineteen seventies feminist and countercultural legacy that has endured in activist politics—whether in the habit of expressing outrage on social media, or in the eight-hour meetings of Occupy Wall Street, in which everyone was allowed to speak.

Consciousness raising was transformative for many participants; early CR activist Lynn O'Connor wrote that women in CR groups

> feel a growing personal strength that is new and exciting. Some of them feel a surge of energy. The talk about men diminishes and

they turn to themselves. They reveal long-hidden secret ambitions and many realize they have never taken themselves seriously. They liberate a vision of themselves as strong, serious people with an inherent capacity for achievement and independence.[364]

The focus group participant talks, too. In contrast to the feminist consciousness raiser, however, she goes home with a couple hundred dollars, but has learned little, and is part of no larger movement for social change. Indeed, in the focus group, the solution to your life's complexities is a better baby wipe, rather than socialized healthcare or egalitarian marriage.

The focus group, in a way, represents a cooptation of some of our most radical impulses as Americans. Despite all the rhetoric of individualism, we like to work cooperatively and to figure things out in groups.

Yet it may not represent a simple appropriation. In some sense, the focus group of today is the ghost of the New Left and second wave feminism. Like any apparition, it is but a shadow of the deceased but also serves as a reminder of its flaws. These movements may have placed too much emphasis on giving voice to the dissatisfied. Political and countercultural expression had shifted from taking power (blocking the trains in a strike, forming a new political party, or shutting down the segregationist lunch counter) to simply giving voice and listening.

Movements that so emphasized letting individuals be heard may have failed to equip people to do much more than express themselves. The New Left confused "psychic first aid with revolution," Russell Jacoby argued. "Endless talk on 'I 'and 'thou,'" he wrote, "forgets that neither can be created out of endless talk."[365]

As it was during World War II, the focus group in the nineteen seventies was powered by political developments from the left side of the spectrum. It was increasingly necessary because of great divides between elites and masses and a healthy, potentially revolutionary mass alienation. The left helped create that situation. But the left's own problems show why the focus group, as a tool of corporate elites, was both so appealing and so successful. The focus group—and the left from which it emerged—showed the limitations of all this talking. The Anglo-American left of the nineteen seventies, and the culture that has succeeded it, fueled a culture in which everyone wants to be heard and few are actually demanding state power, or trying to seize control of corporate profits, a political state of affairs that persists today. Now, we are mostly just expressing ourselves, and it is rare that we occupy the boss's office or smoke his cigars (or eat his dried kale snacks from Whole Foods—as being a boss is not all it used to be).

The contemporary focus group continues to evoke the consciousness-raising past, though to different ends. Not many feminist consciousness-raising groups exist nowadays, though the feminist group Redstockings, formed during feminism's second wave, still uses them, and you can read in young women's Tumblr pages a revival of the impulse to politicize—and converse about—daily life under patriarchy. But the focus group still feels a little bit like a CR session.

In one-way mirrored rooms in Midtown Manhattan listening to animated discussions brought to us by J. P. Morgan Chase and Procter & Gamble, feminism is still a constant presence. Wendy, a young woman in Brooklyn who withheld her last name for professional reasons, was a habitual focus group participant throughout the early two thousand. She says the groups discussing gender were the ones that would get the most heated—and that feminist issues would come up often. "Panty hose," she remembers, shaking her head. "Heated debates between women who never wear it, and women who thought it was unprofessional not to wear it." There were debates in the group over whether it was "sexist to require women to wear it." This led in turn to discussion of leg-shaving, and of race ("nude," of course, does not describe dark skin). Observes Wendy wryly, "Who knew a discussion about panty hose was really about racism and sexism?"

In an echo of some of those early CR groups, Wendy recalled, some women "would tell other women what they should think and what she should feel." Once, she said, in a discussion about bras, one woman said she'd prefer a bra that would look sexy to her boyfriend. "And," Wendy remembers with amusement, "everyone attacked her for wanting to look sexy for a man!"[366]

These are important matters to discuss, but in these contexts, "endless talk" serves only capital, not the conversationalists. The focus group here becomes a literalization of Jacoby's fears about the direction of both psychoanalysis and politics. In the nineteen eighties and nineteen nineties, with the population in many ways already depoliticized by such talk, the culture of consultation would only escalate—and face backlash.

Midtown Manhattan, 2012

I did not expect to be rejected when I auditioned for the focus group for Kelly Ripa's reality show. She was looking for women whose retail tastes are both high-end and low-end—that's me!

Kim, the interviewer, walked around asking us questions as we mingled in the Manhattan hotel lobby. She asked me if I was a big shopper and I said yes (an exaggeration). She asked if I watched HSN and other shopping networks. I said no (true). She wandered away and later circled back to me. She seemed to be critically appraising my outfit, although, in tight black Lucky jeans, fairly expensive boots, and a designer shirt from Loehmann's, I thought I looked pretty good. She asked again, skeptically, if I shopped a lot. I said yes but admitted, "possibly not as much as a lot of people."

When the recruiter called to inform me of my rejection, he explained, "We were looking for very specific answers when Kim was walking around asking questions. It's much more scientific than you might think."

Chapter Six: Entertaining Joe Sixpack

Frasier is pissed off.

His radio show is going to be tested in a focus group. The fictional shrink and radio host explains to his brother what a focus group is: people the studio bring in "off the street." He bemoans the fact that his show could be changed as a result of the opinions of "Joe Sixpack." His brother listens and sympathizes, "How demeaning!"

Yet in the end it is the snobbish Frasier who victimizes the average Joe, not the other way around. The group is told not to worry about hurting anyone's feelings because no one connected with the show is behind the mirror, but it's a lie: Frasier is behind the mirror. Eleven out of twelve of the participants love the show, but one guy—a Middle Eastern newsstand proprietor—"just doesn't like" Frasier. He doesn't explain why. Despite the enthusiasm from the rest of the group, Frasier becomes obsessed with his one detractor, stalking the poor fellow. A madcap series of events ensues, culminating with Frasier accidentally burning down the man's newsstand.[367]

The scenario is a creative person's fantasy about getting revenge on those focus group naysayers. But it's also a spoof on the elitism of those same creatives, who imagine themselves victimized by people who are in fact far less powerful than themselves.

That *Frasier* episode aired in 1996, as the late-twentieth-century hostility to focus groups—from creative and corporate elites—heated up quite publicly. The anger of entertainment industry creatives—and critical audiences—over the incursions of market research was palpable in this period and into the next century. As it does in other industries, the hostility to the entertainment focus group has provided a way for professionals and other elites to blame ordinary people for problems caused by the capitalist class and by an increasingly marketized society.

The entertainment industry uses focus groups to test trailers and gauge audience reaction to specific characters, plot lines, actors, and titles. A focus group is usually performed after the film has been made, and the discussion takes place after a test screening. The practice has been widespread since the nineteen eighties, and by 2004, Hollywood studios were spending at least $100 million a year on market research.[368]

Focus groups are also used to better understand, and often fine-tune or narrow, a movie or TV show's audience. The imagined audience may have sensibilities and tastes that are different from the Hollywood elites. Just as Madison Avenue can be out of touch with the values and mores of mainstream America, so can Hollywood. Ron Howard and Brian Grazer's 1989 feel-good comedy about family life, *Parenthood*, was, to the surprise of the directors, offensive to initial focus group audiences. "The audience told us there was too much vulgarity in the movie," Grazer has said. "We took out a lot of the vulgarity. The scores went up, made us feel better, the movie played better. It didn't offend anybody."[369]

Focus groups helped the corporate suits overcome skepticism about *The X-Files* by revealing that the target audience was as alienated as the show's creators. Top brass at the Fox Network disliked the conspiratorial premise of *The X-Files*, that there had been "widespread covert activity to prevent the public from learning about the existence of UFOs." But when the network consulted focus groups, it made a discovery that would not surprise anyone with sustained exposure to ordinary Americans: not only did the participants not think the premise of *The X-Files* was preposterous, they thought it was realistic. *X-Files* creator Chris Carter has said, "The thing that was amazing to me was that . . . everyone believed the government was conspiring . . . No one even questioned the notion."[370]

Studio heads and creatives are predominantly white, middle-aged, affluent residents of the Los Angeles area, and they need focus groups to help them understand audiences hailing from other backgrounds. Fullerton remarks, on leading groups that touch on racial issues, "That's the kind of stuff I love because you don't know what you are going to find." She worked on a study for a company with several comedy TV shows (she could not reveal which company) attempting to understand the differences between black and white comedy viewers—and what kinds of shows might appeal to both groups. Fullerton, who is black and born in Jamaica, explains, "Like black and white people might watch Chris Rock, but only white people might be more interested in Penn and Teller. What's going on there?" She found that both blacks and whites enjoyed a serious movie with a diverse cast like *The Shawshank Redemption*, yet "in comedy, very little overlapped." White and black audiences had different reactions to humor about social issues, colored by different political views. Black audiences enjoyed social issue humor more than slapstick humor. *There's Something About Mary* was a flop with black groups. The client learned that there wasn't much it could do to get black people to like certain kinds of "white" comedy, a useful insight that may have helped plant the seed for the boom in hilarious black cable comedy of the nineteen nineties and early two thousands (including Dave Chappelle, Wanda Sykes, Chris Rock, the standups on *Def Comedy Jam*, and many others). As Fullerton explains, since black households constitute, as a percentage, more premium cable subscribers, companies were eager to understand and cater to them better. In that case, focus groups could reveal more than simple survey data, and helped the network bridge racial gaps to make decisions that were more profitable, serving more of its audience.

Fullerton also recalls running groups on comedian Chris Rock's image, in the early years of his HBO special. The focus groups loved his humor, but not his look. He wore sweaters—sweater vests, even.[371] As Fullerton recalls, Rock was "not very sharp-looking." Test audiences liked everything about the content of his brutally honest act, she recalls. "Believable, it was credible, it was right on point." They felt he was "telling it like it is." Paradoxically, she explained, with a note of surprise in her voice, "his lack of sophistication in terms of dress" meant people were not as eager to watch him. They felt, Fullerton emphasized, that Rock should "look more put together."

Of course, this was news to the entertainment industry honchos, for whom Rock was an artist and a black man, an "outsider" who could dress accordingly—after all, wouldn't the average person relate to Chris Rock *more* if he dressed like Everyman? Fullerton notes that this often happens with women and black stars—people want to see them looking their best, perhaps to better represent. "They wanted him to look like that aspirational quality," she muses. "They wanted him to be somebody you would want to take home." The focus groups helped identify a problem that the industry hadn't anticipated and had an effect on Rock's positioning as a human brand. "If you go back to his early shows," Fullerton says, "and you look at how he is now—he's much more chic. He's much more put together." Indeed, in 1994, in Rock's HBO special, *Big Ass Jokes*, he wears odd Chinese pajamas (with the abovementioned sweaters). Ten years later, he was wearing a suit[372] (and twelve years later, the lesson still seemed to stick: he wore a bow tie and dinner jacket to host the 2016 Oscars).

In the case of children's programming, the gap between producers and audience is obviously even greater than that between Santa Monica and Columbus, or even than America's well-known racial divide, making the need for testing even more intense. When Fullerton worked for Nickelodeon on kids' programming, she says of her client, "They wanted to be more in the world of the kids." While focus groups are often accused of dumbing down entertainment, it is not unusual in children's programming to underestimate the audience, because adults often assume that kids are less sophisticated than they are. Nickelodeon used its focus groups to figure out how to make the shows more challenging, so there would be, as Fullerton put it, "multilayers of the show so kids could discover certain things beyond what was shown . . . so it was kid-friendly but complex. There was a recognition that kids are not stupid."[373]

A focus group can also help to clarify that the movie makes sense. No one wants to release a movie only to find that critical matters of plot or background were incomprehensible to the viewers. Ron Howard has said,

"What I would hate to do is to put the movie out there, find that the audience is confused about something or upset about something that you could have fixed, and go, 'God I had no idea they would respond that way.'"[374]

It can help filmmakers understand their market, for better and for worse. Some in Hollywood swear by the methodology, for exactly these commercial reasons. Marcus Nispel, director of the 2003 remake of *The Texas Chainsaw Massacre* told *Adweek*,

> What's amazing is I now look at tracking, test results, focus groups with feverish passion . . . Before, you question everything, you think it all doesn't matter. Focus groups? What do people really know? Now that the movie is getting 95 percent approval ratings, it completely validates that focus groups are geniuses.[375]

Our entertainment has been market tested for a long time. In the late nineteen thirties, just before Lazarsfeld and Merton invented the focus group, independent companies emerged to offer market research to film studios. The rise of television posed a competitive threat to movies, prompting a need for better marketing. Television was also a more effective means of advertising movies than print newspapers, but also more expensive, raising the stakes for marketing strategies. Moreover, movies became a business in which serious money could be made, and studios needed to be able to explain to investors who their market was.[376] In the nineteen seventies, these economic changes were amplified by the fact that early generations of studio heads and founders were beginning to die out, according to film scholar Justin Wyatt, to be replaced by larger media conglomerates. The new captains of the movie industry spoke and thought like businesspeople, in the language of markets and profits.

There was, then, much more incentive and drive to make movies that were commercially successful. *Jaws*, the 1975 shark thriller that so terrified Generation X (whether we ever saw the movie—many of us stayed out of the water) was the first film to gross more than $100 million in the U.S. box office (by far, grossing over $260 million[377]). Late nineteen seventies Hollywood was characterized by a mind-set in which projects were increasingly chosen for their marketing potential, rather than artistic merit.[378] That drive for profits from investors and parent companies included demanding that studios perform more market research. Not only did they contract out to independent firms, as studios had always done, they also began hiring more executives with expertise in marketing and market research.[379]

The field of market research itself became more concerned with dividing audiences, not only according to race, gender, or age, but according to taste, sensibilities, and values—a practice that would strongly inform studios' way of thinking about audiences.

Today, focus groups often shape the plot of Hollywood movies, particularly endings. In fact, the "focus group ending" has become an accepted reality for the American moviegoer: the ending that is changed, at the last minute, because of a focus group's objection to the original. Roughly half of movies are re-shot after the focus groups, and about half the changes made concern the way the film closes.[380] It's common to shoot several different endings and focus group–test each.[381]

Focus groups had strong opinions about Glenn Close's temptress character in the 1987 backlash thriller *Fatal Attraction*. Screenwriter James Dearden had made a short film called *Diversion*, based on a short story with a similar plot. Producer Sherry Lansing, an actress-turned-movie-mogul who became chair of Paramount several years later, wanted to make it into a long feature-length film in order to develop sympathy for the single female character. Glenn Close shared that vision, saying years later, "I never thought of her as a villain."

The film that Lansing ultimately made, directed by Adrian Lyne, centers around an affair between a happily married lawyer (Michael Douglas, who was often cast as an oppressed white male during this culturally conservative period) and a sexually voracious book editor (Glenn Close). He tries to break it off, and she becomes obsessed with him. Much worse, she terrorizes his family, boiling his little girl's pet rabbit and threatening to kill his wife. The original ending had the Glenn Close character kill herself, and Michael Douglas's hapless married protagonist arrested for her murder—with a suggestion that he'll eventually be exonerated by a threatening tape that his wife has discovered. Focus group audiences hated this version, feeling that it did not inflict enough suffering—punishment—on the villainess.[382]

They got what they wanted. The movie was reshot so that the murderous adulteress was killed off by the wife.[383] Glenn Close herself fought this change, arguing—with the support of psychiatrists—that psychologically, it was far more plausible for her to self-destruct and kill herself. "When I heard they wanted to make my character into a psychopath, where I'd go after someone with a knife, rather than someone who was self-destructive and basically tragic, it was a profound problem for me," she told Douglas years later on Oprah.

> As I told you I did a lot of research about the character. I felt that even though there were a lot of secrets and people might not have understood all the behavior, I did. So to be brought back six months later, and told you were going to change that character, was very hard. And I think I fought against it for three weeks.

Douglas laughs affectionately, "Oh, you did." Close—who has, in recent years, campaigned to remove the stigma from mental illness—laughs, too, but with a quiet distance: "I was so mad."

Douglas continues, "But you were so good in the part, that everyone wanted you to be killed, wanted someone's hands around your throat."[384]

Fatal Attraction, which was the second highest grossing movie of 1987,[385] shows how the "focus group ending" can be completely at odds with the creative intentions behind the film. Close said she spoke with psychiatrists about whether Alex's behavior really was plausible, particularly the rabbit-boiling, which Close always viewed as "over the top." Said Close, "I always thought that she was a human being in a lot of pain and needed a lot of help."[386] The movie Lansing and Close had envisioned was exactly the opposite of the one that theater audiences ended up seeing.[387]

The feeling that the elite auteur should not have to listen to the people has held sway in Hollywood for even longer than it has in the rest of the corporate world. The entertainment industry has used focus groups since the origin of the methodology—recall that the focus group grew out of Lazarsfeld's radio industry research. And some in the movie industry had been using sophisticated survey techniques since the nineteen forties, with the help of George Gallup's Audience Research Institute.

Hollywood has a venerable history of resisting market research, feeling that making movies is an artistic, not a commercial, pursuit. Indeed, as Caltech English professor Catherine Jurca has pointed out, the role of the public in shaping films—and the industry's desire to find out what the public wanted—is spoofed in several movies of the late nineteen thirties and early nineteen forties. In *The Goldwyn Follies*, Hazel Dawes, a young woman who is supposed to represent the public's opinion, is distressed by the sad ending of the movie shown to her: "I didn't know Romeo and Juliet died," she says with dismay.[388] Some in the industry were inspired to incorporate methods similar to the focus groups developed by the work of Lazarsfeld and others testing World War II propaganda radio programs (discussed in chapter two), but they faced resistance from their peers, who felt that movie-making was an art and should be based on intuition.[389] In 1953, still trying to gain acceptance for his methods, film industry market researcher Leo Handel mocked this attitude as precious and elitist, sneering that the film industry people would rather depend on "the mystic 'feel' of the market which seems to reach its heights of potency in the air-conditioned private dining rooms of Bel Air and Miami Beach."[390]

Many entertainment business observers lament the effect of focus groups on movies and television. *Chicago Reader* film critic Jonathan Rosenbaum, in his book *Movie Wars*, argues that audiences are unfairly blamed for the dumbing down of movies. Studios—and their many apologists in the entertainment press—tell us that since market research "scientifically" proves that people have bad taste, Hollywood is just giving them what they want. Rosenbaum disagrees: ". . . [T]his line of reasoning is even more stupid, self-serving and self-deluded than the worst of these movies."[391] After all, he points out, "Test marketing assumes that an audience confronted with something new will arrive at a permanent verdict immediately after seeing it. But our experience of movies . . . seldom works that way." Our assumptions and expectations shape our initial reaction, and "once we get past them all sorts of delayed responses become possible; a day or month or week later, what initially made us querulous might win us over completely." The focus group, he feels, can only measure that initial response.[392]

The focus group has, over the years, had plenty of detractors among Hollywood insiders as well. Director Robert Altman called it "a process I don't believe in, and I don't think is correct for my kind of films."[393] He got his revenge in *The Player* by parodying a Hollywood focus group–directed process. A pair of writers has pitched a tale of gritty hard luck, in which the protagonist is executed at the end. After a focus group objects, the studio executive changes the ending to a more upbeat one. A colleague asks, "What about truth? What about reality?" Our cynical executive replies, "What about the way the old ending tested in Canoga Park? Everybody hated it. Now we reshot it, and everyone loves it. That's reality."

Altman isn't alone. Says Fullerton, "Especially in the entertainment business . . . creative people don't want to be told what to do by consumers." She explains, "Creative people feel that the audience that they're talking to, they know what's really good for them." Creative talent's war on the focus group is evident from the ways in which the writers in Hollywood, as on Madison Avenue, get their revenge by inventing plots that lampoon focus groups, not only on *Frasier*, but on shows ranging from *King of the Hill* to *Mad Men*.

Broadway uses focus groups, too, though the practice is less accepted in the theater world than in Hollywood. Julie Taymor's infamously disastrous *Spider Man: Turn Off the Dark* production was extensively focus grouped before the show began, and then again, once the musical opened to terrible reviews.[394] (Critics bemoaned the confusing plot and an absurd excess of special effects. *New York Times* theater critic Ben Brantley called its February 2011 opening "an ungodly indecipherable mess . . . like watching the Hindenberg crash and burn." He deemed its re-release that June "just a bore."[395]) After Taymor, who directed the wildly successful *Lion King*, was fired from *Spider Man* in March 2011, she publicly criticized the show's producers for relying on focus groups. She said she had adamantly opposed the focus groups, finding their use in the theater world "very scary." She felt that audiences should not be able to "tell you how to make a show . . . Shakespeare would have been appalled." Her comments echoed those of Steve Jobs and other innovators: "It's just in the nature of things that when you're doing something very new, audiences don't know how to talk about it immediately." She said, of the use of focus groups for live theater, that she "did not believe in it on any level," noting that if she'd used them for the *Lion King*, the show would have been quite different: one of the main characters dies early in the show, and it is unlikely that test audiences would have approved such a sad event.[396]

Auteurs, critics, and fans blame focus groups for everything that's wrong with entertainment. But this is probably wrongheaded. For one thing, says Donna Fullerton, in battles between researchers and entertainment industry creatives, most of the time, the auteurs win.

Fullerton, who has worked extensively as a focus group moderator for entertainment companies, including Nickelodeon, HBO, and many others, says that the influence of focus groups on entertainment is never as dramatic as people fear. Despite the high-profile examples discussed in this chapter, writers still have more sway, ultimately, than the researchers. (She would like to see focus group findings considered more often than they are, to improve certain elements of the story—a character, a plot twist. But of course, she is a market researcher.) This makes conducting focus groups in the entertainment industry far different from research on consumer products; clients are, she says, far less likely to act on researchers' findings.

But whether or not Fullerton is right, focus groups aren't the only reason movies have gotten so bad. Rather, a reliance on market resarch is a symptom of a bigger problem: the increasing importance of the profit motive and greater involvement of financial and corporate elites. Those are the people who should properly be blamed. "Focus groups" can be an easy scapegoat for a sense that our entertainment is too marketized, with not enough space for artistic experimentation or political dissent. Even if studio heads didn't test the movies, the profit motive would dumb down movies in other ways: with the repeated use of commercially successful formulas, the literal recycling of plots and characters in the form

Lobby card for the 1938 film *Goldwyn Follies*. Market research has long been lampooned in Hollywood movies, reflecting resentment of the process in the entertainment industry; this movie was an early example. Copyright allows editorial use. From The Movie Stills Database.

of sequels and remakes, and the pre-emptive underestimation of the audience that accompanies almost any serious attempt to make money from a cultural product.

It's intriguing to consider that one problem might not be too much consultation, but not enough. The entertainment industry's recent experience shows that perhaps it's more creatively fruitful to engage fans on a deeper level than the traditional focus group can.

All these years of market research have primed the industry—and consumers—for a culture of consultation, that, via the internet, can be far more intense than a focus group, leaving creators even more open to public input that is more spontaneous and sometimes more meaningful.

In recent years, blogs and social media have loomed larger and provided alternative ways for the entertainment industry to hear from consumers, especially serious fans. (Of course, one salient difference is that participants in this type of consultation are unpaid.) Blogs, internet discussion groups, and websites for hard-core fans of *Buffy the Vampire Slayer* and other Joss Whedon shows influenced these shows' plots. (*Buffy* had more than one million fan websites.) Sometimes fans let the show's creators know what was working—or not: as Whedon said in an interview when asked how the fans influence the show,

> I think it's really neat . . . sure, I'll read the posting board. I'm always interested to see what people are responding to, and what they're not. To an extent it does [affect me]. For example, when I saw that people were rejecting the Oz character when he was first introduced, I realized how carefully I had to place him. I wrote scenes where Willow falls in love with him in a way where fans would fall in love with him too. You learn that people don't take things at face value; you have to earn them.[397]

The fan sites inspired specific plot developments (such as Buffy and Spike getting married, or Giles and Anya believing they had been married). Many sites include "fan fiction," fiction created by the fans and based on the show. Such creative efforts often inspired the writers, thus blurring the boundaries between consumer and producer.

Some shows have formalized the blurring of those boundaries, allowing fans to actually make the show at times. In 2015, at the end of *Mad Men*'s on-air tenure, AMC launched "Mad Men: The Fan Cut," a contest resulting in an entirely fan-created episode. AMC's executive vice president for marketing, Linda Schupack, described the fan episode as "tremendously well-received," emphasizing not the artistic quality but the feeling of participation. "They're allowing people to engage deeply with the world of *Mad Men* and make it their own . . . a very special thing."[398] There have also been fan-made episodes of *My Little Pony* and *Star Wars*.

The gaming industry is experimenting with these strategies as well, and there are already beloved fan-made remakes of popular video games including *Pokemon* and *Super Mario Bros.* The industry sometime allows fans to contribute ideas and storylines, as well as voting on characters, weapons, and designs.[399] One gamer blog noted that it's an "embarrassment" to the industry how much better some of the fan-made games are, given they are created "for free."[400] Another gaming writer has called it "the future of game development."

We may see the use of focus groups decline in entertainment, not because creatives don't like them—that's always been true—but because technology offers much less formal and, ultimately, more ways to involve the viewer, and many of these are also more satisfying forms of participation. While everyone complains about the "focus group ending," many viewers want even more input into the plot of their favorite TV shows and video games than a focus group ever could have provided. A 2010 survey commissioned by a firm called Diffusion PR found that more than two-thirds of viewers aged eighteen to forty-four would like to use live voting polls to influence the plot of their favorite shows.[401] For the culture industry, new and ever more lively forms of consultation are constantly emerging.

Canton, Ohio, 1980

A group of eleven Americans are gathered in a blue-collar city. It's July of an election year. The discussion has been convened to shed light on Ronald Reagan's presidential campaign. In describing how things are going in America, panelists use words like "confused," "discouraged," "worried," and "brow-beaten."

A man says, "Everyone is struggling so hard to make ends meet."

A man says people are questioning "how strong a country we really are, because with the problems in Iraq and Afghanistan we haven't done anything to show our strength."

Another man says, "Unless things are turned around, we're in trouble."

They agree, "People are no longer together for a common cause or purpose."

"We are looking for someone who is strong, who knows what he wants and who doesn't mind telling people what he thinks—not just what they want to hear."[402]

Chapter Seven: "Where is the Emotion?" The Emergence of the Focus Group in Electoral Politics

The moms are talking about layoffs. Their hours have been cut. Wages frozen. They have been pinching pennies any way they can: cut back on the cable TV, take fewer car trips to save gas, storing up coupons.

Asked how things are going in the country, they use words like "depressing," "scary," "discouraging," "confusing," and "sour." They feel the economy is getting worse. They do not believe news reports that say it is getting better, nor politicians who say the same.

They don't see any evidence of a recovery, not in their own lives. "If I go to the store one more time and see that the price of milk has gone up again, I'll just scream!," one mom fumed.

When it comes to politics, they're not worried about gay marriage or abortion—they are thinking about one thing: jobs. They're worried about how they will ever pay for their kids' college education—even if the kids in question are just one or two years old.

They're trying to stay positive. Faith in God. Also, grateful. They love their families. At least one adult in the household still has a job. The moms are resourceful, doing what they can to get by. They donate blood. They collect cans.

Most of them voted for Obama the last time around. They'd like to think he's doing his best, but they're not sure. They feel he has lost his passion and they are confused about whether to give him another chance.

Some of the moms blame Wall Street and the big banks for the problems in the economy. They're mad that the banks were bailed out, yet no one is helping families like theirs. They don't blame Obama, or Congress, for the country's economic problems, but they're frustrated that politicians haven't done more to help. They mostly don't know the names of our Congressional leaders—like John Boehner or Nancy Pelosi—but they still feel that Congress could bicker less and compromise more. But mostly when they look at the economic situation of the country, they blame themselves and other ordinary Americans like themselves—for living beyond their means, buying houses they could not afford.

Where are we? A discussion group organized by Occupy Wall Street? A labor union? The Democratic Party? A government seeking input on its economic policies? A sociology professor seeking insight into the impact of economic inequality?

No, the surprising sponsor of this encounter group was Walmart.

The "Walmart Moms" focus groups were held in fall 2011 in Orlando, Florida, Manchester, New Hampshire, and Des Moines, Iowa, with women who had children under eighteen and had shopped at Walmart at least once in the past month. Walmart commissioned Democratic and Republican research firms to do the work, and the study was released with much fanfare: LOOK WHAT THE WALMART MOMS ARE THINKING, one typical headline exclaimed.[403] It was accepted by the media as a revealing look into the mind of the struggling working-class woman, and in a way, maybe it was.[404]

Walmart is a company by now famous for discriminating against female workers—the target of a decade-long lawsuit *Betty Dukes v. Walmart*, the largest civil rights class action suit in history[405]—and failing to pay living wages to its majority-female workforce. It's also famous for making staggering profits off that workforce, making the Walton family—heirs of Walmart founder Sam Walton—the richest in the United States.

Women are paid less than men in nearly every position at the company—even male cashiers make more than female cashiers. The company has also been accused of leading a race to the bottom in wages for the retail industry—driving down wages throughout the sector, the majority of whose employees are women. Such criticisms have been dogging Walmart for years, but because the discrimination case had gone to the Supreme Court, the headlines about discrimination loomed especially large the year this focus group convened.

No wonder Walmart wanted to position itself to working-class women—who are, after all, its largest customer group by far—not as oppressor, but as listener.

"Walmart Moms are a big deal," reads the flattering copy on the company's website touting the findings. The groups allowed the company to present itself as the confidant, with special insight into the struggles of the nation's moms.

Walmart simultaneously created a new demographic category and cast itself as a friend of America's struggling women with its bipartisan "Walmart Moms" focus groups. This only ratified what most Americans at some level already understood: that politics and consumerism had become one and the same. Both required the participation and opinions of ordinary people, yet granted big corporations the power to make the important decisions. Just as significantly, it showed that a company beseiged by criticism—in this case, for its treatment of working-class women—could easily change the subject by listening. With the creation of these focus groups, and by labeling them "Walmart Moms," Walmart deftly re-branded itself from oppressor to champion of the nation's hard-working women.

Most of all, the Walmart Moms group—and the public relations campaign surrounding it—enacted one of the central political paradoxes of our time: ordinary people are listened to more than ever, even as they have less and less real power. Only in this sort of political environment could a company notorious for rendering working-class women powerless and exploited then turn around and theatrically display their voices, one in which elites ignore the actual needs of the masses—in this company's case, for living wages, healthcare, and equal treatment—but listen to them endlessly.

How did we get here?

While the early, mid-century focus group had a political purpose—recall that Lazarsfeld was hired to test the government's World War II propaganda, an elite aim in the service of a democratic agenda over the ensuing decades—its use came to reflect a changing relationship between the masses and elites: one in which elites pursued a markedly undemocratic agenda, listening to the people endlessly, with the aim of selling them stuff they didn't need, like Vitamin Water, or policies that are not in their interests.

Over the course of the late twentieth century, the focus group became increasingly central to politics, beginning its ascendance in the mid-nineteen seventies.

Some conspicuous listening had been deployed before that time. When Roger Ailes (who would years later become head of Fox News, and later still be disgraced by a torrent of sexual harassment allegations) was running Richard Nixon's 1968 campaign, extensively advised by admen, he put panels of ordinary people on television with the candidate. These did have something in common with the modern-day televised political focus group. As described in Joe McGinniss's *The Selling of the President*, they were opportunities to demonstrate conspicuous listening, as ordinary citizens like cab drivers (and Ailes always insisted, "one Negro, not two" and no farmers since farmers' issues are boring to everyone else) were rounded up to ask Nixon questions in person. But these were campaign performances engineered to show the candidate having "real" conversations with "real" people—a feat that few Americans were confident Nixon could pull off. The point was not to explore the panelists' opinions—as it is in a contemporary focus group—but to humanize a candidate who was often difficult to love.[406]

Just a few years later, Republican candidates were using real focus groups to shape political messaging. Celinda Lake, now one of the best-known Democratic pollsters, says of her own entry into the world of focus groups, "I learned from Republicans." Her first brush with the method came when working for Republican candidate Gerald Ford in 1976.[407] One of the Ford campaign's significant focus group–guided decisions concerned an ad showing Ford flinching after an assassination attempt.

It was intended to show the candidate's resilience and determination to serve his country despite the dangers he'd faced doing so. But focus groups found it too "shocking" as the memory of the JFK assassination was still raw. The ad never aired.[408]

At the time, focus groups were in wider use by Republicans than by Democrats,[409] perhaps because, realizing they were a party of business elites, they were quicker to grasp the gap between themselves and the masses. But the Democrats quickly caught on.

As James Harding has documented in his 2008 book *Alpha Dogs*, a company called the Sawyer Miller Group was a leader in bringing techniques from the world of advertising into widespread use in politics—revealing not just how people felt, but why. Focus groups were critical to this project.

One of the founders of the firm was Ned Kennan. He had figured out that selling consumer products was more about unconscious than rational communication. The focus group could reveal people's feelings. As Harding describes, in trying to figure out how to sell more Listerine, Kennan discovered through his focus groups that people who used Listerine—a mouthwash—were people who followed the rules. Didn't run red lights. Paid taxes. When they bought an appliance, they would read and follow the directions on how to use it. And they followed the directions on the bottle, fill the cap and gargle. His advice: just make the cap bigger! They'll keep following the directions and they will buy more.

Kennan's first political campaign was for Boston Mayor Kevin White in the nineteen seventies. The mayor and his team felt he was misunderstood—despite all he'd done for the city, no one liked him. Kennan conducted focus groups, then told him, They're never going to like you. Own it. Your campaign is, "Kevin White is crazy but he loves this city and makes it work."[410] White won, and the Sawyer Miller firm was launched as a powerhouse in the political focus group industry. It would expand dramatically throughout the nineteen eighties.

Andy Tuck remembers sitting on the stoop of his Upper West Side apartment building one morning in the early nineteen nineties reading the *New York Times* with a jittery feeling—no coffee needed. Skimming the headlines, he realized that his firm was involved in almost every story on the front page—and page two as well. After years of being mired in the insignificant world of consumer products, the move to political consulting brought a heady feeling of relevance.

Tuck was a market researcher who had been leading focus groups for years. A musician and philosophy professor, he had gone into the advertising industry to better provide for his family.

Everyone admits that consumer focus groups can be boring. Andy Tuck explains that when the topic is consumer goods, "There's often nothing you can do" to make people want to engage. If they are not already passionate consumers of your brand or its competitors, "it doesn't matter what words you use. There's no way to make them care."[411]

Lily Marotta, a veteran focus group participant, says this problem of apathy among participants is widespread. She recalls participating in a discussion of different ad campaigns for a gum brand. The group facilitator wanted to know

> what we liked about them, what we thought of when we saw them, what emotions we had. That's what they were really trying to get—what emotions we were feeling. I'm like, It's gum. I'm not feeling a lot of emotions from this.[412]

This rarely happens in the political focus group.

After years of trying to get consumers to care about, in his words "Excedrin vs. Tylenol," Andy Tuck felt he really lucked out when Young & Rubicam did some work for the first Bush administration, testing people's feelings about invasion of Kuwait, through focus groups. He explains that it is "easier and more rewarding" to run groups on political issues than on consumer preferences, "because people actually do care . . . [politics] affects their lives. It's going to raise their taxes, it's going to lower their taxes, it's going to change who goes to their public schools . . ."

Tuck is a liberal Democrat, so of course he didn't agree with the Bush administration's policies. Yet he found the work riveting, because it explored issues that were actually significant, unlike the color of a Maxi Pad box. He characterizes the project with wry self-deprecation: "I worked with a couple of other nice people on a big report, sent that off, they had a war—I felt a little ambivalent." He laughs, adding with a self-conscious nod at my tape recorder, "Yes, please record, 'He laughed.'"

Despite his ambivalence about the Kuwait war, Tuck was hooked on political consulting: "I just loved it." Having for years deployed what he called "these dopey, banal techniques" for the advertising industry, it was exhilarating to use them for more significant political purposes.

He couldn't wait to do more. Through a Young & Rubicam colleague, he recalls, "I found, luckily enough, a firm who worked only for the Democratic Party." That firm was the Sawyer Miller Group.

The ninety-hour-a-week job with Sawyer Miller, recalls Tuck, "was so much fun, it was the best job I've ever had in my life . . . that was where I saw all these techniques used at their maximum effectiveness."

President Ford flinching at the sound of gunfire during an assassination attempt by Sara Jane Moore in San Francisco, September 22, 1975. Focus groups rejected a similar image for an ad campaign, letting consultants know that voters were still raw from the JFK assassination and not ready for presidential vulnerability. Provided to Wikimedia Commons by the Gerald R. Ford Presidential Library and Museum. Public domain.

Political crisis consulting is exciting because the outcomes matter. Tuck explains,

> When there's very important live-or-die, win-or-lose decisions to be made, that's when strategy matters more, and that's where strategic research matters more. So what you can learn out of two, four, six, eight focus groups is extraordinarily important, and you waste no time. Everything's crucial. Every reaction, every raised eyebrow.
>
> Every time anybody pushes back from the table, you want to understand that because it's going to affect whether you win or lose, whether your candidate gets an extra ten thousand votes . . . or loses those ten thousand votes.
>
> Sometimes a pushback from the table is just a pushback from the table. But you want to find out, you want to ask. So if you're a good moderator you'll actually say, "Hey George. I noticed you just leaned away from the table. Did you have a big meal or is it something that Randy just said?" . . . Does he seem pissed off? Does he seem like he's been insulted? Does he seem like he's pulling out of the group and doesn't really want to be a part of it anymore because he thinks, "I don't want to get in a fight because these aren't my people" . . . And that stuff always comes up really clearly when you're doing politics.[413]

In the early twentieth century, when polling first began to occupy a central place in American political culture, public opinion researcher Paul Cherington celebrated his industry's potential to give the "vox populi" a "voice" and "restore effective democracy."[414]

Advertising pioneer Claude Hopkins wrote in 1927, long before the focus group, that growing up in poverty helped his career and fueled his enthusiasm for market research:

> I do know the common people. I love to talk to laboring men, to study housewives who must count their pennies, to gain the

confidence and learn the ambitions of poor boys and girls . . . My words may be simple, my sentences short. Scholars may ridicule my style. The rich may laugh . . . but in many humble households the common people will read and buy. They will feel the writer knows them. And they, in advertising, form 95 percent of our customers.[415]

This understanding of market research as a populist and democratic project persisted. As the tools for selling consumer goods became more embedded in the political system, we see more language extolling techniques like focus groups as bringing more democracy to the consumer markeplace: CEOs, the men of Sawyer Miller liked to say, were "up for election every single day."[417] The marketing world had convinced itself that its methods of gauging public opinon were actually more democratic than political mechanisms like voting—so therefore, what a brilliant twist to use them to democratize real life democracy.

In the nineteen eighties, the increasingly strategic and central role of focus groups in politics was part of a dramatic expansion in the political polling and influence industries. Reagan spent more than a million dollars per year on polling (including focus groups), while Carter, his predecessor, had spent only $250,000.

The explosion of the culture of consultation was fueled, appropriately, by people called "consultants." Beginning in the nineteen sixties, political candidates began reaching beyond their supporters and volunteers, seeking professional help with public opinion research and media. By the nineteen eighties, this was a huge industry: every presidential and statewide political campaign hired professional consultants.[418] In 1982, the *New York Times* noted that "politicians are relying more than in the past on campaign consultants," and that these professionals were branching beyond their specialties to "take over campaigns completely." The *Times* also noted that such professionals' numbers and fees were growing every year.[419]

One of the most important of these consultants was Reagan's pollster, Richard Wirthlin. A sophisticated political entrepreneur, Wirthlin's business was not limited to the president; in 1982, his polling and strategy firm had eighty employees and was running about one hundred campaigns around the nation.[420] He was not politically far right, though he also worked for

Barry Goldwater and Margaret Thatcher. But he enjoyed Reagan's "innate optimism"—as he would write in an autobiography later[421]—and rhetorical talent, and the two men worked well together. In 1976 Wirthlin devised a public opinion research strategy for Reagan that would lead to his 1980 victory; it included polling, interviews, and focus groups.

Wirthlin was constantly testing the impact of Reagan's rhetoric and making sure he was tapping into shared values—especialy the themes of family, neighborhood, workplace, freedom. This strategy ensured, according to Wirthlin ghostwriter Wynton Hall—himself a communication strategist—that even if Reagan's "policies aren't popular the rhetoric surrounding them can be."[422] This was a critical shift in the use of the focus group: it could be used, not to find out what people wanted, but how to get them to accept things they didn't want at all.

Wirthlin arranged for viewers to watch TV with a dial device, that they could use to indicate whether they liked or didn't like a particular passage of speech. Similar to the Lazarsfeld-Stanton Program Analyzer, these devices had been used to test political campaign ads since the nineteen sixties. Wirthlin, however, was the first to integrate the technology into a sitting president's communication strategy.

"You persuade by reason," said Wirthlin, "but if you want to motivate you have got to do it through emotion. You do that by tapping into people's values."[423] He made "caring maps" to chart how the American people felt about things.

Wirthlin used focus groups at some key historic moments. For example, in 1985, every time Reagan delivered a speech about Soviet relations and disarmament, the president used phrases that had been tested by focus groups[424] with American audiences, and retained the phrases that tested well. He knew what he wanted to do—end the Cold War—but he needed to package it in the right way so the American people would accept it, emphasizing themes like peace through strength, and phrases like "a fresh start."[425] Wirthlin, in a 2010 interview, told the *New York Times* he was proud of the role his focus groups played in helping Reagan set the stage for disarmament—allowing the conservative hawk who had originally called the Soviet

Union an "evil empire" to find a rhetoric of peace that would resonate with Americans.[426]

Both Democratic and Republican consultants in this period were clear that the focus groups did not shape the policies; rather, leaders knew what they wanted to do and used focus groups to figure out how to sell these policies. Indeed, *The Public Mind*, a 1989 documentary, suggests just how little the nineteen eighties' rise in political focus groups had to do with actually listening to people's ideas or concerns. Stanley Greenberg, one of the most prominent Democratic pollsters, in an interview for the film, echoed Wirthlin on feelings: "The goal of the group is really to find out where is the emotion, you know?"[427]

The film shows footage from a group in New Jersey.

Stanley Greenberg: Our goal is really to talk through, as honestly and openly as we can, about the subjects and really get into the kinds of things you feel about the subjects.

Participant: Right now car insurance for me is just an annoyance, it's not a top priority for me, it's just a minor annoyance, I'd rather see them addressing more serious issues, like life, living, and breathing. But I think it's only to get worse, and the New Jersey Turnpike and use of toxic waste . . . there are hot spots all along the New Jersey Turnpike and this area, we are, one of those hot spots for cancer and it's only going to get worse.

SG: What's your greatest fear when you think about the environment?

P: That in ten years we might not be sitting here.

P: Death. Death of the human population. We're destroying everything in sight and it primarily has happened in the past fifty years.

P: Pollution, toxic waste, what they do to foods, where we're gonna put it, landfills, by me we're recycling, but they think that's the biggest inconvenience in the world, but we have to start thinking about this, you know, where we're gonna be putting all of this stuff.

The focus group participants were asked to vote on whether they want a candidate that cares about the environment or about insurance. When the environment candidate won the show of hands, the participants were asked why:

> **P**: Well because once the environment's gone it's all over. You can always work with things that are financial, I mean you can always get a grip on these, but once the environment's gone, it's gone, we're not getting it back, it's not something we can go out and change it, you can always change these other things.

> **P**: If you're dying of pollution, you're not worried about higher rates.

> **P**: Of course I want them to worry about all issues, but if I had to pick one, of course, it has to be the environment, that's your life.[428]

Reflecting on the group, Greenberg conspicuously didn't say that maybe since voters are concerned about the environment, politicians should make it a policy priority. Rather, he mused, "You can address a problem with media. You try to do something with media that offsets that problem. So that you get filmed on the beach showing you care about the environment."[429]

The political focus group took off in this period in part because it was needed more than ever to bridge the widening gap between masses and elites. With the experiences of the haves and have-nots increasingly diverging, so were their political agendas, meaning that the goal of the focus group became, increasingly, not to find out what the people need but to determine how best to sell them on policies at odds with their interests.

After all, in this period, as the Cold War wound down, the class war escalated—with the ruling class on the offensive. During the nineteen seventies, capitalist elites had been concerned about the predictability of their profits and about whether they could continue to dominate the world. The Soviet Union supported communist countries in Latin America and in Africa. At home, in the United States, workers were going on wildcat strikes and unions were strong in many sectors. Ralph Nader's consumer movement and a growing environmental consciousness had corporate America scared. Although voter participation was not especially high during this period, all other forms of political participation were—whether attending protests or working on electoral campaigns.[430] Economic elites feared that they—and their privileges—were under attack.

In 1971, Lewis Powell, a corporate lawyer Nixon would appoint to the Supreme Court the following year, wrote a memo to Eugene Sydnor, the director of the Chamber of Commerce, in which he eloquently expressed these fears. While conspiracy theorists have no doubt made too much of the Powell memo, it does offer a window onto elite thinking; it was ahead of its time, but helped to catalyze a new way of thinking for the ruling class. Powell wrote, "The assault on the enterprise system is broadly based and consistently pursued. It is gaining momentum and converts." He worried that both the media and the universities were dominated by opponents and skeptics of free enterprise, and that business elites had been too passive, too willing to appease its critics, and needed to mobilize and fight back. "The time has come—indeed, it is long overdue," Powell exhorted, "for the wisdom, ingenuity and resources of American business to be marshaled against those who would destroy it." He plaintively demanded in a sub-heading in the memo, "WHAT CAN BE DONE ABOUT THE PUBLIC?"[431]

In 1975, Samuel Huntington and a group of other elite thinkers wrote a similar report called *A Crisis of Democracy*. The Trilateral Commission, described in *Foreign Affairs* magazine the following year as "an organization of influential private citizens,"[432] had been formed in 1972 at a meeting at the Rockefeller family's 3,510-acre estate in Pocantico, about half an hour north of New York City. Overlooking the Hudson River, the estate, built by oil industry profits, boasts terraced beaux arts gardens, a nine-hole golf course, a collection of classic cars and horse carriages, and a major private art collection including works by Picasso, Calder, Warhol, and Chagall. The meeting was hosted by David Rockefeller, chairman of Chase Manhattan Bank and grandson of oil tycoon John D. Rockefeller, who told those in attendance that it was time for elites to organize: the governments of rich countries were drifting "aimlessly." "Now," he admonished, "is a propitious time for persons from the private sector to make a valuable contribution to public policy."[433] The Trilateral Commission was founded to promote a foreign policy more favorable to the global economic elite, and more coordination among the elites of Western countries, in reaction to what some saw as the Nixon administration's unilateralism. They were concerned that increasing coordination among oil-exporting countries and, especially, "Third World militancy" were threatening their economic and political dominance.[434] But they were also worried about their ability, as elites, to maintain hegemony and order at home. It turned out that their idea of a "crisis of democracy" was actually an "excess of democracy." They worried that all this popular empowerment had gone too far and wondered, "Is political democracy, as it exists today, a viable form of government for the industrialized countries of Europe, North America, and Asia?" They fretted that the people had been participating too much and had gotten too much of what they wanted. As a result, government was too big, while the authority of those holding state power was not respected. The Trilateral Commission suggested that the cure for this excess of democracy was a little less democracy, or, as they put it, "a greater degree of moderation in democracy."[435]

Such warnings were heeded, and the capitalist elites mobilized against popular will. The result was a tremendous consolidation of elite power in the nineteen seventies and nineteen eighties. Lobbying firms to advance capitalist interests increased; a study by the Greater Washington Board of Trade showed that while there were 1,700 lobbying organizations in 1977, there were 2,000 in 1980, and that one or two new ones emerged every week.[436] In *Lobbying America: The Politic of Business from Nixon to NAFTA*, Benjamin Waterhouse argues that in this period, American business began to translate its economic power into political influence and to far more aggressively shape policy.[437]

For all Wirthlin's "caring maps", and increasing attentiveness to the feelings of the average American, recall that in 1981, President Ronald Reagan fired air traffic controllers who refused to call off their strike and broke their union—an action that would embolden employers everywhere and thus permanently reshape the workplace in their favor.[438] Corporate power was on the rise, and popular power was under attack—no matter how attentively Reagan's advisors listened to the people.

As the real political power of the American public declined—whether we consider Americans as citizens, workers, people who breathe air and drink water—they were, paradoxically, listened to more than ever. They could give their opinion freely in a focus group, and feel the frisson of having influence. But increasingly, the average Americans could not join a union, or expect to be paid decently and fairly for their labor with some measure of job security—all things that give people real power.

About a decade into the political consultation explosion, in an article describing the pervasive influence of focus groups on political campaigns, the *New York Times Magazine* noted this paradox:

> It has become a commonplace of American political discourse that so-called ordinary people have no say in the process, that the average citizen's opinion counts for less and less in a system dominated by special interests. Yet nearly every day, somewhere in the country, conversations . . . are being staged among people who have been chosen precisely because of their ordinariness. These people are encouraged to say exactly what's on their minds. They are treated with great solicitude and even paid a fee for the trouble of expressing their opinions, and their thoughts and feelings can end up, sometimes verbatim, in policy speeches and campaign literature. These sessions, called focus groups, are becoming ever more influential, even as the power of the "little guy" allegedly evaporates.[439]

The *Times* was right to note the tension, though wrong to suggest that the rise of focus groups cast doubt on the "commonplace" narrative. There was nothing merely "alleged" about the evaporating power of the little guy.

Then and now, the opinions of average people appear to have had little effect on policy. In a 2014 paper, Martin Gilens and Benjamin Page, political scientists at Princeton and Northwestern, respectively, studied 1,779 policy cases between 1981 and 2002, examining the opinions of Americans at the fiftieth income percentile, those of Americans at the ninetieth income percentile, and those of interest groups listed on *Fortune* magazine's "Power 25." Gilens and Page found that while their better-off fellow citizens and business interest groups had a significant influence on policy outcomes, average Americans enjoyed little to none.[440]

Toward the end of the century, the "average" American's opinions were avidly sought after, but they mattered very little. Ordinary people were eagerly listened to, but they had no power. Indeed, the focus groups were needed precisely *because* actual ordinary people were so marginal to the political process; as politics became more controlled by elites, the gap between the political class and the average person grew. Thus, the spread of the focus group was a symptom of the estrangement between politicians and the rest. While the *New York Times Magazine* writer, in 1992, saw the rise of the focus group as somehow at odds with—perhaps even contradictory to—the narrative of the common person's declining political power, it was not. The focus group was an elite solution to that problem. Ordinary people had been shut out of meaningful policy-making, but to win their votes, politicians still needed to hear from them.

New York, 2012

Today we are a small group—only four people—of middle-aged professionals discussing financial services. The moderator, Bob, introduces himself, but he cannot reveal the name of the client. This is often the case in a focus group.

He tells us he has led every kind of focus group. He has interviewed four-year-olds about TV shows—cute but exhausting—and (his favorite) he has spent time on the links chatting with groups of elderly people about golf carts.

Bob gets reflective discussing his work:

> **When I say I travel a lot for this job, people say, that sounds like fun. But the truth is that travel is the least fun part of my job. I'm always on airplanes. I went to San Francisco and sat for two weeks in windowless rooms!**

But talking to people is the fun part. I talk to every imaginable person about every imaginable topic.

If I'm not interested one week, I know I just have to wait another week and it will be another group and another topic.

Our topic is personal finance.

We introduce ourselves. Ana's husband lives in Virginia. "It's wonderful," she says. "We never have time to have any problems." They have no kids and two cats. She designs luggage and he is a statistician. They are doing well. But she thinks she needs some financial advice. She has been with Chase forever. It seems like a lot of trouble to switch banks.

Steve is also married with two cats and no kids. He and his wife run a small achitectural engineering firm.

I'm a married writing professor with one kid and one cat. I don't say that I'm writing about focus groups.

Joanne is an opera singer. She wishes banks would provide an advocate who would translate all their offerings into what she calls "my language." She banks with Citibank and gets no interest on her checking account.

Bob shows us some promotional copy. Joanne finds the bank's claims unrealistic. Steve agrees, pointing out that the bank seems to be promising good returns without risk.

Ana and I are swayed by their skepticism. Some would say this is, therefore, not our "real" opinion.

But this is precisely why group discussions are useful to marketers: we rarely make decisions in a vacuum. We are influenced by others, and the way we can work and think together is part of what they can reveal.

Chapter Eight: "God and Coca-Cola": The Story of New Coke

He has an eccentric, rumpled, and professorial look, with a large, bohemian Afro, but he's a lot more square than he looks. Because much of his work illuminates business practices, he is paid substantial sums for addressing corporate audiences. Malcolm Gladwell, *New Yorker* writer and author of such best-sellers as *Blink* and *The Tipping Point*, is probably the most famous and prominent mainstream critic of the focus group. He feels that "focus groups generally fail"[441]—an argument he makes often but never presents any data to support.

In his TED talks, books, and other offerings of punditry, Gladwell often uses New Coke as an example of the failings of focus groups. He finds, in the story of New Coke, "a really good illustration of how complicated it is to find out what people really think."[442] In his version of this narrative—which has become conventional—Coke asked consumers, in blind taste tests, which cola they liked better. The problem with this approach, in Gladwell's view, is that we have different reactions to the taste of a beverage after a sip than we do after drinking an entire can. It also disregards, argues Gladwell, an important marketing concept called sensation transference—the insight that the taste or feeling of a product is intertwined with the packaging. That is, part of the reason we like the taste of Coke is that (back in the day) we loved the bottle, and we still love the logo, the red, the squiggly lettering. *"In the real world,"* Gladwell admonishes (the emphasis is his), *"no one ever drinks Coca-Cola blind."*[443]

In the nineteen fifties, as we've seen, critics like Vance Packard worried that market research techniques were used by corporations to manipulate the people. But at the turn of the century such criticism came even more often from within the corporate elite. Many began, increasingly, to worry that they were listening too much. The leader who refused to listen, who disregarded the carping masses, became a new ideal, a sort of corporate and neoliberal incarnation of the romance novel hero, who eschews sensitivity (and consultation), simply sweeping our heroine off her feet.

Focus groups became, in the nineteen nineties and early two thousand, a frequent subject of mockery, as Ruth Shalit noted in in Salon in 1999.[444] In one ad that year, for Little Caesars pizza, eclectic groups were asked whether they wanted more cheese and more toppings on their pizza, including "Star Trekkies, clowns and a Brazilian rain forest tribe" and finally culminating in a herd of orangutans.[445] It's a joke about the extent and reach, by this time, of the culture of consultation. There's also a sense of weariness in the ad—do we really need to ask *everyone* what they think?

One person's weariness is another person's anxiety—and this was part of the emotional landscape of the nineteen nineties elite as well. Where Packard tapped into the fear that the public was manipulated by elites, by the end of the century, the fear about focus groups that was most often publicly articulated was almost the opposite one: that the elites would be led astray by the public.

Gladwell is pithy. He also has a knack for telling elites what they want to hear. When it comes to New Coke, as is so often the case, the story is more complicated than a TED talk. The story of New Coke is one that emerged specifically from the zeitgest of the nineteen eighties, a time in which, as we have seen in the previous chapter, focus groups had become increasingly central to political as well as commercial life. Corporate spending on focus groups had grown steadily since the nineteen seventies. Elites were beginning to chafe at having to consult the people so much, and more importantly, the public increasingly resented the inauthenticity of the focus grouped world.

There are some facts that everyone can agree upon. For decades, Pepsi had been beating Coke in blind taste tests. The upstart rival hammered Coke with this fact in advertising, urging consumers to "Take the Pepsi Challenge"—that is, try Pepsi and Coke without knowing which is which, and see how much better they end up liking Pepsi. This campaign was not only humiliating to Coca-Cola, but was also helping Pepsi to lure away significant chunks of Coke's market share, though Coke was still the industry leader.[446] After extensive laboratory work and taste testing, Coke decided to change its ninety-nine-year-old formula to a sweeter and less fizzy one—in short, a beverage that was just a shade less distinguishable from Pepsi.

New Coke was rolled out with fanfare on April 23, 1985. Middle America's then-favorite[447] black man, Bill Cosby, gamely presented himself in TV ads as a Coke drinker who liked New Coke even better—assuring the customer that if she liked the old Coke, she was really going to love the new one.[448] Television announcements blared at the nation around the clock, as if for a declaration of war. ABC News even stopped an episode of *General Hospital* to break the news. This was no small news judgment call: General Hospital is the longest-running daytime soap opera in history, and its plotlines have been of such importance to many viewers that in the pre-Tivo nineteen seventies and nineteen eighties, KISS 108, a Boston radio station, would summarize the episode every day for those who'd missed it. But the network officials rightly judged that a change in America's favorite soft drink was worth interrupting one of its favorite shows.

Coke executives announced the new product in ways that implicitly credited the market research, and by implication, the consumer. In the press conference announcing New Coke, company president Roberto Goizueta said,

> Some may choose to call this the boldest single marketing move in the history of the packaged-goods business . . . We call it the surest move ever made because the new taste of Coke was shaped by the taste of the consumer.[449]

He repeated this mantra throughout the press conference.[450] Within forty-eight hours, about 80 percent of Americans knew about the change to the nation's favorite soft drink.[451] That's many more than, even in today's information-saturated environment, can name a single Supreme Court Justice or the U.S. vice president.[452]

But America was not pleased. For three months, angry consumers— about 1,500 a day by June—called Coca-Cola headquarters, sometimes in tears. They wrote some 40,000 letters of protest, including one that said, "Changing Coke is like God making the grass purple or putting toes on our ears or teeth on our knees."[453] Some customers stockpiled bottles of old Coke, by the hundreds, knowing that they'd never get used to the new formula. One customer remembers buying so much old Coke that after the debacle was over he had to repair the floor in his spare bedroom: "because of all the weight, the floor had sunk. It was well worth it."[454]

The intensity of the objection far surpassed public reaction to much more deliberate corporate wrongdoing. It's worth noting that people didn't get nearly as angry over reports that Coca-Cola conspired with paramilitary groups in Colombia to execute workers in their bottling plants that were trying to organize unions.[455]

One customer proclaimed, "When they took Old Coke off the market, they violated my freedom of choice. It's as basic as the Magna Carta, the Declaration of Independence. We went to war with Japan over that freedom."[456] This was not as idiosyncratic as it sounds; the idea that the freedom to choose Coke over Pepsi was *the reason* we'd repeatedly gone to war in the twentieth century came up again and again in media interviews with Coke loyalists from this period.[457]

Others similarly equated Coke loyalty to patriotism, calling the change "un-American."[458] One letter to the company said, "I don't think I'd be more upset if you burned the flag in my yard."[459] Another said, "Next week, they'll be chiseling Teddy Roosevelt off the side of Mount Rushmore."[460]

A psychiatrist hired by the company to listen to some of the messages on the company hotline said the consumers were reacting as if a family member had died.[461] Perhaps most disturbingly, one Coke enthusiast wrote to the company, "There are only two things in my life: God and Coca-Cola. Now you have taken one of those things away from me."[462]

But many people did more than leave messages or write letters. A deliveryman was beaten by a woman with an umbrella as he stacked New Coke onto a grocery shelf. His assailant yelled, "You bastard! You ruined it! It tastes like shit!"[463] Others went so far as to organize a social movement of sorts, with protest rallies and an advocacy group. Demonstrators carried signs in downtown Atlanta (home of Coke headquarters) that read "We want the real thing" and "Our children will never know refreshment."[464] Karen Wilson, then twenty-eight, who led a demonstration against Coke's calumny in San Francisco's Union Square, described her reaction to New Coke to a *Time* reporter: "At first I was numb. Then I was shocked. Then I started to yell and scream and run up and down."[465] Another original Coke partisan, Gay Mullins of Seattle, Washington, started an organization called Old Coke Drinkers of America, attracting media attention by publicly dumping New Coke down the sewer.[466]

Sales were fine before the vocal backlash, but tanked as hostility to the product spread across the nation. Clearly some people liked New Coke—they bought it, after all. But the fans never organized nor managed the passion of the new beverage's detractors. This was the most dramatic rejection of a product in the history of mass consumption. It wasn't that New Coke was inherently disgusting—remember, the blind taste testers liked it. Rather, those who hated it were emphatic and compelling, and people listened to them.

Company officials were bewildered. On July 11 of that year, less than three months after the launch of New Coke, Coca-Cola attempted to appease the traditionalists by launching Coca-Cola Classic, which was the same as the Old Coke. The very first case was presented to Gay Mullins, in person, at a press conference announcing the launch of Classic, "in appreciation of his message." Classic Coke's return led two TV networks newscasts and made the front page of almost every major newspaper.[467] One former member of Old Coke Drinkers of America has proudly described Coke's reversal as "a real grassroots campaign that made a difference!"[468]

Less than a year later, New Coke had disappeared from many markets.[469] It would vanish completely by 2002.[470]

As with the Edsel, the credit that the company had initially afforded the focus groups turned to blame, once the public started vocally rejecting New Coke. Top officials at Coca-Cola blamed the focus groups in terms that flattered the broader public, suggesting the market research simply couldn't measure our feelings about Coke because those feelings were just too profound to be understood by such crass methods.[471] Company president Donald R. Keough said,

> The passion for original Coke caught us by surprise. The simple fact is that all of the time and money and skill poured into customer research on the new Coca-Cola could not measure or reveal the depth or emotional attachment to the original Coca-Cola felt by so many people . . . It is not only a function of culture or upbringing or inherited brand loyalty. It is a wonderful American mystery. A lovely American enigma. And you cannot measure it any more than you can measure love, pride or patriotism.[472]

The relaunch was such a success, and so hugely helped a company that had been struggling for market share, that some people have wondered if the whole New Coke fiasco was a conspiracy to restore Coca-Cola's dominance in an increasingly competitive soda market. But there is no evidence to support this. Responding to a questioner who wondered if it was all a plot, Keough said, "We're not that dumb, and we're not that smart."

A more specific variation on Keough's requiem for New Coke emerged in the late nineteen eighties, in marketing circles, and has thrived ever since. This was the "wrong question"[473] story: that people interviewed by market researchers were never told that the New Coke would be replacing the old Coke, the one they knew and loved[474] and had endowed with all sorts of childhood associations, like Marcel Proust and his famous madeleine cookie. In this narrative of the story, Coca-Cola disregarded the importance of *loss aversion*—an important concept in behavioral economics with loads of implications for marketing—the observation that people don't like to give anything up, even if invited to replace it with something better.

Conventional wisdom continued to heap scorn upon Coke's research process, and does so even today. Douglas Rushkoff joins Gladwell in blaming them for the New Coke debacle, ranking it among "marketing's greatest mistakes."[475] "Everyone knows" why New Coke failed. The *New York Times*, in mid-2011, characterizes New Coke as a "focus group debacle,"[476] suggesting that the research failed to capture consumers' deep feelings about the brand, even quoting a Harvard Business School professor to sanctify this received wisdom.

Yet it's not the case that focus groups can't measure our feelings about brands; in fact, that's one of the things they're best at. While it sounds nice to say that our deepest desires and emotions can't be divined by market research, in this context, it's also sentimental and wishful thinking. Much of the time they can. And the emotional relationship of consumers to brands is exactly the sort of thing focus groups are best equipped to illuminate.

The problem with blaming the New Coke debacle on focus groups is that it's completely wrong. The New Coke disaster can more accurately be blamed on the company's failure to listen to its focus groups,[477] which in fact revealed deep attachment to the Coke brand. Not only did focus groups foreshadow the passion for old Coke that would later doom the new, but the way in which they revealed this actually showed how valuable the focus group method can be. That's because focus groups can mirror the group effects that are an important part of the real marketplace. The groups revealed profound opposition to changing Coke, and the ways in which consumers could affect each other's opinions about such a change.[478]

When Roberto Goizueta became company president in 1980, he greatly accelerated market research on Diet Coke (which he would eventually launch in 1982). During the market research on that product, marketing head Sergio Zyman ran a series of focus groups. During one of these sessions, Goizueta asked Zyman to slip his moderators a note—a common practice during a focus group—asking them to pose one more question:

> The last question on the docket today will be a fake story—the Coca-Cola company is about to launch a brand-new cola. As

a matter of fact, this new product is already on the shelves in Denver, Colorado. The product is similar to Coca-Cola and as a matter of fact it has replaced Coca-Cola. Denver is madly in love with the product. We'd like to get a sense of how you'd react.[479]

Some of the focus group participants flipped out. "What do you mean you're taking away my Coca-Cola?" one said. Asked how they felt about changes to other well-known products, one consumer said, "We don't give a shit about Budweiser or Hershey, but you can't take Coke away."[480]

Later focus group research revealed equally strong feelings—with a fascininating additional lesson in group dynamics. In two thousand one-on-one interviews conducted in 1982, about 10–12 percent of the customers fervently opposed tampering with the Coke formula, and half of those said they would never get over it.[481] Focus groups—conducted between 1983 and 1985—then showed that even though the serious dissenters were a minority, they were so vocal that their anger tended to influence others in the group. Like the Diet Coke discussants who'd been asked to weigh in on New Coke, these focus group participants had no problem with the idea of improving an unknown "Brand X," tampering with Pepsi, or altering Budweiser—but they did not want to see Coke change. "It was like saying you were going to make the flag prettier," said Zyman, a young genius in his field who'd previously worked at Pepsi, describing some of the distress in these focus groups.[482]

As Rutgers University marketing professor Robert Schindler makes clear in his much-overlooked piece of revisionism, "Coke's researchers started out asking the right questions, and in the right way." There was no "wrong question" problem, and the company certainly did not fail to probe consumers' feelings about the brand. The groups accurately foreshadowed the entire ensuing saga.

It was not so much the number of hard-core dissenters that should have bothered the company, but their passion and their potential to influence others. In real life, the New Coke haters were so vocal that they turned the rest of the buying public against the product. The more people heard about New Coke, the more they disliked it: the company's research showed that 53 percent of shoppers liked New Coke on May 30, 1985, but by the following year, as it was coming off the market, only 30 percent liked it.[483] The same thing had happened in the focus group,[484] that exposure to the vocal opponents of New Coke could change the minds of others in the group.

This frequently happens in focus groups: a few dissenters can turn the group against a product. That dynamic is sometimes seen as a weakness of the method. Former moderator Kara Gilmour laments that "there [is] always this dominant voice that kind of leads the conversation,"[485] and one person with a strong negative opinion can influence the whole group. Kara Jesella, former *Teen Vogue* editor (now NYU PhD candidate), felt this often happened with focus groups testing that magazine:

> Quickly one or two girls became the leaders . . . the two who were the loudest, and everyone else kept falling in line behind them, and you could sort of see them changing their opinions in accordance with what these two girls were saying.

Jesella felt that the nuances of these group dynamics were often ignored by those interpreting the results, who would concentrate on the consensus—"no one liked this page"—as opposed to the process, which was that

> People seemed to be sort of into it and then these two girls said they didn't like it and everyone was like, "Oh, I don't like it, either." So it was really, like, what we were being told was not what I saw. It was totally two different things.[486]

This line of thinking—an understandable frustration coming from the client behind the mirror—is one that greatly annoys some veteran market researchers. Andy Tuck says, rolling his eyes, "Everyone believes this is a problem with focus groups, but it is so not a problem."

When clients ask Tuck about the danger of the "controlling respondent," he says,

> Oh, my God, I hope he'll be there. Because that's fantastic. It makes the group so much better. And then I explain. In real life, those people exist. We want to see the group effects. We want to observe.[487]

Tuck is right: the fact that a couple dissenters can influence a group isn't a weakness of the methodology. As Coca-Cola learned too late, this is an important insight of group dynamics (long recognized in social science) and valuable information for the client. After all, markets are social, not a series of monadic individuals making choices all by themselves. Indeed, in the case of New Coke, the groups showed exactly how social influence can affect consumer behavior, as Schindler's research convincingly demonstrates. If company officials had paid more attention to that dynamic—the way a little bit of negativity and complaining can be hugely influential—they would have gained much insight into the risks of launching New Coke.[488]

But focus groups are only one of many factors influencing a business decision. And as often happens, the client—Coke—failed to heed the focus groups. This isn't always a bad idea when focus groups, taste tests, and survey research conflict—in fact, it's usual market research practice.[489] Veteran focus group researchers say clients ignore their results all the time. But in this case doing so turned out to be colossally stupid.

Coke assumed that the naysayers in the focus group simply didn't represent the larger population. This, as we can see with brilliantly clear hindsight, was true. Even after all the publicity, one researcher found that consumers rated new Coke labeled as old Coke more highly than old Coke labeled as new Coke.[490] Yet it was irrelevant what most people felt—because most people's feelings lacked intensity. Even on Facebook, where all sorts of strange enthusiasms flourish—Pop Rocks, which were dogged for years by persistent and baseless rumors that they would cause children to explode, are "liked" by 16,678 people—New Coke has at this writing only 196 fans, while Coca-Cola has more than 31.5 million.

The taste tests could not capture Americans' feelings about Coke, nor could they capture the power of social influence. But the focus groups could—and did. They simply weren't taken seriously. Rather than being a cautionary tale about the ineffectiveness of focus groups, the New Coke fiasco shows that the focus group is a unique way for a company to learn how consumers can be affected by each others' opinions.[491] As James Harding writes of New Coke in *Alpha Dogs*,

> The quantitative numbers were right: seven out of eight people
> were happy for the company to launch New Coke. But one pas-
> sionate opponent could change that . . . The qualitative research
> hinted at an important dynamic in American public opinion, the
> contagion of public anger.[492]

At the time, the president of Pepsi—which celebrated the roll-out of Coca-
Cola's innovation by giving all of its employees the day off[493]—christened
New Coke "the Edsel of the nineteen eighties."[494] He was right, though not
for the reasons he intended. Just like the Edsel, New Coke's demise has been
blamed on focus groups—insistently, confidently, and without evidence.

What's going on when most commentators—including corporate
America's favorite pet intellectuals—get a story entirely wrong? Why do
we hold focus groups responsible for the twentieth century's most dire
marketing snafus? Probably these myths—along with the appeal of the
men who resist the culture of consultation, from Malcolm Gladwell to
Dubya Bush—persist because of a deep ambivalence about focus groups
in our society. Corporate clients, creative artists, and political elites need
to listen to people all the more as gaps in our experience widen. Yet elite
distance from ordinary people breeds entitlement. Increasingly, these
elites feel they should simply be able to do as they please without consultation. They resent having to listen to "the people," because they think
that they know better. As "the people" we also feel resentful, at some level
understanding that the culture of consultation cannot substitute for our
lack of real power.

But the focus group is the wrong target of popular resentment; we
should be upset about our lack of real political power and the dominance
of a corporate elite. As for the elites, their hostility to the focus groups they
commission and pay for is revealing; market research is a compromise in
an unequal society, but as our elites become more entitled, they don't feel
they should have to compromise even slightly. They don't feel they should
have to spend *any* time listening to the people. Indeed, any opportunity
to blame focus groups for corporate failures is an opportunity to blame
ordinary people, and this opportunity is always eagerly seized.

What would make so many of the leading business intellectuals of the early oughts get the New Coke story so wrong? Just as the New Coke story itself was a window on the nineteen eighties, its reinvention by TED stars like Gladwell at the turn of this century revealed much about that time: upper-middlebrow culture had grown weary of "the people," instead falling in love with the myth of the lone genius entrepreneur.

Salad Dressing Group, 2007

"Now we're talking about a more premium salad dressing," **the moderator explains. "You seemed to like the flip cap on** **the standard salad dressing. What did you think of it on this** **one?"**

"Same thing," a woman enthuses. "I like the portion control. **Well, at least the fact that it's not going to gush out. I like that.** **And I like that flip-top feeling."**

A serious-faced bleach-blond has an especially practical angle:

"When I unscrew this, I'm really going to pour too much and **I'm going to end up wasting the product. Eventually I'm going** **to save money by using this, because it's channeled."**

A slightly younger woman adds, "It looks like some thought **went into this cap. Someone said, 'This is a better way to do it.'"**

A fellow respondent concurs enthusiastically: "This is a new **design concept that someone thought about." She builds on** **her fellow respondent's point: "It's updated. More modern-** **ized. More contemporary." She smiles approvingly.**[495]

Chapter Nine: "A Faster Horse?"
The Entrepreneur Strikes Back

Addressing the crowd of corporate bigwigs at TED in 2004—looking cerebral in slightly worn jeans and sneakers—Gladwell held forth:

> If I asked all of you what you want in a coffee, you know what you'd say? Every one of you would say, "I want a dark, rich, hearty roast." That's what people always say.

But in reality, Gladwell reveals, only about 25–30 percent of consumers want the dark roast. "Most of you like weak, milky coffee," he smiled impishly. "But you will never ever say, to someone who asks you, that you would like a milky weak coffee."[496]

The Marketing Research Association, one of the main industry trade groups, has estimated that from 1990 to 2002, usage of focus groups doubled (from 110,000 to 218,000 sessions per year).[497] Yet elite critique of the practice got especially intense in the first decade of the aughts, with a new ideal of elite manhood. This vision of leadership celebrated as revolutionary anyone who loudly rejected the idea that ordinary people should be listened to, ever.

At the same TED meeting, Gladwell expounded on the food industry's long road to extra chunky spaghetti sauce. For years, he explained, Ragu and Prego would hold focus groups and ask consumers, "What do you want in a spaghetti sauce?" For twenty, thirty years, "no one ever said they wanted extra chunky. Even though at least a third of them deep in their hearts actually did! People don't know what they want."

In a 2005 speech to American Association of Advertising Agencies called "Focus Groups Should Be Abolished," Gladwell regaled his audience with the story of the Aeron chair, which also makes an appearance in his best-selling 2005 book, *Blink*.[498] The designers at the Herman Miller company, on the theory that office chairs would be more comfortable if you could adjust their lower backs, devised a new chair that could do this. Then they tested it.

Focus groups loved the comfort, but there was a problem: they found the chair hideous. Gladwell explains,

> The aesthetic scores suck. They are some of the lowest scores ever. Now normally, in the real world, when you come up with an idea and the people who are supposed to buy it hate it, you go back to the drawing board, right? If your customer hates it, it's suicide.

> But Herman Miller said, "You know what, we're going forward." Over the course of the next two years, this chair that everyone said that they hated, turns out, they didn't really hate it. Sales start to go up. People start to look at the chair and say, "Well, actually it is comfortable and I think it's kind of cool-looking." Suddenly this chair, called the Aeron chair, becomes a cultural and commercial phenomenon and one of the greatest-selling chairs in the history of office chairs.[499]

Gladwell thinks the process of discussing their preferences just biases people further against the unknown:

> They say they don't like the chair, of course they don't. The chair is nothing they've ever seen before, but that was the whole plan in designing the chair. But that's what's wonderful about it, that's why this chair will make billions of dollars for Herman Miller, but it's also what dooms that chair in the focus group . . .

The more breakthrough, the more revolutionary and the more innovative an idea is, the longer it will take for people to come to appreciate it.[500]

Many decades earlier, Frankfurt School theorist Theodor Adorno worked with Lazarsfeld on the Princeton Radio Project, a predecessor to the Bureau, from 1938 to 1941. Adorno found the work extremely alienating, particularly the Lazarsfeld-Stanton Program Analyzer, the device that would provide the technological underpinning, several years later, for Merton and Lazarsfeld's invention of the focus group. Adorno was having none of it:

> [I]n order to grasp the phenomenon of cultural reification according to the prevalent norms of empirical sociology one would have to use reified methods as they stood so threateningly before my eyes in the form of that machine, the program analyzer.[501]

Adorno did not even see the point of studying listeners' opinions and reactions, referring constantly to the project on which he had been hired as "the so-called Music Study."[502] He disagreed with the whole concept of audience research, feeling that since people didn't know anything about music, why study their opinions about it? He hated that he was asked to track the "likes and dislikes" of radio listeners, objecting on grounds almost exactly the same as Gladwell's, though far more eloquently: "To like it is almost the same thing as to recognize it."[503] Adorno's objections—though articulated a few years before the first real focus groups—would be among the first of many such objections to qualititative market research from cultural elites.

Because of Gladwell's *New Yorker* job, and his intellectual image, many readers assume that such critiques come out of this sort of left-leaning interest in how corporate America crushes the human spirit, even to its own detriment. However, Gladwell's background, and continuing livelihood, suggests otherwise. All he shares with Adorno is a horror of the masses.

As investigative journalist Yasha Levine revealed in his much-overlooked exposé, during college Gladwell attended journalism trainings at the National Journalism Center, a tobacco industry PR project, and to the delight of the industry, he recycled many of its talking points in later coverage of smoking. Among other doozies, he blamed children for taking up smoking and explained why rising smoking rates among youth weren't the fault of industry advertising. A 1996 tobacco industry memo named Gladwell as one of its key media assets.

He remains an "asset" to a variety of other industries as well; at over $40,000 per speech, Levine estimated that Gladwell makes more than a million dollars a year addressing corporate audiences, a fact that for years went undisclosed even in his stories about business issues.[504] Right or wrong, his critique of focus groups—or anything else for that matter—comes not from the from the artsy left, as his readers might assume, but from the alpine heights of the business elite.

Who does know better than the focus groups, according to Gladwell? "Experts"—entrepreneurs and other creative elites—he finds new ways to say over and over, in a chapter of *Blink* dedicated to criticizing market research.[505] Thus when Gladwell critiques focus groups on the grounds that people don't know what they want, that they just don't understand the profound coolness of new innovations, what he's saying is that ordinary people are stupid and elites know best. Ignorant folks should not be telling our smart, creative intellentsia what to do. It's an "edgy" critique that a tobacco CEO would love.

Gladwell's cheeky manner and bohemian look belies his profound conventionality. His critique of focus groups misses the point; our confusion about our desires, and our resistance to imagining new ways of doing things, can be valuable information for marketers. But what's even more conservative—and more obviously wrong—is his assumption that only elite geniuses have good ideas. Elite critics of the focus group tend to have this in common.

Douglas Rushkoff positioned himself as a "maverick" on this subject—by saying exactly the same thing as Gladwell. A similarly sought-after author and speaker on business topics, he criticized recent business practices for discouraging creativity, writing in 2005, "We innovated by focus group consensus, removing our own creativity from the equation."[506] For entrepreneurs, the problem with paying too much attention to customers, he explained, is that "the source of innovation is quite disconnected from their own expertise, sensibility or passion, and turned toward trying to decipher the sensibilities and passions of strangers."[507] On the other hand, Rushkoff writes, "While the big brands were busy conducting focus groups to determine which celebrity to artifically link to their products, entrepreneurs like Mary Kay, Martha Stewart, and even George Foreman were busy launching products based, to varying degrees, on their expertise.[508]

Remember Don Draper on *Mad Men*'s 2007 debut episode,[509] ripping up the focus group report and throwing it in the trash: the gesture establishes the bold, independent masculinity of his character, and also allows the show's writers to get a dig in at the focus groups they so resent in their own industry. The episode revealed little about the nineteen sixties but much about the twenty-first-century context in which it was written and consumed.

Such re-imaginings of history were in vogue during this period. In another personification of this ideal, a made-up version of Henry Ford (who was a real person) emerged, also in the early two thousand. "If I'd asked the people what they wanted," the iconic inventor of the Model T is supposed to have said, "they would have said, a faster horse." In the first decade of the twenty-first century, in business circles and in the media, this quote was circulated extensively, always attributed to Henry Ford, and always used to dismiss the idea of focus groups. It was a frequent way to articulate the idea that elite experts know best, and that asking the people anything is a waste of time.

Because he invented the first lasting mass-market car, Henry Ford is an appealing mouthpiece for this sentiment.

There's one problem. There is no evidence that Henry Ford ever said this. Although he died in 1947, the quote itself did not exist until 2002, according to a well-researched essay by entrepreneur Patrick Vlaskovits on the *Harvard Business Review* blog.[510] The quote surfaced at precisely the time that elite criticism of focus groups was growing particularly shrill.

Vlaskovits noted that it does seem to be true that Ford disdained popular opinion. But rather than simply helping his business, as those retailing the probably apocryphal quote assume, his contempt for consumers eventually hindered his business success.[511] When more competition entered the market, and customers wanted better cars and easier financing for them, according to Vlaskovits, Ford was slow to respond and this hurt him competitively.

Though Vlaskovits doesn't mention it, Ford also published the anti-Semitic classic "Protocols of the Elders of Zion" in his Dearborn, Michigan, newspaper, [512] and received a "Grand Cross of the German Eagle" award from the Nazi regime, refusing many exhortations to reject and return this award. (Harvard PhD candidate Stefan Link has argued that Ford's politics were not developed enough to be actually fascist, and that Ford

1910 Model T Ford, Salt Lake City, Utah. Photo by Harry Shipler of Shipler Commercial Photographers, April 11, 1910. Public domain.

and Fordism were just as popular with the Soviets and others seeking an alternative to liberal capitalism as they were with the Nazis.)[513] Still, Ford's anti-Semitism and ties to the Nazis are well known. It is perhaps a disturbing sign of how far we have gone in lionizing elites, that these unsavory attitudes and relationships have apparently not made Ford's contempt for the masses any less charming to the many who quote this fake axiom (nor have many drawn the obvious connections between Ford's cozy relationship with authoritarians and his hatred of the vox populi).

As political scientist Corey Robin has observed, misattributed quotes of this kind are common, and often better and pithier than whatever the "great man" in question actually said.[514] But because such made-up quotes are often crowd-sourced products of collective fantasy, they say more about the culture at a given moment than about the people to whom they are attributed. The "faster horse" quote is a great example of this: it reveals nothing about Ford, since he never said it, nor about market research, but much about the anti-popular feeling among elites early this century and their resentment of the ordinary citizen.

The invention of this quote effectively remade Ford into an archetype, not of his own time, but of the last turn of the century: the macho entrepreneur, whose disdain for focus groups demonstrated his independence from the sluggish, unimaginative masses.

This archetype was everywhere, and much celebrated. When Chuck Jordan, legendary car designer for General Motors, died, obituaries remembered his disdain for focus groups, expressed, as such disdain often is, with hostility to the ordinary folks who comprise them. "A good designer doesn't need Mr. and Mrs. Zilch from Kansas telling him what to do," Jordan, the artist behind the flamboyant tailfins on the 1959 Cadillac Eldorado, said in 2006.[515]

No one better personified this early twenty-first-century idea of the elite genius than the late Steve Jobs. And no one has been more lionized for his contempt for focus groups than Jobs.[516]

At first glance, Steve Jobs seems like an appropriate messenger for the don't-listen-to-the-stupid-masses lesson that Gladwell and others have trumpeted. An *Onion* headline after his death said simply, "Last Man in America Who Knew What The Fuck He Was Doing Dies."[517] Like Henry Ford, he was beloved. Apple is one of the most innovative companies on Earth, and people adore its products with almost-religious passion.

Jobs did indeed speak out against focus groups, and often, at one point saying,

> It's really hard to design products by focus groups. A lot of times, people don't know what they want until you show it to them.[518]

Saying the same thing another way, when asked how much market research went into the iPad, he said, "None. It's not the consumers' job to know what they want."[519]

He often quoted the "faster horse" observation of "Henry Ford's" in interviews:

> So you can't go out and ask people, you know, what's the next big [thing]. There's a great quote by Henry Ford, right? He said, "If I'd have asked my customers what they wanted, they would have told me 'A faster horse.'"[520]

He appears to have been serious about this. Plenty of people in the corporate world—especially in the technology sector, where such sentiments enjoy a kind of hip cachet—talk tough about focus groups, but don't manage to put the critique into action. "My research department doesn't know it, but I'm killing all our focus groups," Cammie Dunaway, chief marketing officer at Yahoo! Inc., said with typical bluster at a 2005 Silicon Valley conference.[521] Five years later, I participated in a Yahoo! Inc. focus group in a windowless conference room in Manhattan. Because of Steve Jobs, the fantasy of "auteur-driven" tech innovation has been prevalent in Silicon Valley,[522] but the reality is that conventional market research is also prevalent. Just about every Fortune 500 company uses focus groups at least for branding and marketing, and in the tech world, they continue to play a role in product development at many companies, too.

But many at Apple have confirmed that Jobs' no-focus-groups principle was real.[523] John Sculley, who was, in the nineteen eighties, co-CEO with Jobs, remembers Jobs asking, "How can I possibly ask someone what a graphics-based computer ought to be when they have no idea what a graphics-based computer is? No one has ever seen one before."[524]

How does Apple innovate? In an excellent essay called "You Can't Innovate Like Apple,"[525] Nielsen Company product manager Alain Breillatt explains that Apple can get away with not doing market research because of "the cult-like customers who adore them." They design the products for themselves, and they have customers they know will love everything as much as they do. But how did they get there?

It turns out that the Apple experience doesn't prove what the elite market research haters would like it to prove. If anything, Steve Jobs's Apple shows that more consultation can lead to even more innovation. It's just that in Apple's case, the consultation took place within the company. Apple's design decisions, under Steve Jobs, were made not solely by one very smart guy, but by its workers.

It was Apple's working conditions—for engineers, not, infamously, for Chinese factory workers making Apple products, whose conditions have often been awful[526]—that made innovation possible, not its bold indifference to the opinion of its customers. In fact, a little piece of Jobs's Apple suggests the way the world should work: the company listens to (some of) its workers, whose tastes and interests are quite similar to its market.

Apple under Steve Jobs apparently enjoyed more, not less, input from customers than most companies: they allowed their own employees— who were also Apple consumers—lots of influence. The employees were the focus group. This is a strategy known as "market immersion," having employees who are deeply immersed in the firm's markets, or are customers themselves.[527] The fact that Apple's employees—from designers to salespeople—are exactly the type of people who would buy its products made formal market research unnecessary.

As Steve Jobs has explained, Apple's product developers do not assume that their customers are so very different from themselves. iTunes, and the iPod, he told *Fortune* magazine, came about because

> we all love music . . . Then we all wanted to carry our whole music libraries around with us. The team worked really hard. And the

reason that they worked so hard is because we all wanted one
. . . the first few hundred customers were us . . . [I]t's not about
fooling people, and it's not about convincing people that they
want something they don't. We figure out what we want. And
I think we're pretty good at having the right discipline to think
through whether a lot of other people are going to want it, too.
That's what we get paid to do.[528]

Of course, as Breillatt explains, Apple owns its entire system—its oper-
ating system, software, and hardware—so it is able to conceive and execute the whole consumer experience in a way that few companies can.[529]
But Apple also invests in innovation. Breillatt points out that

the vast majority of CEOs who say, "I want to be just like Apple,"
have no idea what it really takes to achieve that level of success . . . they want to be adored by their customers, they want to
launch sexy products that cause the press to fall all over themselves, and they want to experience incredible financial growth.
But they generally want to do it on the cheap.[530]

That last cannot be done. Apple's teams under Jobs were given plenty
of time to work, and if their work wasn't perfect, it was rejected. (In
addition to his managerial virtues, Jobs was a temperamental maniac,
and a total perfectionist: after the iPod was designed, Jobs complained
there were features he still wasn't "in love with" and sent them back to
work harder.)

Apple recruits the very best people, and Breillatt explains that the
company's designers are paid 50 percent more than their counterparts at
other companies. But that's not the only reason they stay with Apple. As
Jobs has also said, employees love Apple because they get to do amazing
things there. As Breillatt puts it, the rewards include "being able to do
challenging work that satisfies the mind and allows the creative muscles
to stretch."[531]

Breillatt has, of course, a material interest in defending consumer
research. His livelihood depends upon it. But his argument should be
compelling to those who would like to see a more democratic world, as it

suggests the answer is more consultation, and more egalitarianism, not more snotty elitism of the kind that so many media commentators use the Steve Jobs legacy to advance.

Far from showing that we should all defer to a few elite, rich geniuses, Apple's success demonstrates instead how productive a little bit of horizontality can be. If focus groups have been driven by the past century's divide between the experiences and sensibilities of the elites and those of the masses, the iPhone is the product of something else: a sense of commonality between the creators and the consumers. If focus groups have emerged as a necessary way to make both consumer capitalism and democracy work despite vast inequalities, the Apple workplace under Jobs hints at the necessary conditions for its abolition: a flatter and less divided world (and again, let's remember that Apple surely doesn't look this way at the manufacturing level, to the Chinese worker losing his fingers to make the creatively brainstormed iPad). Apple's privileged Silicon Valley employees—and their innovations—suggest that the world might work better with more consultation. Indeed, in contrast to the elitist moral that persistently emerged from the Steve Jobs obituary, the Apple experience suggests that consultation is not enough: that sometimes those affected by decisions improve the outcome not just by being heard, but by participating.

There are other companies besides Steve Jobs's Apple that have avoided getting bogged down in market research—but again, through more consultation rather than less. Such companies are, as one marketing professor recently observed, "increasing in number and so successful they can no longer be viewed as lucky exceptions to the rule."[532] Tupperware has long relied on its most enthusiastic customers to sell the products. There are other companies that do conventional market research, but engage in extensive formal consultation with employees first. Kraft, for example, uses an online community of some two thousand employees to test preparation methods, ads, and even product names.[533]

The facts don't support the mythology around the genius entrepreneur and his disregard for focus groups. Most of the companies discussed above don't reject the culture of consultation—they improve upon it. They have succeeded because of the collaboration of many creative minds, not the solitary inspiration of one man. Just like the New Coke story, companies like Apple, upon close examination, suggest the value of horizontality and listening—in sharp contrast to the lesson that mainstream elites would have us draw from them. Such subtleties were easily lost in the early twenty-first century's cultural worship of the unique wisdom of the entrepreneur. Indeed, so great was this worship, that the machismo of not listening to anyone was elevated into politics, becoming a cornerstone of political, especially conservative, rhetoric.

Fox News, 7/29/14

"Barack Obama is like a steady Eddie. He has kept the country out of war," a black man explains.

An older white guy disagrees, and begins enumerating a host of problems with Obamacare.

"Oh so let's bring back George Bush." A bleach-blond white woman gets sarcastic, and everyone begins yelling at one another. "Oh so it's all George Bush's fault?" "George Bush lied!"

The sarcastic bottle blonde pleads for everyone to "take it down a notch."[534]

Chapter Ten: "The Decider"

The Bush campaign was worried.

As then-Democratic consultant Bob Beckel told Dan Rather on the air in August 1988, the Reagan Democrats—working-class white Democrats who had defected from that party to vote for Ronald Reagan in 1980 and 1984—were "facing real economic pressures. They've been convinced it's because of poor people. But now they're thinking it's the country club set. If that takes hold, Bush loses."[535]

Fortunately for Bush, Lee Atwater, Republican chief political strategist, was a pioneer in the field of opposition research; in fact, the opposition researchers were the only campaign employees required to report directly to Atwater. What they learned about their opponent was a political strategist's dream. The way they used it would go down in history.

Bush's opponent was Massachusetts governor Michael Dukakis, a liberal Democrat. While governor of Massachusetts, Bush's people had learned (because Dukakis's then-opponent Al Gore raised the issue in the primary) he had supported a weekend furlough program for prisoners. While on furlough, convicted murderer Willie Horton raped a woman.

Throughout the campaign Bush's chief pollster, Bob Teeter, had been conducting focus groups all over the country. But it was those in Paramus, New Jersey, that would make history. (Paramus is, perhaps appropriately given its place in retail politics, a city whose other major claim to fame is that it is one of the largest shopping destinations in the nation, raking in more money in retail sales than any other zip code.) Talking with two groups of Paramus voters (twenty in each group), all of them Reagan Democrats leaning toward Dukakis, Teeter's researchers discovered that the furlough story had serious legs. Told that Dukakis allowed a furlough policy for convicted felons who showed good behavior, the (otherwise rather phlegmatic) participants reacted quickly. One man said, "That would be bad. That would be awful." A woman said of Dukakis, her voice full of feeling, "I'd like to ask him why."[536] After learning about the Democratic candidate's furlough policy and hearing the Willie Horton story, about half the participants decided to vote for Bush. But as usual with focus groups—which are not a quantitative method—what was revealing was not so much that number as the fact that the issue had such intense emotional resonance.

The Bush campaign, and PACs associated with it, acted quickly on these findings. The ads showcased Willie Horton prominently,[537] and contrasted Bush's support of the death penalty for murderers with the stance of Dukakis, who "allowed murderers to have weekend passes" from prison. They showed the scary, scowling face of Willie Horton, while a quietly appalled voiceover explained that he had robbed a boy and stabbed him nineteen times, and that on furlough he had kidnapped a couple, stabbing the man and raping the woman. The text on the screen read "Kidnapping. Stabbing. Raping. Weekend Prison Passes. Dukakis on Crime."[538]

And that is how the the now infamous Willie Horton ads came to be. Candidate Bush quickly made the distress of those Paramus focus group participants his own and it was an issue tailor-made for his reassuring paternal manner. "I think of the arrogant face of a criminal, back on the streets once more, because of a permissive plea bargain or some furlough."

A flyer given out in Illinois read, "All the murderers and rapists and child molesters in Massachusetts voted for Michael Dukakis. We in Illinois can vote against him."[539]

The ads were criticized as racist. Horton was black and the victimized couple were white, and for many white Americans, especially in the

South, the image of the black man as a dangerous threat to white woman-hood resonated. Black writer Ishmael Reed said in an interview for a 2014 documentary, "I was angry," noting that one of the ads shows a crowd of criminals going through the revolving door, but only the black man looks menacingly at the camera. At the time, Lee Atwater called race "totally irrelevant" but you didn't have to be a black public intellectual like Reed to disagree. Said Tom Turnipseed, a white former state senator from South Carolina, against whom Atwater had run a famously dirty campaign pub-licizing his struggles with mental illness as a teenager, "I don't believe that. Like Lee said before he died, you don't holler 'Nigger, nigger, nigger' like you did thirty years ago. You gotta be more subtle than that. But he warn't very subtle at all, to me."[540]

Dukakis had enjoyed a 17 percentage point lead over Bush that summer, but Bush went on to win the election. Horton's presence in the campaign was widely credited. (Some have argued that his electoral impact has been exaggerated by future generations of journalists and consultants,[541] but no one disputes his effect on the Bush campaign's strategy—or on political discourse.) Although, as we have seen, Reagan had used focus groups to test rhetoric and language, scholars and polit-ical observers seem to agree that the Willie Horton moment marked the first time focus groups shaped a national electoral campaign in a publicly visible way.

"Focus groups give you a sense of what makes people tick," said Atwater at the time, "and a sense of what's going on with people's minds and lives that you simply don't get from reading survey data."[542]

Atwater's was a dramatic achievement: some voters who'd been pre-pared to turn on the country club elite were quickly convinced to turn on the poor instead. Even more improbably, they were now ready to believe that one of that same elite was their savior. Not only could focus groups let the elite know what ordinary folks were thinking, they could help that same elite at the expense of those same ordinary folks. By giving the people more influence, they could deprive them of power.

Though the Paramus groups were the first to significantly shape a national election, George H. W. Bush was never comfortable with the culture of consultation. Once in office, he tended to ignore the polling and focus group data that the Republicans collected. He spent less on public opinion research than Reagan—a total of about $1.3 million during his first two years in office.[543] White House spokesman Marlin Fitzwater recalled in a 1999 interview with communications scholar Wynton Hall, who specializes in presidential rhetoric,

> I believe that President Bush's attitude toward polls must have been about the same as it was toward speeches and other things, that it was not legitimate, that it was not real leadership, that it was somehow phony and artificial. He wouldn't do those kinds of things for PR [public relations] reasons. He didn't like to be told where to stand, which directions to face, which profile to give . . . He thought doing was how you showed leadership.[544]

In an era in which the political consultant already held considerable sway, Bush Senior's resistance to his consultants was notable. Advisor Andy Card observes,

> As president, if he were to see a document that said, "Mr. President, this is how you should say this [because the polls say so]," I think that his knee-jerk reaction would say, "Well then that is the way that I WON'T say it!"

Bush approached the 1992 campaign in just that way. He thought he knew better than the ordinary voters. As is now well known, of course, he lost to Clinton, who proved to be a world historical master of the focus group.

Clinton spent more money on public opinion research—$4.8 million in his first two years as president—and used focus groups to shape his rhetoric more than any other president before him, both in the campaign and while in office. Stan Greenberg, Clinton's pollster, still famous for his focus groups, said that when working on Clinton's 1992 election campaign from June to Labor Day he did one national poll a week, increasing it to three a week by October. Focus groups were done twice a week until Labor Day. After that, they were conducted twice a night.[545] By contrast, during Reagan's entire 1980 campaign, Wirthlin had conducted a total of fifty focus groups.[546] (Bush's pollster, Fred Steeper, conducted only a couple more: fifty-four focus groups throughout 1992.)[547] David Gergen, who served as a top advisor in both administrations, has described the difference. With Reagan, "Wirthlin [Reagan's pollster] had a seat at the table, and it was an important seat, sometimes more, sometimes less . . . The difference (with the Clinton administration) . . . is that the pollster increasingly [was] at the head of the table—the seating chart had changed. It's a shift that's important."

Veteran GOP pollster Frank Luntz marveled in 1994 at Clinton's use of focus groups: "The words he uses come right out of Stan Greenberg's focus groups. Greenberg literally pulls the words out of the mouths of ordinary Americans and puts them in the mouths of the president. The result is Bill Clinton speaks like real Americans speak."[548]

During the Clinton presidency, Republicans begin to catch up again in the race to use focus groups effectively. Luntz helped Republicans to sell their largely unpopular policies to the American people by testing language with focus groups. He helped Newt Gingrich, Republican House Speaker, to craft the "Contract with America," and eventually would help George W. Bush market himself as a "kinder, gentler" conservative.[549]

Luntz also helped introduce Americans to the live, staged focus group, in which focus groups became televised performances, putting our fellow Americans on display for us. This was the moment in which we the public become conscious of focus groups as a part of our political life. In 1992 Dan Rather explained to viewers what "focus groups" were, assuming that the public had never heard of them before. (Such explanations are never given in television reports today, of course, because we are assumed to know this term very well.) In Rather's report, as in many similar news stories that appeared in print at that time, the fact that politicians used focus groups was news. Focus groups are used, Rather explained, when candidates "get down to fine-tuning their message."

CBS had asked Democratic consultant Paul Maslin to run a focus group just for the segment. An anchor put it in Goffman-esque terms: "In an unremarkable shopping mall in suburban Detroit, a modern political rite is underway."[550]

"I'm not real pleased with what we have to choose from," said a woman in a striped shirt. A fifty-something woman wearing a big, green headband concurred. "I agree. It's like we're in a rut."[551]

These women, both Reagan Democrats in Macomb County, Michigan, were probably the first focus group participants most viewers had seen. Others in the made-for-TV group included a couple auto workers, a letter carrier, a hospital worker, a grandmother, a cafeteria worker, a saleswoman, a small businessman, and a petroleum industry employee. Maslin explained that the point of the method was to explore voters' feelings: "You can hear from the tone of their responses. It can tell you much more than a cold hard poll about the actual standing of the race at any given time."

That Macomb discussion gave viewers the feeling of going behind the scenes, but was more convincing than the televised focus group of today, because it was not in a TV studio, but in a brightly lit conference room, as a real focus group would be. The segment centered on a group of Macomb County voters—appropriate because during the nineteen eighties, these voters, being Reagan Democrats, had been extensively interviewed in focus groups. Democratic pollster Stan Greenberg, conducting groups in 1985, had made a dispiriting discovery: many working-class white people blamed black people for just about everything that had gone wrong in their lives.[552] Bush had won some of them over with Willie Horton, but the Clinton campaign had hopes of getting them to come back to the Democrats.

A worried, tired-looking woman in late middle age shook her head. "George Bush doesn't know how to run the country." A blond woman with exposed black roots and a lot of eye makeup complained, "Basically I'm impressed with his moral issues, disappointed in his political stances."

They weren't sure about Clinton, either. A man with a mustache said, "I don't think he's proven himself yet." A round-faced man in glasses felt "nervous" about Democrats and "special interest groups."

But a man in a striped shirt conceded, "I kind of like the guy. And the more I hear and see him, I'm beginning to respect him as well." And others seemed open to Clinton, too.

When Maslin played them a clip of George Bush promising "Read my lips: No New Taxes," the group openly cracked up at the notoriously broken promise. The round-faced man said, "That's the only commercial Clinton needs to run from here to Election Day."

They were not particularly upset about Clinton's draft-dodging, either. The man with the mustache reflected, "I'm a veteran. It doesn't particularly offend me that some people didn't want to go over there and get shot at." A forty-something man in a striped shirt dismissed the Republican attacks, "They're just digging deeper and deeper for things that don't matter."

In closing, the anchor intoned, "Ten people on this dark Michigan night seemed to sum up the national mood. And what gets said in groups like this will in large part determine what you hear from the candidates in the coming months."[553]

With such discussions televised, the method entered the public sphere during the nineteen nineties in a more high-profile way than ever. Focus groups were often explicitly contrasted with the political and media elites who usually dominate television, their averageness celebrated. They allowed us, the American people, to see ourselves (just as historian Sarah Igo has argued that polling did earlier in the century) but more vividly, with our flaws in appearance and reasoning heartlessly on display. They were often billed—as they still are on Fox News and CNN—as the "voice of the people." They permitted ordinary folks to "talk back" to politicians and directly challenge the commentariat. Tom Frank, describing the ideology of market populism that dominated this period, has described the nineties as "the age of the focus group, the vox populi transformed into flesh . . ."[554]

Later, during the Clinton administration, reporter Bob Kur introduced a televised group on the Monica Lewinsky scandal, conducted in Towson, Maryland, as people who dwelt a "healthy distance outside the Beltway."[555]

Towson is only fifty miles from Washington, D.C., but it was true that these participants' perspectives were so far removed from those of political elites that the conversation might as well have been taking place in Oklahoma. As pundits gassed on about Clinton's peccadillos and their supposed implications, polls showed that ordinary people didn't care. The televised focus groups allowed them to put that highly sensible indifference into words. Carol, a middle-aged white lady, shrugged and said with a smile, "We knew he was Slick Willie when we elected him and he's still Slick Willie." Erica, a black woman in an austere brown dress, wearing a cross around her neck, concurred: "He summed it up the best way he could. He admitted that he did wrong. But he's right, he needs to concentrate on his family and we need to back out of it as far as the American public is concerned." A woman named Cheryl said, "I agree with Erica. He admitted he was wrong and I'd like to forget about it." "Enough already," someone else agreed.

At moments like this, we are reminded that some voice is better than no voice at all. Sometimes the most reasonable opinions are found outside the political-media industrial complex. But focus groups in politics—especially as performed on television—also serve an important ideological purpose: letting us know that we have no one to blame but ourselves and our fellow citizens for the dismal condition of our politics. Because the people often seem to be such jackasses! It's understandable, as one Reddit commenter did, to dismiss the Iowa focus group convinced that president Obama is a Muslim as a bunch of "ignorant hicks."[556] In one of many shocked reactions, one blogger wrote of the same focus group, "I'm no supporter of President Obama, but good grief. I think we're already living in the film *Idiocracy*?"[557]

Partly because of such attitudes, in the nineteen nineties and early two thousand, listening to focus groups was often seen as a sign of political inauthenticity, and an alarming sign that the vox populi was out of control. In *Interface*, a 1994 science fiction novel by Neal Stephenson and J. Frederick George, a political candidate, after suffering a stroke, has a chip implanted in his brain that so closely wires him to public opinion that the reactions of certain select members of the public—a focus group of ordinary Americans—begin to control him in real time. One of these focus group participants—Floyd Wayne Vishniak, an unemployed Midwestern factory worker dubbed "Economic Roadkill" by the cynical political consultants—figures out the conspiracy and goes on an assassination spree in an effort to shut it down.[558] The distance between Floyd's reality and that of the political elites is palpable:

> The yachts of the rich and powerful were tied up in the water only yards away from the private jets of the even more rich and powerful, and Vishniak could plainly see that if you were the right kind of person, you didn't have to waste your time with parking lots, or even cars.[559]

Yet it's only Vishniak's downtrodden status as a casualty of industrialization that interests the campaign, and is the reason he is chosen to influence the candidate, who can read his brainwaves. In one creepy moment, Floyd is watching a speech, begins thinking some skeptical thoughts, and the candidate begins to address "the unemployed, down-and-out factory worker in the midwest."[560] The novel is a dystopian fantasy exploring, among other themes, just how much focus groups—and their participants—control our politicians. Unlike in the nineteen fifties, the prevailing worry in the nineteen nineties—especially as telegraphed by creative elites—was not that focus groups were a tool for industry to manipulate the people, but that they allow the people too much influence.

These fears had particular traction because of Bill Clinton, who was not only criticized but widely mocked for his extensive use of focus groups, especially by conservative commentators. In a 1996 article, a *Weekly Standard* writer called out "The Focus-Group Fraud."[561] In 1999, Robert Manning, who had been an advisor to the first Bush's defense department, called Clinton foreign policy "more spin than reality," deriding the Kosovo intervention as a "focus group–friendly war."[562]

Gerald Ford, one of the first politicians to use focus groups in the nineteen seventies, had by the early two thousand joined the tradition of rhetorically distancing himself from the method. Accepting the John F. Kennedy Profile in Courage Award in 2001, Ford said,

> To know John Kennedy, as I did, was to understand the true meaning of the word. He understood that courage is not something to be gauged in a poll or located in a focus group.[563]

George W. Bush rode this wave of hostility, but took it to a far more dramatic level. He theatrically rejected focus groups, even lumping any show of public participation into that benighted category. He famously and illiterately proclaimed himself the "Decider," even dismissed the February 2003 antiwar protests as a "focus group," and proudly declared his intention to ignore it: "I don't govern by focus group," he scoffed.

It's the contempt that matters in these statements. Bush was dismissing the opinions of ordinary citizens, but framing his disrespect in language that established him as ruggedly independent of shallow marketing. He was too much of a man to listen to anyone.

With the triumph of neoliberalism and the unchallenged reign of elites, Bush—along with his entrepreneurial and media counterparts, Steve Jobs and Malcolm Gladwell—expressed a relationship to public opinion that sharply contrasted with that of the mid-century political class, which was fearful that the masses might be manipulated, but hopeful that by listening to them, elites might be able to make market democracy work for all.

George W. Bush embodied the opposite of such democratic hopes. He also occupied a strange niche in this history. Despite his professed scorn for focus groups, Bush used them heavily (though not as much as Bill Clinton did). In fact, while Clinton used them to figure out how to craft and talk about popular policies—supporting school uniforms, scaling back welfare programs, balancing the budget, putting 100,000 police officers on the street—in the words of the liberal *Washington Monthly*, Bush used them to spin unpopular ones—"arguably a much more cynical undertaking."[564] And perhaps one that was more elitist and more contemptuous of the popular will.

The second George Bush needed, therefore, more than his predecessors, to deny the use of focus groups, because because he was using them to thwart the desires of the masses. The use of focus groups under George W. Bush was far more secret—a choice that was likely encouraged by focus groups (indeed, as Josh Green of *The Atlantic* has written, one of the most dependable poll results is that people don't like polling).[565] At the same time, since he wanted to ignore the public's wishes without facing rebellion or revolt, he needed even more to listen to the public. In this, his administration reflected a deepening elite predicament.

Privatizing Social Security is an unpopular policy, according to independent polls, when respondents are fully informed. But Bush's focus group expert Fred Steeper found that using words like "choice," "opportunity," and especially "savings" could sway even ardent opponents.[566] Phrases like "school choice" and the "death tax" were also generated by focus groups to sell unpopular Bush administration policies.

The pervasiveness of focus groups and marketing research in consumers had long represented a compromise between democratic promises and class society. But the culture of consultation, as an increasingly significant force shaping the political process, was a sign of something more disquieting than a compromise. Focus groups became not just a way to negotiate class division, but a soft weapon of class warfare, as they were used to spin policies that only benefitted the elite. In this way, their use by George W. Bush and his team constituted a new low point in focus group history.

When we look at our current political landscape, it is remarkable how much of our everyday language and concepts we owe to focus groups. Celinda Lake, one of the most prominent of the Democratic pollsters, who has been part of the political focus group industry since the nineteen seventies, told me that according to her focus groups, voters love the "We are the 99 Percent" message of the Occupy Wall Street movement, but don't like the more threatening sound of the word "Occupy."[567] Republican focus groups were clearly saying the same thing, resulting in nonsensical rhetoric from both parties. For example, the rhetoric of the "99 percent" focus grouped so well that even the Republicans took it up, for a time. During Mitt Romney's campaign for the presidency, Republican pollsters on Fox News expressed skepticism of the rich private equity mogul in precisely those terms, saying now is the era of the 99 percent and this guy is the 1 percent—even though it is hard to identify even one policy item these Republicans agreed with the Occupy Wall Street protesters about.

Just as focus groups at times affected the actual policies that Bill Clinton pushed, they also help determine which policies we are debating and the way we debate them. Celinda Lake has run focus groups on health-care for Service Employees International Union and for Democrats. The groups always find that people don't want a Canadian-style system, they want an "American system." And, Lake explains, "They don't like the sound of 'universal' because they don't want to insure the whole universe."[568] So while a handful of unions—including one representing workers who know more about healthcare than anyone, the California Nurses Association—have argued that other countries save money and have better health out-comes by simply having the government cover everyone, SEIU ran focus groups and, following its findings, instead offered "We need an American system" as a talking point, and never pursued any public conversation about socializing health care or using a single-payer structure that could bring down its costs. In the healthcare reform debate leading up to the passage of Obamacare, focus groups were often used to limit the policy choices in ways that were not in the public interest.

Because there are plenty of examples like this, of the ways that focus groups have been used to limit our political language and ideas, many people, even political consultants, feel that focus groups dumb down politics. Democratic political consultant Doug Usher agrees with this. Opinion research, he says "keeps politicians from taking positions at odds with the electorate," thus keeping policies centrist. You don't see many Democrats pushing for single-payer heathcare—nor are Republicans pressing for a federal law banning abortion. As a Democrat, he wishes more leaders would ignore the research and ask, "What exactly are we progressives offering?"

But others question whether focus groups are really to blame for that. Democratic consultant David Atkins insists that the problem isn't focus groups, but their poor execution by too many Democratic practi-tioners. Bland campaign slogans—"the persuasive equivalent to Muzak," he grumbles (think of John Kerry's "Let America Be America")—"give focus groups a bad name." Qualitative research is necessary, powerful, and the left ignores it at its peril, Atkins says. "Republicans use it to figure out what drives people's passions," he observes (remember Wirthlin and Reagan?), while progressives haven't been as good at that. The Obama

2008 campaign, he notes, was an exception: "an insanely good piece of branding. It didn't matter what he was saying. People were able to graft themselves onto it."[569]

Furthermore, the problem with research finding that "the people" resist policy innovation is that such findings often have more to do with the researchers and their clients than with the people. Take Lake's research on single-payer, for example. Many polls have found that depending on how you ask the question, many Americans do favor some kind of socialized medicine program. In fact, in 1993, Lake's focus groups did, too. Why were her 2008 findings so different? Most likely, as the advocacy group Physicians for a National Health Program pointed out, because she was hired to conduct them by the Herndon Alliance, a group specifically formed to oppose single-payer and advocate for market solutions, which was intent on advancing the idea that Americans didn't want Canadian-style healthcare.[570]

Atkins notes how well the private sector has used focus groups for marketing—think of how vodka manufactures are able to create distinct brands even though all vodka tastes pretty much the same—and remains far more innovative than the policy realm. The private sector doesn't ask its focus groups what they like best, he notes: "What matters is that they get emotional."[571]

Despite the populist rhetoric that's always been associated with focus groups, we suspect that there's something wrong with using them to decide anything important. That probably reflects our discomfort with the marketization of politics and the sense that the commercial world has blended too seamlessly with the state. It's probably also that we know intuitively that being heard isn't the same as having power.

But Celinda Lake points out that politics would be even more elitist and even less relevant to ordinary people without focus groups.[572] Lacking such contact with people, politicians would be even more out of touch than they are.

Indeed, focus groups can provide a useful corrective to elite assumptions about people who never get invited to the opinion-makers' cocktail parties. Remember the Towson voters who didn't care what Slick Willie was doing on his off hours? In a similar example, Stan Greenberg studied Tea Party sympathizers in 2013 and found, contrary to what many liberals and folks in the media thought, while race played a role in their resentments of Obama, it was not the whole story; they vehemently disagreed with him on the role of government.[573] Focus groups can't give you a definitive sample of the population, but interviewers can ask "Why?" and explore motivations in a way that is not possible, or at least not as fruitful, in a survey. You cannot possibly ask people in a survey, "Are you racist?" and expect to get anywhere, but you can lead a conversation to explore the issue.

Lake, of course, has a vested interest in the focus group industry, but Stanford University political scientist Morris Fiorina, a senior fellow at the conservative Hoover Institution, tends to agree with her. He has extensively researched and documented the gap in political opinion between the political elites and the masses. Media and Beltway insiders, for example, feel much more strongly about "culture war" issues like abortion and gay marriage, while most ordinary Americans are more concerned with the economy. He thinks focus groups sometimes usefully bridge such divides, offering elites who spent their lives inside the Beltway "a deeper sense of how people think." In an interview in his Hoover Institution office, he muses, "Bill Kristol [conservative thinker and founding editor of the *Weekly Standard*] should probably spend more time sitting in focus groups."[574]

Indeed, the problem with American politics may not be focus groups or even their misuse, but class: the elites who control both parties don't want to see major policy innovation. In a political culture where class interests other than the ruling class were represented, distinctions between candidates wouldn't have to be invented like those between vodka brands.

The phrase "listening tour" was first coined during Hillary Clinton's 1999 Senate campaign. The former First Lady was running to represent New York, but faced skepticism and charges of carpetbagging, since she had never lived in the state. She spent four months touring New York and listening. She met people in small groups at farms and diners upstate, nodding her head and taking down their comments in notebooks to demonstrate that she was listening.[575] One newspaper headline mocked the ritual with the headline "Now Playing in Our Area: Nodding Hill" (playing on the 1999 movie, *Notting Hill*).[576]

Sixteen years later, running for president, Clinton was listening again. "The strategy going in was to focus on small groups—rather than stage big rallies—and to cultivate more intimate experiences," wrote *Politico*'s Annie Karni.[577] Like the news coverage of Hillary's 1999 listening performance, Karni's account suggests the ways that listening to ordinary people, for elites like Clinton, has become an important performance. Walter Lippmann, newspaperman and World War I government propaganda artist, emphasized the importance of elites using controlled environments to disseminate messages to the masses.[578] "All told," writes Karni of the listening tour, "[Clinton] met with less than a few dozen Iowans who weren't pre-selected."[579]

Still, the idea that she was listening loomed large in her campaign rhetoric. In New Hampshire, the *Wall Street Journal* reporter observed a lot of nodding and note-taking. Furthermore, she seemed eager to emphasize the salience of these conversations to her policy positions and thinking. Recall Madison Avenue's efforts to make focus groups visible in order to send the message that the company cares about ordinary people's opinions. Clinton echoed such efforts, making repeated reference to "what some people have told me."[580]

Meanwhile, Clinton's schedule was packed with a different kind of listening tour. She was mainly listening to people who could donate large sums to her campaign. In May 2015, *Politico* was reporting that the Clinton campaign planned to raise $2 billion, and that she was spending "significant personal time" talking to mid-level donors—people who contribute the maximum to the campaign ($2,700) but can't write a $1 million check to the SuperPAC.[581] These chats with the "millionaire next door"—as well as tête-a-têtes with Democratic billionaires—are the conversations that will have far more influence than any listening session in an Iowa diner.

Our politicians do need to hear from us. The problem is that all this listening does not make make our system democratic.

It is curious that in a democratic society the idea that people should have a voice on political matters would be so widely derided. Rage at the focus group participants who insisted that Barack Obama was a Muslim is understandable, as is politicians' efforts to distance themselves from the focus group, a ritual always under such vehement attack. It is in politics that the contradictions surrounding focus groups intensify, as it's the area of life that we most believe should be democratic and include many voices, yet where we most strongly resent the influence of the misguided or stupid. Indeed, internet discussion often reveals broad resentment of focus groups by the ordinary people to whom they are supposed to give voice. But it's in politics that we should most strenuously insist on real power and real participation for all, not simply focus groups.

The problem isn't that we hear from people like ourselves too often, nor is it that the consumer is too powerful. The problem is that we are *merely* consumers even when it comes to crucial matters of civic life. The hostility to focus groups is a misplaced populism—which really looks more like elitism. We should instead turn our hostility to the profound political and social inequalities that have given rise to the focus group in the first place.

Neither the stay-at-home moms in the brightly-lit conference rooms, nor the shufflingly confused undecided voters on TV are the problem. But it is worth asking who participates in focus groups. For the past couple decades, the industry has been hearing from the same people—again and again—and, often, can't even be sure who they are.

White Plains, NY, 2011

I'm in White Plains, in Westchester County. Much of the surrounding area is leafy and horsey, filling any upper-middle-class aspirant with desire or at least a bit of envy. White Plains isn't like that. It's the kind of place whose residents work very hard in the hopes that they might be able to take a vacation and escape it now and then, one of the few towns near New York City with a Walmart right downtown.

When I arrive at the waiting room for the focus group in which I'm participating, I find it is full of overweight, depressed-looking people. The pay here is less than in Manhattan, the receptionist crabbier, and the recruiters seem more desperate and less organized (on my way back to the train station, after I've participated, they will call me again).

We are testing paper plates through "simulated eating." We are supposed to put the meals on the paper plates but not actually eat them; each participant will waste three meals this way. It's lunchtime, and I particularly resent not being allowed to eat the the spaghetti and meatballs.

A woman in late middle age gives us directions, but it is hard to make out what she is saying. I ask a young assistant if we need to be able to hear her. "Well, that's her volume," I'm told.

We are testing the plate on a variety of measures. Do they make it easy to keep your food separate? To keep food on the plate? When you cut the food does "plate material" get into your food? Does it leave a residue on the placemat? Does it protect you from heat? My plate performed admirably on most counts, though it left a little grease and I had to admit it did not compete with a "permanent plate" (a term I'd never heard before).

I was not very efficient. I struggled to fill the forms out quickly, and to serve myself burgers and spaghetti without embarrassing spillage. Then I struggled to understand whether the problem was with the plate or with me.

Chapter Eleven: Bartender in a Lamborghini: The Professional Respondent

"I have a sickness. I need help!" read the caption. The memo, faxed from one focus group facility to others all over the New York City metro area, resembled the fliers that police place on deli cash registers in urban neighborhoods, with a fuzzy photo warning the public to avoid—and report—a miscreant.[582]

But the man in this photo hadn't committed any crime. He'd simply participated in too many focus groups.

Most recruiting firms prohibit participating in more than one focus group within a six-month period. The memo enumerated ten studies within the last year that he'd attended, and showed a copy of his driver's license and birth date. "If you see me," it commanded, "kick me out of your facility!"[583]

Focus group facilitators tend to speak fondly of the participants, for the most part, and will defend them passionately against their detractors. But there are panelists that market research professionals are less enthusiastic about: people who participate too often. They seem to challenge the market reseachers' idealistic desire to hear—and corporate America's profit-driven need to understand—the sincere and unscripted opinions of the "average" American.

The phenomenon of the repeat panelist is widespread. In any given focus group, you'll find people who join groups regularly for the money, and exercise widely varying levels of deception to do so. Known as "professional respondents"—also called "focus groupies"—such people can cause intense anxiety in the field.

Concern that participants might take advantage of the market research process is not new. The J. Walter Thompson agency, once the largest advertising company in the world, pioneered the use of consumer diaries. A "panel" of consumers would keep records of everything they purchased, and in return, would receive $50 of free merchandise a year. Participants would accumulate points for their diaries, and exchange these points for gifts, selected from JWT's Premium List, a catalog of various desirable objects (pinking shears, croquet sets, and Bibles were all popular).[584] In a 1958 article in *Printers' Ink*, critics of this practice—usually partisans of other market research methods—fretted that such incentives would turn the panel participants into "professional" consumers, marring the accuracy of the diaries.[585]

JWT's system bred some ambiguities: was the panelist a "customer"? After all, she was not only expressing views on consumption, but needed to be constantly supplied with goods. In a 1945 speech to the "premium industry," Lois Gilbert, who was in charge of premiums for the JWT Consumer Panels, reinforced this idea when she emphasized the need to "protect ourselves from running out of merchandise and disappointing our customers." Yet there was, even in JWT's non-monetary system, a sense that the panelist was not only a customer but also someone who was providing labor; a participant joins the panel, Gilbert explains, because she wants to be compensated for her "work." Panelists clearly considered the points they accumulated to be a kind of a currency: "Women are as economical with these points as they are with money or with ration stamps," Gilbert explains. "If an article does not seem worth the number of points charged for it she tells us about it."[586] In a subtle way, the questions surrounding these early panels foreshadow those surrounding focus groups and today's "professional respondents." Do focus groups consist of consumers, or of workers performing a job?

In recent decades, such questions have grown more fraught. Market research professionals became convinced that the problem of respondents "gaming the system," leading to dubious and even useless research, was getting worse.

In a 1990 special issue of *Applied Marketing Research*, a trade journal, editor Marshall Ottenfeld bemoaned the dearth of "virgins" in the field in plainly moralistic (yet tongue-in-cheek) terms. Ottenfeld spoke for many when he decried (in harshly if quaintly gendered terms) the participants who were only in it for the cash:

> [T]here has arisen a new group in the underground economy—the professional respondent. These individuals must be discouraged. Members of the industry who have been able to determine how to stop this deception must come forward and share.
>
> While virgins are a vanishing breed and we must adjust to that reality, it is nowhere written that we have to accommodate our businesses to ladies (and gentlemen) of the evening who only seek out participation for its monetary rewards, and in so doing, disrupt and destroy the organized inquiry that is marketing research.[587]

In the same issue of the journal, Susan Pogash, president of her own Chicago-based market research firm, made clear that the field had already given up on the search for "virgin" focus group participants—those who had never participated in a focus group—and was concerned only with rooting out the "cheaters," e.g., those who were outright lying to get into groups. Pogash said,

> Increasingly, cheater respondents are showing up in focus groups with great regularity. Their appearance used to be a rarity.

Putting together a focus group involves a variety of different companies and workers. First, recruiting firms, staffed by low-wage workers (usually women) call and screen potential participants who have entered themselves into a market research database, usually by phone. When the participants show up, they are welcomed by the staff of the focus group facility. These facilities are generally undecorated office suites, made to look as generic as possible, outfitted with conference rooms that are bugged with high-tech recording equipment and a one-way mirror so clients can observe undetected. The facility staff will look at participants' IDs and size them up to see if anyone looks too familiar. Once participants get into the conference room, they meet the facilitator, who may have a background in advertising or academic qualification in psychology or anthropology. At each level of this process, the industry professionals are on the lookout for the repeat respondent.

Focus group participants are now almost always paid, and the fee has, over the last couple decades, risen at a rate far outpacing inflation.[588] The money—$75–300, depending on the city, the length of the group, and the demographic desired—gives some people an incentive to make a small side business out of participating in focus groups. It's hard to make a living in this way since there is such a huge element of chance governing when recruiters will call, and often there is significant travel time involved. Still, repeat respondents can supplement their income by up to $3,000 per month.[589]

"Once a day, at least," estimates Nadia (who works at a focus group facility and did not want to use her last name for fear of upsetting her employers), asked how often she recognizes a respondent who participates frequently. "I'm sure there are more," she adds.[590]

In a trade publication article, one marketer describes a "nightmare situation." Working on one research project that ran several focus groups in Manhattan on different nights, using different screening questions and intending to explore different demographic groups, he was dismayed to find that of the eighteen people who showed up to participate in the second night's discussions, nine of them had been there on the first night. "If it were two or three," he wrote, "you'd be pretty embarrassed. But NINE? I was shocked and dumbfounded as to how this could happen."[591]

For the person who wants to make money participating in focus groups, advice on how to begin is easily available. Stay a Stay at Home Mom (SSAHM), for example, provides extensive guidance to the would-be focus groupie. SSAHM is a blog brimming with cheerful advice on how to survive on one income in a "two-income society." Its author, Rayven Perkins, has written several self-published e-books on this subject, including *Make More Money Mystery Shopping* as well as *How to Become a Gestational Surrogate Mother* (a better-compensated but far more emo-tionally and physically wearing scheme). Her advice for would-be par-ticipants on focus groups is sensible: she cautions that they are not a dependable source of income, but do pay well, and offer "instant cash," when you qualify for a group. She goes on:

> It is an extremely good idea to network at any focus groups that you attend. Often, other paid research study participants will know of additional research firms in your area that you are unfa-miliar with. [592]

She also suggests that, when asked, "when was the last time you par-ticipated in a focus group?" it's smart to answer as she does by speci-fying when she last participated in a group with that particular firm.[593] Others give similar advice. "They don't want to hear that you were just in a group," a middle-aged woman who lives in Midwood, Brooklyn, and takes part in Manhattan focus groups often, tells me.[594]

Indeed, the answer recruiters are looking for is, "more than six months ago." To learn more about focus groups, I myself participated in many, and must confess that I lied about this question in order to qualify. (You could view this as a lapse in journalistic and personal ethics; I see it as a particularly thorough form of participant observation.) Other chronic participants also admit to being untruthful to get accepted into groups. "You have to lie a little bit," because of the six-month requirement, admits Wendy, who was a frequent focus group participant in her twenties, as a graduate student in need of cash. At one point, she says, she participated in an average of three a month, usually for about $100 each time.[595]

Perkins also offers subtle advice to would-be focus groupies on finessing the phone interview with the recruiter:

> Words like "always" and "never" can disqualify you for a study very easily. You don't want to be indecisive, but saying you would "never" try a particular brand isn't the best idea.

> It helps to listen to the person qualifying you as well. Sometimes, they give you little "clues" along the way, based on their tone of

voice or inflection. Pick up on these clues (don't lie) and you may qualify for more studies.[596]

Wendy has some advice of her own to add: "When you don't know the answer to a question, give a quick answer."[597]

Wendy didn't, however, engage in deception about her identity, or the nature of her consumer habits. "I wasn't saying that I was black or Asian, or drove a Ford," she insists. In fact, it was important to Wendy that she told the truth in the discussions themselves.[598] I felt as Wendy did; while I did lie about the six months, I was mostly honest answering the other questions, and scrupulously truthful about everything I said during the group itself. I didn't want to compromise the actual research and, like so many focus group participants, I liked the idea that my mundane consumer experiences could be helpful or interesting to someone, even if that someone was ultimately the shareholders of Procter & Gamble.

But many aspiring focus group participants tell untruths about more than just their past focus group participation. They lie about the very consumer habits under investigation.

When I met Lily Marotta in a coffee shop in Bushwick, Brooklyn, she was frantically busy on her cell phone. A performance artist, she was also working as a booker for a reality show. Today, the producer needs her to find someone with a disfigured face who wants free surgery—the catch, of course, is that the person has to be willing to have surgery *on the show*. No takers yet, and it's getting down to the wire. The process mirrors the sort of dilemma a focus group recruiter might endure in its intricately strange and weirdly specific criteria. And, in fact, we're here to talk about one of Marotta's many experiments in fluid identity: her life as a professional focus group respondent.

Marotta, who participated in focus groups constantly as an art student in Chicago throughout 2008 and 2009, is nothing like a marketer's vision of the "average" person. Yet to get into focus groups, she was always determined to sound as much like the average consumer as possible. To that end, whatever the question, Marotta would answer, "a medium amount." This, she recalled, laughing, "mostly seemed to work for the liquor ones." If a recruiter asked, "How many times do you drink Stoli vodka?" she said,

"I'd be like 'three to five times a week.'" No matter what the product, she explained, "I'm always like, 'three to five.' Usually that worked." Marotta hardly ever drinks liquor, she admitted: "It's certainly not like I'm drinking all those different varieties three to five times a week!"[599]

One Bank of America study examined whether people would be more likely to become customers if the bank were affiliated with a popular charity or sports team. Marotta, though not an avid sports follower, found an ad on Craigslist seeking focus group participants and filled out the survey: "I was like 'I'm a fan of all sports' and listed random teams." When the recruiter called and asked her about volunteering habits, she says, "I was like 'Yep, I volunteer twice a month.'" (She never volunteers.)

Recruiters also ask what Marotta calls "weird getting-to-know-you" questions, like "If you had any three superpowers what would they be? If you were invisible for a day, what would you do?" These test whether a person can answer questions in a way that is engaging but not too offbeat, and whether you are able, on the spot, to think of something appropriate to say. (I've been asked by such recruiters what famous person I'd like to have dinner with, and I usually mention someone safe like Michelle Obama, even if I might prefer to dine with Iggy Pop.) When they'd ask Marotta, "'What would you do if you won a million dollars?'" she said, "I just gave a nice answer like 'buy my mother a house' or something like that."

Sometimes Marotta's dogged efforts to make herself seem more average have backfired. Once, when asked which beers she drank, Marotta said, "I tried to say all popular beers." The study was actually about craft beer, so she was excluded. Most of the time, though, the strategy of appearing as normative as possible worked for her.

Marotta clearly enjoys exploring different identities. In this way, her focus group involvement mirrors her performance art: in one of her video installations, she plays four different women riding the Staten Island Ferry.[600]

While Marotta is unusual in being an actual performance artist, other "professional participants" share her feeling that there is always an element of performance to the focus group. Wendy described the focus group as "putting on a performance, how do we represent ourselves."

She liked to experiment with this: "I'm someone who looks kind of nice . . . Sometimes I'd be a little bitchy, trying on different aspects of my personality."[601]

Some professional respondents go vaudeville with the performance, resorting to extreme levels of deception in order to get into focus groups. "Some people have no shame at all," says Nadia, a moderator as well as a longtime facility employee. "They come in different outfits, different styles, sunglasses, hats." I'm startled to hear this, and she laughs at my surprise: "Oh my gosh, there *totally are* disguises!"

Of one imposter spotted frequently in her workplace, Nadia says,

I've seen this person in a mustache. I've seen him in like, wigs. Eyebrows. Totally different styles of clothing. One day it will be a three-piece suit. One day a track suit. Hats. Just totally different styles that one person would not wear.[602]

He must figure out different ways, he must have friends that have numbers he can call from, maybe he has call routing, I don't know, it's really hard to say. Every facility, every research company has this problem.

Many professional participants will even have fake IDs. Nadia says,

They have different identities, different addresses, different emails. They'll get a phone number from a friend, they'll call, they'll just leave a message, then they'll call back and say I'm calling for this study.

Nadia describes the impossibility of patrolling the identities of participants who are determined to deceive:

This one guy, I have no idea who he really is. I mean, I know his real name. But I have no idea what he really does, what his home life is like. There's no way to profile someone like that because you can't trust anything they're saying to you. Like, this guy has been in for every group under the sun that he could possibly qualify for. One day he'll be here for a finance study in a business suit talking about banking. Another day, he'll be like a bartender. A third day he'll be a luxury sports car owner. Depending on what study it is he's a different person. He's a person that suits the study.[603]

Some deceptions are too preposterous to sustain, of course. Kara Gilmour remembers a man showing up to a group on feminine hygiene products.[604] Nadia's facility is afflicted by a mother/daughter duo of imposters who visit often. Like the sports car–driving bartender, they embrace a range of incompatible identities; "One day they're a housewife," says Nadia, "the next day a nurse." The fake nurse was unmasked in a group on insulin, when, as Nadia related, she claimed to have given out "twenty times more than anyone, more than the busiest nurse at the busiest hospital. The client was like, 'That's amazing, but something is clearly wrong.'"[605]

In a situation like that, the host at the facility will generally call the fake panelist out of the room, taking care not to confront them in front of the rest of the group, or the client (who is, remember, often behind the mirror). Usually, the imposter will be paid for their participation and asked never to come back. "But of course they do!" laments Nadia. "We really don't have security. There's nothing we can really do to threaten them. They leave, and come back as someone else."

Nadia keeps a folder of information on the worst offenders and is on the lookout for them in her facility: "There's this one woman who wears so much of this certain perfume," she muses. "As soon as she comes into the facility, everyone can smell her. Even if I don't see her right away, I know she's here."[606]

A "professional panelist" confession by *New York* magazine writer Will Leitch, Augustinian in its elaboration of wrongdoing, provoked hand-wringing among market researchers. He was the "person that suits the study" that Nadia complains about. In his words:

I have been many men in my career as a focus-group member. For a travel study, I was a hardy adventurer who'd backpacked through Mongolia. For a deodorant group, I claimed a glandular problem that caused me to sweat profusely, no matter the conditions. On other occasions, I have grown up on Long Island, lived in southern New Jersey, suffered from long-term asthma—and, for a brief few hours, been of Italian descent.[607]

The reaction in the field was one of despair. Large trade organizations like the Market Research Association (MRA) saw the *New York* piece as a deliberate assault on their livelihood, and condemned Leitch. As MRA executive director Larry Hadcock complained in the group's press release,

> Billions of dollars are expended annually based upon the outcome of survey and opinion research. To suggest ways to sabotage this process puts countless businesses that are critical to the U.S. economy in jeopardy.[608]

A coalition of market research professional organizations wrote a letter to *New York* magazine to protest Leitch's essay:

> Printing the article is akin to telling readers how to cheat on the law boards, falsify medical credentials or steal from their employers. For your publication to further this unethical behavior is unconscionable.[609]

Clearly, professional respondents cause tremendous anxiety in the market research world. Many people who work in the field become visibly angry and upset when talking about them.

What, though, is this anxiety really about? Of course it makes sense to worry about the quality of information: people who don't drink Stoli don't have anything valid to say about its flavor. Oddly, though, what seems to most disturb market researchers—many of whom admit they themselves went into this line of work to make money—is that these respondents are participating "just for the money." Mark Goodin, president of Aaron-Abrams Field Support Services, a recruiting and fieldwork firm, writes in a web article, "These respondents aren't interested in helping companies improve their products and services. They're interested in the cash. Nothing more."[610]

The professional respondent drives the industry crazy because she challenges a core belief in the field: that focus groups represent average people. Part of the reason the "averageness" of the participants is so desired and fetishized is that often the reason for conducting focus groups at all is to bridge the gap between elites and "ordinary" consumers or voters.

The professional panelist seems to thwart this quest. "I have a Hall of Shame of people who try to trick us," Shelly Bogetich, president of C2 Consumer Research in Roseville, a suburb of Sacramento, told the *Sacramento Business Journal*. "We're looking for the average person's perspective . . ."[611] However, if you attend any number of focus groups, one thing quickly becomes clear: there's nothing "average," or even necessarily representative, about many of these people. Says veteran moderator Kara Gilmour, "They're all crazy!"[612]

Many focus group participants are, like Marotta, eccentric people pretending to represent an elusive "average American." Marketers are always searching for that average consumer, and the focus group often exposes that project as little more than a joke.

Then again, perhaps part of the reason that the focus group keeps working, no matter how many people game the system, is that none of us are as unique as we think we are. Even if focus groups are full of eccentrics and liars, they end up being useful for confirming or challenging marketers' hunches because consumption habits simply don't vary that much. Almost any group of people, however unscientifically assembled, should give you some window onto how "people" will react to your product.

Clients' instincts are probably confirmed more often than challenged by focus group research, and that's often its purpose. In fact, moderators say they are hardly ever surprised by the results of a focus group.

"I think none of the findings are terribly surprising," says Julia Strohm, the former ARC researcher, "nor should they be."[613] Those of us outside the industry might assume that if you put ten people in a room you'll get ten different opinions, but actually, that's rarely the case.

"Often they'll use the same exact words," says Nadia. "How they feel— if they're in the same demographic—is they all feel the same way."[614]

Julia Strohm agrees, adding, "If they don't, they're an anomaly, and you don't care about them."[615]

Indeed, Strohm's former boss, Andy Tuck, used to laugh when his clients would ask him to find out what the focus group participants read: "They read what everyone else reads," he'd chortle, with professorial amusement at the illogic of the question.[616] Strohm elaborates: "If *Vogue* has the biggest circulation, that's what most of them are reading. Or *Martha Stewart Living* or *Oprah.*"

(This is much more true of cultural and consumer tastes than of politics, Andy Tuck points out. People do, of course, still think differently about politics and social values in Texas than in Massachusetts, as we all discover each national election cycle.)

ARC takes the insight into our cultural homogeneity further than many market research groups—to the extent that they don't think it's usually necessary to hold groups in different parts of the country. Strohm explains,

> If you start doing a couple focus groups, normally you will see very similar patterns of response, and you do not have to do many of them, and things don't really vary from region to region . . . I think back in the day there might have been more regional difference than there is now. Today I think the country is really quite homogenized and what you can access in New York you can access in Phoenix.[617]

Tuck agrees, "We have the same stores and the same malls all over the country. We have at this point all seen the same ads . . . Basically everyone has more or less the same relationship to Starbucks."

Tuck laughs at the idea—common among clients—that "there's a perfect focus group in Kansas City."[618] Columbus, too, is often called "the test market of the USA" because it is in the Midwest, yet is also ethnically and culturally diverse.[619] In recent years Sacramento has become another mecca for marketers, for similar reasons.[620]

Tuck points out that it is ridiculous to insist on conducting focus groups in such supposedly normative places, not only because we are all not so different, but because there is no way that ten to twelve people, or even a couple hundred, could "represent" anyone. The focus group study is always too small and too arbitrary a sample, so you may as well talk to anyone.

He explains:

> No focus groups are projectable to a larger population, it doesn't matter how many focus groups you do. You could do a thousand focus groups. Don't project that, because it's not a quantitative exercise. The questions are asked in different ways. There's different tone of voice, different context, there's different people in the room.[621]

We are a lot more homogeneous than we like to think, a state of affairs we can blame on competitive capitalism, according to French sociologist Pierre Bourdieu. We think that competition produces diversity but it actually breeds sameness.[622] If we really were the intrepid individuals we believe we are, market research just wouldn't work at all—and it does work at least some of the time. And the focus group works because even people who are lying about their averageness are still basically pretty unremarkable.

Of course, most of us hate this idea. While some focus group participants, like Marotta, fake their own averageness, others totally reject it. The consumers participating in focus groups are not content to be paid for being average—they feel they have more to offer. In their 1999 book, *Under the Radar*, Jonathan Bond and Richard Kirshenbaum, founders of legendary ad agency Kirshenbaum, Bond and Partners (KB&P), note that focus group participants, by the time of their book's writing, would delight in dissecting advertising messages:

> We often hear focus group participants trying to play brand managers by saying, "The strategy on this ad is bad, it should be this . . ."[623]

Donna Fullerton says it has become a struggle, in recent years, to convince focus group respondents to think of themselves simply as consumers. "They're putting themselves in the marketer's shoe rather than in the consumer's," she says with some amusement. To a company, the value of a focus group participant is simply the fact that she is a shopper.

But she tends to feel she is an expert on advertising and all sorts of business matters, and she's got advice to give. The participant is "educated about advertising," says Fullerton, and wants to tell Madison Avenue how to do its job.[624] As one client put it, "Someone starts talking and you think, 'They could be working for us!'"[625]

Fullerton says she tries to redirect participants away from that line of conversation constantly, always toward more personal territory: "Well, we don't have to worry about that now. How do you feel? How do your friends feel? Always coming back to that place." No one wants to speak as an average, passive recipient of consumer culture anymore. Says Fullerton, "That's been a big change [in her several decades as a consumer focus group moderator]. Everyone's an entrepreneur, everyone's a marketer, everyone's a corporate person."[626]

Many Americans don't want to think of themselves as average, and go to ridiculous lengths to deny their averageness. Behavioral economists have found that we ignore data—whether in choosing investments, buying a house, or making any important life decision—believing that we are special and things will work out better for us than for those sorry old "average" folks. In an absurd fulfillment of Garrison Keillor's imagined Lake Wobegon, where all the children are above average, New York City parents work so hard to prepare four-year-olds for school entrance tests that the gifted programs can't accommodate all the children who score in the ninety-ninth percentile. All this sounds crazy, but makes sense if you look at the way we've structured our society. Why would we want to be average? In the weirdly gleeful words of New York Times neoliberalism cheerleader and columnist Thomas Friedman, "average is over." The average Jane's prospects in the United States are depressing. Her kids attend mediocre schools. Her retirement portfolio's performance, if she even has one, is lackluster. If she starts a business, it will fail.[627] If she loses her job, she doesn't have enough money saved up to survive for more than a couple months. Who wants to be that person? We all want to be special, not only because we're raging narcissists, but because here in the U.S., unlike in more equitable societies, the penalty for being merely average is so harsh.

A practical downside of the professional respondents, for companies, is that they make the process more expensive than it otherwise would be. The paradox is that while participants' value lies in their amateur status, they feel entitled to be well-compensated and treated as sought-after professionals—evoking the J. Walter Thompson Consumer Panelists who griped indignantly if they didn't like their gifts. This problem is spoofed in a cartoon by Tom Fishburne, which shows participants in a waiting room complaining about the amenities. "Cabernet but no pinot," one grouses, while another wails, "Only two wifi bars??" A third "groupie" declares, "I cannot work under these conditions."

That's a joke, of course, but in 2012, Republican congressman Mike Kelly introduced legislation to clarify that participants in market research are not employees of market research companies—to protect the companies from government labor law investigations on behalf of these participants. It was unsuccessful, but the market research industry continues to lobby for such protections.

Other worries are less tangible, and speak to the long-running industry fantasy that the focus group is a platform for the voice of the innocent, uncorrupted "ordinary person." Susan Pogash warned decades ago that the professionals "tend to be jaded about the subject matter and the process."[628] This feeling is shared by many market research professionals: that the "focus groupies" can't respond sincerely or authentically because they have seen it all before. They have, writes Jonathan Hilland, president and CEO of Mindwave Research, been "over-stimulated, and no longer have a reaction that is 'spontaneous' to anything. Nothing surprises or impresses them anymore."[629] (Of course this comment is also frequently made about consumers in general; it's hard to market anything to us anymore because we're so over everything.) The groupies are also familiar with the process, and with some of the methodologies, which makes it harder for them to engage genuinely with assignments like, "Make a collage about how 7 Up makes you feel."

Additionally, since professional respondents are lying to get into the groups, it's hard to know if anything they say is true. Talking about the man with many disguises—a sports car–owning bartender—Nadia insists,

"A person like this contaminates a group. Then everything in the group becomes questionable."[630]

"The 'professional respondent' is a problem not because he attends a lot of groups per se, but because in doing so he is more likely to lie when he gets there," explained writer Damian Lanigan in a 1997 investigation for Campaign, a web magazine covering the marketing and advertising industries."[631] "This is either to remain consistent with his earlier answers or because he's just a liar, but either way the results aren't much good."

Once in the group, even if they'd lied to get in, many people will then be honest about what they say, since as research shows, it is harder to sustain a lie face-to-face. But Lanigan is right that many do feel they need to keep up the charade; having lied to get in, they need to keep their comments in the discussion consistent with their questionnaire answers. Agrees Marotta, "I still kept it up like I was drinking those sodas," even though she rarely drinks soda. If they asked what kind of liquor she'd order in a bar, Marotta said she made sure to order something she'd mentioned in her phone interview.[632]

Even when the professional respondents aren't really lying, there's often an artifice or element of theater inherent in the situation. Says Susan Pogash,

You have a professional playing an amateur's game . . . the frequent repeater will be an actor playing a role.[633]

Professional participants recognize this element to the focus group, and enjoy it. Marotta says she often exaggerates her emotional relationship to the product, saying, for instance, "I love 7 Up because my mom used to give it to me when I was sick." For Marotta, it's "fun to get into that mode, not lying about it but feeling what you feel and timesing it by ten. Which is what they want you to do."[634] Wendy agrees that focus group participation often involves "putting on a performance."[635] One frequent panelist writes that participation involves creating a persona: "'Focus group mom' isn't exactly me, but she's enough like me that I can pull her off."[636]

Sometimes, participants say that it's hard not to lie in focus groups because they just haven't ever given the product any thought. "Sometimes you have to pull it so much out of your ass," admits Marotta. "I know I'm making up stuff, like, 'This truck makes me think of the freedom I feel when I drink the soda.'"[637]

Pressures in the industry allow professional respondents to flourish. One problem is that the scientific pretensions of market research create fertile ground for the imposters. Often clients want to be able to tell their bosses that they talked to a certain number of people, feeling that number gives their "findings" more validity. Sometimes when the facility staff screen the people again, that is, ask them the same questions, they don't qualify. This isn't as mysterious as it sounds. As a focus group candidate, I've more than once forgotten how I answered the questions the first time, and thus disqualified myself in the second round. (This isn't usually because I'm being dishonest: sometimes I simply don't know how often I buy, say, moisturizer, or breakfast cereal, and therefore, can't remember what guess I hazarded the first time around.) When this happens, the workers at the focus group facility are in a bind; should they put the dubious respondents in the group anyway and hope everything will be okay? Or should they admit that these two people aren't really qualified and tell the client just to do a six-person group? The client reaction may vary; while some will appreciate having the sketchy panelists weeded out, others may demand to have everyone included. That's because they want, Nadia explains, "full sets of data that are equal in all cities. It's something to put down on paper but it's not true. There's no point."[638]

This pressure to produce a certain number of participants can make it hard to find people between the ages of thirty and forty who suffer from irritable bowel syndrome and make more than $100,000 a year; mothers who buy juice drinks infrequently but not never; people undecided about the presidential election who do read newspapers.

Many also blame the dynamics of the industry, in which people are often demanding and downright mean to one another. "One of the biggest things I hate about this industry is it makes people crazy," Nadia says. "Like, where were you brought up that you're talking to another person like this, over shampoo?" Later, she returns to this idea that fear of client rage forces recruiters and others in the industry to cut corners: "I think if people behaved better, things might come out better. But one of the hardest things about research is the client reaction because they go insane. It doesn't matter who you are, they go insane." Pressure from the client, she says, puts pressure on those in charge of the research and recruitment, and in turn, affects everyone involved in the process.

Recruiters don't get paid well, and they work on commission. "So they're really pressured to seal the deal and find these respondents," adds Nadia. "And they're on the phone *all day*."[639] While moderators tend to be educated, recruiters are often high school graduates or other people without great employment options. Their job is demanding, and they frequently lack either the motivation or the skills to do it with much subtlety.

In my own experience as a focus group candidate, recruiter desperation—and thus, willingness to stretch the group's requirements for admission—is commonplace and quickly turns to cynicism. Many people working in this job seem to actively encourage deception.

Recruiters will tell you—the potential focus-group participant—how you should answer the questions when someone at the facility calls for a second screening. For one group, I was a little uncertain of some of my answers, and the recruiter assured me she'd email me to remind me how I'd answered, so I'd give the "right" answers when another recruiter called to repeat the screening process. I've even been coached by recruiters about what to say in the groups in order to make sure my answers were consistent.

A mother with an eleven-month-old baby tells me she does a lot of focus groups "for extra money." If I want to get into more groups, she advises me, I should call a recruiter named Sharon, because "Sharon is always desperate. She changes your answers to fit the group. You say yes and she says, 'Let's say no.'"[640]

I was recruited for a group on paper plates, not an item to which I've ever devoted much conscious emotion (other than environmental distress when they're thrown away). The facility called me much more frequently than most, and seemed far less selective. The recruiter asked if I bought plain paper plates, or plates with patterns on them. I thought about it, and realized I bought them most often for a kid's birthday party, requiring appropriate decorations. The recruiter was quick to redirect me: "But normally you'd buy the plain white plates because those are cheaper?" I got the message, and hastily answered as suggested: "Yes, of course!" The next day, I was on the Metro North commuter train, headed to a desolate office park to test—and discuss—the porosity of a diverse range of plain white paper plates.

Professional participants experience this sort of thing often. Marotta reports, "I'll be asked the number of times I go to the movies or see a show and I'll say 'about XX many times' and they're like, 'do you think you also maybe go drinking this many times?'" On the Bank of America charity study, the one in which Marotta exaggerated her volunteerism, she says, the recruiter "egged me on to say I volunteered more." Other recruiters will ask about "the chips you eat or something like that, and then they're like, 'well, what about this kind of chip?'" Marotta would happily agree that she did indeed consume the suggested chip.[641]

Sometimes recruiters go so far as to perpetrate farce. One commenter to a market research blog wrote: "My husband and I managed to build our holiday fund quite nicely by attending various focus groups." In one group, she reported, "we were told to pretend that we did not know each other."

Clearly, improving the working conditions of the recruiters would help. Describing how his firm took steps to rid its own groups from "cheaters," Jonathan Hilland writes that, among other measures, his firm invested in the recruiters; they are now "salaried at a good hourly rate with benefits and paid vacation." (This is definitely not standard practice.) The recruiters are given more time to recruit—clearly critical, since so much of the fudging seems to happen when people are trying to meet unrealistic deadlines—and also get a bonus when everyone in their groups turns out to have been well-screened and truly qualified.[642]

While most market researchers view the professional panelists as a menace, there are alternative views. Some market researchers point out that everyone is savvier these days, and that the panelists who "know more than we want them to know"[643] are simply part of this phenomenon. In this view, the search for the ingénue, the receptive innocence of the average person, is outdated. The professional panelist is just part of a more knowing culture in which everyone is in on the charade of advertising.

Julia Strohm is lighthearted about repeat participants. "I don't even worry about it . . . I think I saw [one] once," she recalls, "and she was a great respondent so I was glad to have her."[644]

She's not alone in feeling that the presence of a professional participant in a group doesn't have to be a crisis. After all, some people are good at being in focus groups. Even Nadia admits,

> I've definitely selected people, that, if the group needs more people and I remember them to be a good respondent, I will overlook [the six-month requirement] . . . [if] they're responsive and they're a normal person, we'll ask them to come aboard.[645]

Andy Tuck is emphatic that the presence of repeat participants doesn't matter. Asked if such people tell the truth in the groups, the former philosophy professor says mischievously, "I don't even know what the truth is."[646]

In a sense, researchers' view of the "professional panelist" problem is informed by how they feel about all the panelists: do they feel grateful, or do they feel constantly suspicious? Do they feel that the participants' presence is a gift, or something more like a transaction? Pogash feels it's the latter, which may account for her rage at the "professionals":

> Respondents are paid for their time. In agreeing to participate they enter into a contract. They are NOT doing us a favor. For us to view the relationship as a set of reciprocal favors is crazy.[647]

Obviously, someone who is lying in the group probably isn't too useful. But when they are representing their own experiences and opinions more or less accurately, what's wrong with people trying to make a living by giving their opinions?

When pressed about the professional respondents, even Nadia admits that "their opinion might be valid."[648]

The market researchers' anxiety about professional respondents may, then, have less to do with their impact on the research and more to do with the way in which their existence calls into question the mythologies at the heart of focus group research. That is, focus groups are supposed to represent the authentic voice of the people. "The person who suits the study" deprives the project of populist virtue.

Then again, though it is for many the major draw, money is not the only reason people participate in focus groups. Most important, says Julia Strohm, is the desire to help:

> One of the reasons why I have a great fondness for the respondents is because they really want to help. For the most part, they really want to go in there and do a good job for you . . . I do think that most people really genuinely want to be of service to the moderator in particular and there is a bond that is created.

Strohm says, "Very, very rarely do you get someone who is in it for the money."[649] Though her take is intriguing, it's not widely shared. Most clients and researchers feel that the money is important to the focus group participants, and certainly most participants I spoke with agreed. But she certainly is right that there are other motives.

For many there's the lure of having one's opinion valued—having our "expertise" as consumers recognized and valued, perhaps by powerful people. One frequent participant writes of her first experience that, as part of a group evaluating an exhibit at a San Francisco children's museum, for that hour, "I became an expert in museum planning." She explains,

> It was up to me to tell the group coordinator that it didn't matter to most parents whether the exhibit had interactive play elements or presented the risk of lead poisoning, as long as it had parking, clean changing tables and cost less than $20 for a family of four. Furthermore, I told him, if the museum made us cross any of the Bay Area's costly and crowded bridges, it had better entertain the kids for more than an hour, or there'd

be bigger demand for refunds than Super Bowl tickets. A tape recorder was rolling. A camera had been set up. There was a two-way mirror. The curator, architect, director—and, for all I know, the ten biggest donors to the museum—were all going to see me and hear me telling them how I thought they should run their museum. They wanted my input. I was their public. I didn't have to know beans about museums. I just had to know what it would take to get me to go to theirs. I got family passes and $80. It was instantly addicting.[650]

Moderator Kara Gilmour agrees: "The whole point is to make the participants feel like they're the experts, that they're in control . . . , and you try to not let them notice that you're guiding the conversation."[651]

The blogs that encourage signing up for focus group databases also tout the appeal of having "influence," highlighting how the focus group taps into our desire to be more powerful in the world, and to make a difference. Julia Strohm explains,

I think people feel very powerless in their lives, and I do think that coming to a forum like a focus group is a little stab at changing their world or having an impact on their world in a little way, and I think that feels good.[652]

A focus group also taps into our desire for community, something many of us are lacking in our daily lives. Getting in your car and driving to a focus group offers an instant social milieu: you might even like some of the other people present.

Strohm points out, too, that the fact that the focus group is moderated gives the discussion a sense of meaning and purpose. While there is no doubt that many people don't get enough time to hang out and have a drink with their friends, the focus group also feels more directed, and for some, more useful, than discussion at, for instance, a bar. Strohm comments drily, "It might be overstating to say that it helps people if the peanut butter company decides to—what do they add these days? Yet another jam flavor."[653] But she feels strongly that most participants do enjoy this sense of having an effect on the public world.

Both Marotta and Wendy also cited a fascination with other people's psyches and lives as a draw of participating in a focus group. Said Marotta:

> I think it's funny, just the weird details you learn from other people talking about their lives. Just hearing about this girl who is like such a wigger talking about her Bacardi days with her ex-boyfriend. And just little things, some woman talking about redoing her basement or talking about their favorite TV show and I think that's fun to hear.[654]

Participants also love giving their opinions—a draw mentioned on every blog on the subject. We're accustomed to seeing pundits on TV who, in one way or another, make money by sounding off about their—often quite insupportable—views. The focus group offers ordinary people the chance to do the same. Says Kara Gilmour,

> For me, the thing that made [focus groups] really fun consistently was, I feel like for a lot of these people, it is so important to have somebody listen to them . . . and I think for a lot of people, that's very rare in their lives.[655]

Professional and frequent focus group panelists agree. Says Wendy, "There's something nice about someone asking you how you feel and what you think, even if it's about an advertisement for cat food. It might speak to a desperation to be heard."[656]

Others echo that sentiment. In an essay for *SF Gate*, "Hear Me Roar: Focus Groups are One Mom's Desperate Attempt to be Heard," Turi Ryder uses almost the same words, confessing an "ugly little secret . . . I need people to listen to my opinions."[657] Being a stay-at-home mom, she explains, she feels she doesn't have many opportunities to hold forth. The focus group has returned the pleasure of opining to her:

> Let my older son watch as his one-year-old brother throws the toy train cars out the window one at a time. Who cares if I'm driving around listening to the shower radio because I have no

time to get the stereo fixed? My opinion matters once again—
about every six or seven weeks for an hour and a half.[658]

There is a justice in the "professional respondent" problem: this
industry hell-bent on persuading us to buy stuff we don't need, and
believe political candidates who are lying, is being hoodwinked by ordinary people on a daily basis. There's also something surreal about the
fact that imposters who are lying about the opinions, consumer habits,
and perhaps even their genders are, every day, shaping almost every
aspect of our daily lives and political discourse. But the lure of making a
living from one's opinions is profound for other reasons.

Just as the industry fears, some chronic participants do nourish a
fantasy that focus groups could provide an alternative to a real job. Many
bloggers encourage the idea that market research studies can be part of
an income stream that supports a person or even helps support a family.
Used in combination with other strategies, one exhorts,

> you may find you no longer have the need to go out and look
> for a job working for someone else . . . Focus groups can be
> conducted in person, as well as over the phone or online from
> the comfort of your family room while you sit around in your
> pajamas. Beats listening to you [sic] boss![659]

One woman I talked with after a focus group, a Midtown Manhattan
office worker headed back to her home in Midwood, Brooklyn, said she
participated in a focus group at least once a week. She imagined doing
focus groups nightly, eventually being able to quit her job. She sighed with
delight at the thought: "Wouldn't that be awesome?"[660]

Industry spent so much of the twentieth century convincing people to
think of themselves as consumers, rather than workers. Rather than fight
for a society in which work is humane and industry's profits are shared
with those who perform its labor, people were gradually convinced, as
historian Stuart Ewen has argued, to instead accept social arrangements
that allowed ordinary people to enjoy the fruits of capitalist innovation
as consumers.[661] Throughout the second half of the last century, workers
enjoyed fewer rights on the job and a diminishing share of capital's riches,

a state of affairs that was always justified by an appeal to the welfare of "the consumer," who did indeed enjoy cheaper and more plentiful goods and ever more convenient shopping—whether at her twenty-four-hour Walmart Supercenter or through Amazon.com, from the comfort of her very own bedroom—but didn't she ever have to go to work? Of course she does, if she has a job. And that's made it a flawed tradeoff.

But given this aggressive re-branding of our entire culture as one in which the welfare and dignity of the worker is easily exchanged for that of the consumer, it made sense that some people would decide to make a *living* from consumption. Why not? They have realized that being consumers makes them "experts" whose insight is worth something. In a sense, the reviled "professional respondents" are implicitly calling corporate America on an invidious set of promises. If our value to you is solely based on our consumerism, they ask, why can't you pay us for that?

Fox News, 2011

"There's no coherent policy," a Republican voter in the Fox News focus group complains, discussing President Obama's approach to international affairs. "No one seems to know what's going on."

A woman weighs in. ""I believe Barack Obama's religious beliefs do govern his foreign policy."

The moderator, Frank Luntz, looks surprised. "And what are his religious beliefs?"

"I believe he is a Muslim," she answers promptly.

Murmurs of assent fill the room.[662]

Chapter Twelve: "Who Are These Appalling People?"

Watching a focus group often forces us—any of us—to face our our discomfort with our fellow citizens. This queasiness becomes particularly acute during an election season.

Every other time you turn on the TV, Frank Luntz is "taking the temperature" of a group of middle Americans. During one such session in election year 2008, I watched with a friend, mesmerized, as demonstrated with a wiggly green line, how Luntz's dogged band of stalwartly undecided voters felt about a debate between John McCain and Barack Obama. Did they like it when Barack Obama said "energy independence"? (Ooh, yes, quite a lot!) Or when John McCain said, "the surge is working" or "Bill Ayers"? (Hmm, not so much—the line had a bit of a sag at such moments.) We were so concerned about the green line that at times we couldn't properly concentrate on the debate.

But the focus group's actual discussion made even more compelling, if awkward, television. We didn't necessarily want to know how undecided our fellow Americans were on crucial issues of the day. "Who *are* these appalling people?" gasped my companion, after we'd watched in horrified silence for a few minutes. It may sound unkind, but she was simply putting into words what many other viewers—myself included—felt.

Who indeed? They're you and I, in some sense, which explains why they're neither as pretty, nor as articulate, as most people on television.

It also explains why we regard them with a distressed mix of recognition and alienation.

Not everyone can be Steve Jobs. But heaping scorn upon the focus group and its participants is an equal opportunity form of elitism, shared throughout the population.

The most intense hostility comes from the very people the focus group is convened to help. Clients' hatred of focus groups is so common that it is joked about in the industry. When I told Andy Tuck, partner in Applied Research & Consulting LLC, a market research firm based in Manhattan's now-stylish meat-packing district, about my friend's worried comment about the Frank Luntz groups, he was delighted. "We're going to put that on a sign in here!" he chortled, gesturing at his conference room. "'Who Are These Appalling People?'"[663] He recognizes the sentiment instantly, because it's one that his clients express all the time.

As Malcolm Tucker, the fictional director of communication and strategy for a cabinet minister on the satirical British TV show *In the Thick of It*, puts it in a 2010 book written by the show's writers,

> Are focus groups helpful? In a word: absofuckinglutely not. Fuck no . . . The problem is that focus groups are made up of members of the public and are therefore intrinsically unreliable/lop-sided/racist/mental.[664]

Tucker is a made-up character, but his sentiment is broadly shared in the real world. As for Andy Tuck's laughter, he can explain. Clients who contract for focus groups, whether in corporate America, advertising, or the political world, Tuck says, "always hate the participants."[665]

For market research professionals like Andy Tuck, the clients' hatred seems to validate the process—demonstrating that focus groups really do represent the public at large. Says Tuck of the corporate clients watching the consumers from behind the mirror, "They're meeting their masters."[666] In his view, the clients hate the focus group participants because elites hate to listen to people. The hatred itself ratifies market democracy, proving that the consumer, rather than capital, rules the world. Hatred of focus groups legitimizes focus groups.

"There's a lot of condescension," agrees another veteran market researcher, Julia Strohm, musing on client attitudes toward focus group participants over tea with me in her Manhattan apartment, which is minimally and pleasingly decorated with artifacts from her extensive travel in Asia.

A practicing Buddhist, Strohm feels that clients make too much of the fact that the participants are getting paid. (There are market researchers, too, who feel that most participants are only there for the money, an issue explored in the previous chapter.) She explains,

> The clients feel that because they're being paid that's the contract, and that that negates any need to have respect or gratitude for them. At least, that's what I sense. Many, many clients say how much [the respondents] are being paid. They're really hyperfocused on that.[667]

Clients also resent the fact that they, accomplished experts, have to listen to people who do not know what they're talking about and know nothing about their field. It is not only the process that they hate, but the participants themselves. Former *Teen Vogue* editor Kara Jesella—who has been on the client side of the focus group process for several media companies—describes the teenage girls that regularly tested that magazine as "vicious." She continues, "You know what? In all the ones I've seen, people really like to criticize. There's way more criticizing than saying, 'I like this.'"

Jesella recalls the awkwardness of the fact that "We're sitting right there, and they're critiquing something they know we created."[668] The negativity can be painful for the client to hear. But some participants view it as their obligation. Writes Tori Ryder, the San Francisco housewife:

> These sessions are sort of like therapy—one must be brutally honest, or it doesn't work. If the website's new logo is ugly and looks vaguely sexual, it's my duty to say so. I'm helping the company succeed. It would be wrong to be diplomatic. Think of all the money they're paying to get it right.

It's also true that the relative anonymity of the focus group participants makes it safer for them to make negative comments than for people within the company who might share some of their misgivings. As Ryder puts it:

> I fly under the radar. They only know about me what they have on the profile. The people on the other side of the glass will never see me again.[669]

Like internet commenters, some no doubt abuse this anonymity just to vent and be assholes. In his list of "types" of focus group participants, the fictional Malcolm Tucker names the Disillusioned Voters, aka the Grumpy Cunt:

> This guy is pissed off about everything. The immigrants. The economy. The NHS. The roads. Erectile disfunction. The fact that he's just won the lottery. The fact that he's a grumpy cunt.[670]

Another common client sentiment is that the people in the focus groups are not the target consumer, an attitide that is not new. Joseph J. Paul, manager of marketing research for feminine care products at Kimberly-Clark, told *Marketing News* in 1976 that during a focus group,

> the people from the agency would sit behind the screen and when it was over they would say, "Boy did you bring in a bunch of stupid consumers. Our consumer isn't like that. Our consumer is young, sophisticated, and bright. You brought in a bunch of dummies . . . They don't know anything about this product."[671]

Sometimes recruitment for the group has indeed been slipshod. Jesella recalls in a *Teen Vogue* group one girl who was "one of the loudest" who "said in the beginning that she didn't like teen magazines, so of course she's not going to like this." Another girl "kept making the point that she's a tomboy . . . she's never going to like a fashion mag. You know? It makes no sense to take her opinion. She probably really won't buy this magazine."

Such consumers may in fact be ill-suited to discuss a particular product. But Andy Tuck feels that most of the time, clients hate the participants because these ordinary people offend their elite narcissism, providing an unbearable reality check: "[Clients] can't believe that their customers don't care about them or their product."

Many clients also resent the arrogance of focus group participants, feeling that they have way too much confidence in their own opinions, and too little humility about their own lack of expertise. (This may have something to do with the how rarely most people are listened to by anyone with power; once people get in that conference room, that feeling of influence goes to their heads.) Market researchers say that participants generally have to be deflected from telling the client what to do, and gently encouraged to talk instead about their personal habits or reactions.

The market research industry tends to defend focus groups against the haters in populist as much as commercial terms. For them, the clients' hatred of the focus groups is part of what legitimizes the method.

Market researchers often love the participants and feel protective of them. "We tend to hire nice people here," says Andy Tuck, "and they are really shocked by how mean the clients are about the consumers."[672] Julia Strohm, who has worked for Tuck at ARC, was one of those nice people. Her attitude toward the participants is almost one of reverence:

> I go in with enormous gratitude to the participants, because I think they're very kind to show up and give us their time and energy and ideas and responses and really sometimes some very deep personal feelings. And I think it's a real kindness on their part . . . I go in really enjoying the people and really, really appreciating them.

Strohm observes that participants bond with the moderator and feel committed to helping that person do their job: "For the most part, they really want to go in there and do a good job for you."[673]

But the researchers' emotional investment in the participants goes beyond their empathy: the moderators tend to feel invested in an idealistic vision of their profession. They believe that that they are truly listening to the voice of the people, making the ordinary person's opinions matter. Even when they are ambivalent about aspects of their work, market researchers feel that there is something ennobling about letting the people speak. "I think of myself as an advocate for the consumer," says Donna Fullerton. Later she observes, "There's stuff that people are saying that is going to be manipulated and be used to promote products and services that one may not need. It's true. But I think my value comes from being the ear for people and seeing what they think. That's really where I live in the whole process."[674]

Being the consumer's representative imbues market researchers with a sense of purpose, and it enrages them when clients don't want to listen to the focus groups. Pat Tobin, a longtime focus group moderator specializing in children, says when clients ignore the research, she feels it is just typical of the way our society ignores children and their needs. "Nobody listens to kids," she fumes. "It makes me so angry."[675]

Of course, the market researchers' populism can be self-serving. In New York City, I've noticed that more than half the participants in some focus groups are actors, hardly a representative sample of Americans—though they are voluble and not shy, making them "good respondents." Yet many focus groups are a closer microcosm of society than many in corporate America are otherwise likely to encounter; where else do lady truck drivers mix easily with housewives and white collar workers?

This narrative of market research as a populist project, then, contains just enough truth to resonate. The hostility from clients fuels that narrative. Market researchers feel the clients hate the groups because the groups are doing something right: giving voice to the people.

The hostility comes from an elite fearing the masses, but sometimes it resonates with the rest of us, which is why we turn on the TV and feel appalled by the Luntz groups. Ordinary people tend to blame one another when things go wrong, instead of blaming the ruling class. Focus groups are one of many ways that we scapegoat our fellow citizens. Focus group participants are supposed to represent our own deepest feelings and opinions about everything from baby wipes to the war in Iraq, but the rest of us often resent them—wondering why anyone pays attention to folks who plainly don't know what they're talking about.

In the case of political groups, they have, gallingly, been selected for their *inability* to make up their minds about critical issues of the day. We resent the focus group participants because we feel they are doing a poor job of representing us. We blame them for our shallow and often toxic political culture, and for useless products we don't need. In a typical rant, one blogger reacted to 2011 Des Moines, Iowa focus group discussants—televised on Fox—who agreed that the churchgoing president of the United States was a Muslim: "Willful ignorance . . . complete idiots totally devoid of knowledge, fact and truth." Listening to these same pasty-faced Iowans, so confident in their baseless assertions, so certain that the president was a Muslim, even the conservative moderator, Frank Luntz, was momentarily gobsmacked and could only manage a "Wow."[676] Many of us would agree, and we're enraged that elites listen to these people.

It's not unusual to find hatred of focus groups and their influence—blaming them for bad politics, bad movies—whether in blogs and internet comments or casual conversations. A typical discussion on a gamer blog reveals one rant after another along these lines:

I really really hate focus groups. I think my biggest gripe with a lot of games these days is that they are so focus group tested that it's a detriment to the creativity of the designers.

It's getting to the point that every game feels like it was designed for the *Idiocracy*.

Another person in the thread dismisses the participants as "uninformed randos."[677]

Hostility to focus groups is frequently embraced by the left as a shorthand for everything that's wrong with contempoary society and politics. A 2014 editorial in the *Australian Financial Review* typical of this stance argues (referring to Down Under's leftish party), "Labor needs philosophy, not focus groups."[678]

All this reflects the extent of the focus group's reach and its paradox: as ordinary people increasingly lost real political power, the culture of consultation dramatically extended its reach, becoming central to the political process. Thus, while ordinary people had less and less power, their voices were more often heard.

But hatred of the focus group is the populism of fools,[679] because it's really a kind of elitism. Malcolm Gladwell has been writing apologetics for corporate wrongdoing for his entire career—no wonder he doesn't want to hear from ordinary people. Besides, he benefits richly from the cult of expertise—his hefty revenue in speaking fees wouldn't exist without it.

Hatred of the focus group is understandable as a visceral reaction to the marketization of everything. But ultimately, it makes more sense as a position for representatives of the elite like Gladwell, George W. Bush, and the late Steve Jobs, than for ordinary folks, left-of-center critics, or anyone else. The problem with the culture of consultation isn't that elites hear too much from the people. The problem is that consulation is not enough: in a better world, the people would have much greater power, and far more avenues for participation, whether in culture or politics.

Fox News, 2016

Frank Luntz has convened, on Fox News, a live focus group of Michigan Democrats to share their impressions after a March 2016 debate between Bernie Sanders and Hillary Clinton.

"I can relate to Bernie," says a light-skinned black woman with slightly gray hair. "Just on a personal level. I'm just confident in a lot of the things that he says. There's a level of comfort that I think all of America wants to feel. We just don't feel comfortable, and we want to feel comfortable with each other and with the people that lead us."

Luntz plays some clips from the debate, and the participants eagerly weigh in.

"To me, when he said, healthcare is a right because we're all human beings," a white man in his thirties muses, "to me, that was really powerful and I think it would echo what Pope Francis has been saying, about how we need to take care of

people more. Instead of building walls we need to build bridges."

"Bernie has that human touch," a young professional-looking white woman interrupts. "He's got that human touch. As much as I want to believe Hillary, when she speaks I think, yes, yes, Hillary, you're qualified, but you're lacking that empathy that Bernie Sanders supporters feel when he speaks."

"Yes," a young black man says. "It goes along with the trust aspect that Bernie has. He's someone we can all relate to and trust."[680]

Conclusion: Are Focus Groups Dead?

When a *New York Times Magazine* reporter asked Donald Trump if his campaign conducted focus groups, he responded in the well-worn fake populist tradition of George W. Bush. "'I do focus groups,' he said, pressing both of his thumbs to the front of his head, 'Right here.'"[681]

Like all such cowboys, his implication was macho and authoritarian: he knew better than the people. Why would he ask them about anything? His supporters loved him for it. In response to Federal Election Commission numbers showing that Trump spent less than any other candidate on political consultants, Trump's Reddit fans exulted:

> He doesn't need focus groups and consultants telling him what to say.
>
> The lack of overly polished, group tested party approved nonsense is exactly why Trump is winning. People are sick of shiny political robots built to not offend.[682]

Of course, like most theatrical focus-group-rejectors, even Trump had his own consultation strategies. He admitted to the same *Times* reporter that he tested out epithets like "Lyin' Ted," or "Crooked Hillary" at campaign rallies, seeing which ones ellicited more applause. But still, Trump's presidential victory might be a sign that the hegemony of consultation is beginning to crack.

Trump's election represents an extreme moment. Of course it is a symptom of many things—including the worldwide rise of right-wing nationalist movements. But it may also represent a shift in communication between American elites and the masses. Elites have been uncomfortable with focus groups—their own creation—for a long time, because they have long been ambivalent about hearing from the people. In Trump's case, a billionaire boldly asserted that he didn't care what people had to say.

Ordinary people have been uneasy with all the market-testing, too. Hillary Clinton did seem like a "shiny political robot built not to offend." They liked Trump (well, some people did, let's remember that he didn't even win the popular vote) in part because they were tired of elites pretending to listen. They know perfectly well that the culture of consultation has degenerated into a concerted effort to sell them products they don't need and policies they don't want. Like any populist impulse, this suspicion can have either progressive or reactionary implications.

People are always hoping that the culture of consultation will die. It probably won't until it is replaced with something more meaningfully democratic. In the 2016 election, its limitations came dramatically to the surface. Hillary Clinton's tightly scripted, heavily focus-grouped campaign was a failure. Meanwhile, Donald Trump and Bernie Sanders, both candidates whose personalities and political positions veered far from market research–tested centrism, were popular sensations, routinely drawing crowds in the tens of thousands. The enthusiasm of these crowds was a dramatic departure from the typical reception given to mainstream American presidential candidates. At one Sanders campaign rally I attended in Washington Square Park in New York City, more people showed up than could be allowed into the park. To get close to the stage, my son and I would have had to camp out all day like Deadheads of yore—or consumers today in line for a new iPhone. Most important, Sanders and Trump both won votes far beyond what anyone expected. In Trump's case, he astonished almost everyone by winning the presidency.

Unlike Trump, Sanders didn't make blustery public statements rejecting focus groups, but he barely used them. Campaign insiders told me emphatically that Sanders was not a fan of the method and did not find it useful.[683] Sanders' rejection of the focus group had a different ideological context than Trump's. "Let's not insult the intelligence of the American people," Sanders insisted at one point, "People aren't dumb." He seemed, in his atypical message and self-presentation, to reject the condescending relationship underlying the culture of consultation: one in which elites view the people as stupid and listen only in order to manipulate us.

As an authoritarian, Trump had little to say about political participation. But Sanders seemed to be demanding of us that we do more than consult or tweet, that we be more than either focus groupies or data points. Decrying the influence of money on politics, he showed it was possible to run a strong campaign without big money, with small donations (averaging $27 each). Sanders called for a political "revolution," explaining that even if he became president, change could not come from the top, but by grassroots organization. Obviously his was not a perfect campaign, since he didn't win the Democratic nomination, much less the presidency, but his widespread appeal might signal a shift in American politics. Sanders's campaign, far from being a sales pitch, was a constant call for more political action from the voters themselves. Sanders's persona—from his disheveled appearance to his open identification as a socialist—felt very unmarketed. But his rejection of the culture of consultation ran deeper than image or word choice, rooted as it was in the radical assumption that in a democracy, people should not merely hold opinions, but power.

What's heartening is not that a politician ran for national office with Sanders's message—though it's unusual—but that his call for a movement resonated with many people and seemed to tap into a growing desire for more meaningful participation. One contender for New York state senate the same year told *The Nation* she would be an organizer as much as a legislator, expecting her constituents to take power with her: "I want people inside my office every day. I want the community to make the decisions."[684]

The culture of consultation may be hitting some roadblocks; inequality makes us angrier and less amenable to elite persuasion.

Consider, too, the trajectory of the elite itself—from social democrats in Red Vienna or New Deal America trying to persuade the masses to listen to opera or fight the Nazis, to a nihilistic, self-centered ruling class that wants to sell us kombucha and avoid paying estate taxes. The culture of consultation has not been serving the interests of the masses. For all these reasons, we might expect that people would continue to be attracted by populist calls to reject it, whether from left-wing insurgents like Sanders or right-wing nationalists like Trump.

But let's remember, elites and the rest of us alike have been suffering from consulation fatigue for a long time. Trump's theatrical rejection of the focus group is nothing new, nor is mass suspicion of the form. Indeed, the story I tell in this book suggests that these tensions have simply been incorporated into the culture of consultation, which will be with us at least until we find a more egalitarian way of organizing our society.

The political revolt against the culture of consultation is taking place in the context of its dramatic expansion. Jobs in the market research industry are expected to grow by 19 percent from 2014 to 2024, much faster than the average job growth in the United States.[685] When we consider that the purpose of market research has always been to help elites understand the majority, it stands to reason that in an era of rising inequality and alienation, such listening strategies would be needed more than ever.

The masses and the elites occupy dramatically different worlds now. Listening across these divides has always been the aim of the culture of consultation, and the chasms between us are becoming more treacherous to navigate in this way. But, for now, the elite solution is a dramatic expansion of consultation's technology and strategies. Even as rebellion against the culture of consultation simmers, that culture has become more pervasive than ever, becoming a kind of Panopticon that we may never quite escape.

The demise of the focus group has been frequently announced in recent years, even by market research insiders. "Focus groups are dead," declared keynote speaker Mike Volpe, chief marketing officer of HubSpot, a firm specializing in online analytics, at the 2011 Social Media FTW[686]

(For The Win was a bit of internet lingo that has at this writing become obsolete).

Volpe wasn't alone in his projection. The slow expiration of the focus group has been loudly and frequently heralded in recent years in the media and by people like him who are always hawking some higher-tech way to understand the consumer.[687] Numerous articles and blog posts over the past decade have challenged the continued relevance of the focus group and implied that its use was in decline.[688, 689] A 2013 blog post from Greenbook, an organization tracking the future of market research, even suggested that the traditional in-person focus group was an "endangered species."[690]

A March 2016 New York Times story breathlessly declared focus groups over, because the cutting-edge method is apparently now "crowd-sourcing." The source for this claim was, of course, a person who runs a small market research consultancy specializing in subjecting technologies to large numbers of online users. But the definition of "crowd-sourcing" in the article was oddly plastic; the entrepreneur featured in the lede seemed to intend that word to mean "sending out surveys," a methodology that would not even have seemed novel to Frances Maule in the nineteen twenties.[691]

The data does not support these eulogies. In 2007, marketing scholar David Stewart estimated that the use of focus groups had grown steadily since the nineteen seventies, and that the business world's spending on focus groups was estimated to account for at least 80 percent of the $1.1 billion spent annually on qualitative research.[692] ESOMAR, a market research trade group, has found that the percentage of market research dollars that companies are spending on focus groups has remained relatively stable—11 percent in both 2007 and 2013 (actually increasing by a few points in 2011 and 2012).[693] Other industry organizations agree that the use of focus groups remains robust. Greenbook—despite the blog post cited above—reports no significant change in focus group spending from 2013 to 2014.[694] In 2013, almost half the companies responding to Greenbook's survey reported using the traditional focus group more than any other market research method that year.[695] And in 2014, the Market

Research Association estimated that at Fortune 500 companies, almost 70 percent of market research dollars were spent on focus groups.[696]

The focus group is often declared dead because of technology, whether the internet or neuroscience. Yet the unpredictibility and potential insight yielded by face-to-face conversation, and by real-time group dynamics, are still valuable. The traditional focus group, as it emerged in the middle of the last century, will probably be with us for a long time.

Not only does the focus group remain significant, the culture of consultation it spawned is more robust than ever, has taken on more forms, and occupies far more of our daily lives as consumers and as citizens.

"Citizen engagement" is now regarded by policy-makers as so important that firms specializing in it now often manage public debate over local policy decisions. Focus groups, town meetings, and numerous other forms of mediated conversation now accompany the hiring of a school superintendent or the redevelopment of a downtown area. There has been extensive research on what forms of "engagement" work best, but small groups led by a facilitator are common and a burgeoning industry of consultants has emerged. Some of the groups include Public Agenda, Everyday Democracy, and America Speaks.

In part, this use of focus groups reflects the way in which private sector language and processes have affected the public sector. At a focus group in Southington, Connecticut, seeking input on what sort of school superintendent the town should hire, the consultant repeatedly referred to the public school system as "the biggest business in town." But they also reflect a lack of public confidence in the existing democratic processes. At the same focus groups, parents of special needs children said they'd been urged by a school board member to come. They were glad they had attended the focus group, because otherwise their concerns might not have been heard.[697]

Why would people be more compelled by the culture of consultation's trappings than by actual democratic mechanisms? It would seem that the parents of special needs children would be better served by showing up to their (elected) school board meeting than to a focus group.

The mechanisms of the culture of consultation seem to have displaced some of the traditional structures of participation—in our minds as well as in reality. Jennifer Berkshire, a communications consultant for labor unions, says that when a union holds a focus groups, members are often more likely to come than if the union held a membership meeting. "They take it more seriously," she says. "They feel more confident that their opinion is going to be heard."[698]

But being part of a focus group feels satisfying; people know that such groups have some influence, while the workings of actual democratic processes feel murky and unclear, and most of us are cynical about them. Furthermore, at least they know that in a focus group, someone is listening.

This is what we should be mad about: that our democratic institutions can't be trusted to represent our interests. When a focus group feels more like democracy than the real thing, we need to ask how well the real thing is functioning.

Usually, the idea behind such "citizen engagement" strategies is to allow those affected by the proposed policy to feel heard, but a focus group is quite different from a partnership. It allows decision-makers to find out what people think about a plan that elites have already made, rarely to allow ordinary citizens to shape or change the direction of policy. With divisive issues—most recently, plans to privatize public education—the "citizen engagement" process often aims to help a contentious community find common ground—as a "citizen engagement guide" from the Gates Foundation, used in Seattle, suggests.[699] Put another way, these tactics make an elite agenda seem collaborative and uncontested, thus allowing the agenda to move forward with minimal reputation damage to the elites.

The process is particularly salient as a strategy to avoid class struggle. The city of Ypsilanti embarked on an extensive citizen engagement process, including many focus groups, called Shape Ypsi, to address some city planning and other policy issues facing the community. Ypsilanti has a declining tax base, and has long been struggling with a decline in manufacturing jobs. It is also plagued by inequality and racial segregation. There have been controversies over whether to build more affordable housing, raise taxes to fund the public schools, and build more discount retail. Megan Masson-Minock, the consultant who led the Shape Ypsi focus groups, says community engagement tends to be most emphasized in "really distressed communities . . . everybody has to be engaged and everybody has to agree at the table just because there has been years and years of abuses."[700] Put another way, the less social and political power people have, the more important it is to make them feel listened to—or they might revolt.

Now and then, such processes are criticized. Recently, the Chicago Public Schools embarked on a public engagement campaign on its controversial practice of closing poorly performing schools. The Walton Family Foundation funded the initiative. In spite of claims by a CPS spokesperson that the funds went toward the most "rigorous and inclusive" campaign to engage parents the district had ever embarked on, there was a major public backlash against the meetings, with local media highlighting the foundation's connections to the charter school movement.

The methods have been evolving, sometimes getting more creative than simple focus groups. At the beginning of Bill de Blasio's transition to mayor of New York City, citizens could show up to a "Talking Transition" tent, where they could voice their wishes for the next administration, or write them on a Post-it.

As laughable, and in some cases disgraceful, as such consultation efforts are, they may be better than simply not listening, which is why elites continually rethink and reinvent them. Strategies of "public engagement" can also feel inclusive, which is why those in power often see them as more effective than traditional forms of propaganda. Richard Edelman, CEO of Edelman, the largest public relations firm in the United States, hails them as part of a new and smarter public relations, allowing citizens to "co-create" the message.[701]

In a related trend, "participatory budgeting" has become a popular way to involve ordinary people in decisions about one of the most contentious areas of politics: how our money is spent. Citizens show up, debate, and and vote directly on how parts of the city budget should be used. People really love being able to do this. But do such projects expand the reach of democracy? Celina Su, a Brooklyn College political scientist who has studied participatory budgeting, observes that the process tends to favor those in the community with social power.[702] They are more likely to hear about the meetings, and to have the resources to campaign for their pet projects (a gym in their own children's school, for example). Gianpaolo Baiocchi, an NYU professor who has also studied participatory budgeting, has noted that it can distract social justice activists from actually trying to gain more power in the system of governance.[703] It is also true that participatory budgeting affects only a small piece of any budget, making it a token power grab even for those able to use it effectively. Yet as with every form that the culture of consultation takes—but perhaps even more than the traditional focus group—participatory budgeting is drenched in democratic affect.

Of course, citizen engagement and participatory budgeting are micro-trends compared to the biggest recent shift in the culture of consultation: the internet, which has expanded consultation to breathtaking scale. Nathaniel Wice, a former Time Inc. editor who now works in technology and marketing, says media companies needed in-person focus groups two decades ago far more than they do now. "Twenty years ago you didn't know what readers were thinking unless you asked them," he explained. When he worked at *Time* in the nineteen nineties, Wice said, other than through focus groups, editors "never engaged with readers."[704] The internet has allowed elites to learn about the thoughts, feelings, and habits of the masses better now than any other time in history. Innovations that already seem old—Yelp and Amazon reviews, blogs and the comment function on news media sites—have yielded an enormous amount of data, both qualitative and quantitative, for companies seeking to understand the public mind. The voices of our fellow citizens are sold back to us in new ways; Angie's List, a platform for finding local vendors based on user recommendations is touted as "people just like you."

But it is the emergence of social media that has transformed the culture of consultation most profoundly of all, by bringing it into our daily lives. In 2012, the *New York Times* reported on how data from Facebook, Twitter, and Foursquare were giving companies more information than ever about consumer behavior and desires. @WalmartLabs, a unit of the retail giant devoted to extracting valuable marketing data from social media, had discovered that people were all abuzz over cake pops (little bites of cake on lollipop sticks) after Starbucks began selling them. @WalmartLabs discussed the finding with the company's buyers, and Walmart began to sell cake pop makers in its stores. The product was a hit.

A software firm called MicroStrategy had created an app that could access private Facebook profiles. As has been widely reported elsewhere, such data mining means that we are giving companies, and political candidates, access to our thoughts, feelings, consumer purchases, habits, opinions, and comings and goings all day long. In the course of a couple weeks, by using social media, I routinely let big data collectors know what I think about Hillary Clinton, the Confederate flag, racism, media bias, and the plight of Haitians in the Dominican Republic. I also let them know that I went to Target, Modell's, the Family Dollar, the gym, the library, and my kid's public school, as well as which city buses I take regularly, and how I feel about the service on these buses. If they monitor my private chats—which we know they do—they will also learn about plenty of things that I would not post on my public timeline, including my sexual practices. Corporate America knows all of these things about me, and about millions and millions of other people.

The political world knows these things, too. Barack Obama's 2012 reelection campaign was run by his online data analytics team, which had an office the size of a football field.[705] Rather than simply using polls, interviews, and traditional focus groups to stand in for the electorate, Obama's data nerds were able to track each potential voter as an individual and figure out what was likely to change her behavior.

David Simas, director of opinion research, explaining the importance of the analytics to *MIT Technology Review*, said,

> What that gave us was the ability to run a national presidential campaign the way you'd do a local ward campaign. You know the people on your block. People have relationships with one another and you leverage them so you know the way they talk about issues, what they're discussing at the coffee shop.[706]

Indeed, the data was precise—telling them exactly who should contact whom and with what pro-Obama message—but what was also brilliant was social media as a vehicle for those messages. Social scientists ever since Paul Lazarsfeld have known that the people we hang out with influence our politics more than any propaganda does. "People really trust their friends, not political advertising," Obama campaign digital director Teddy Goff told *Nation* reporter John Nichols.[707] (Social media was not the only source of this massive information flood: the campaign used many other technologies, like our cable boxes,[708] or MiniVan, an app used by campaign volunteers to record data about people they talked to while canvassing.)

Throughout the history of market research—including focus groups—many political consultants have believed that their field lagged behind the commercial world and had yet to use market research methologies as effectively. (Democratic consultant David Atkins notes that while liberal Democrats have often struggled to sell basic elements of their agenda to the public, corporate America has succeeded in getting us to buy Vitamin Water and to distinguish between indistinguishable vodka brands.[709]) Yet the age of big data has changed that. Many private companies have lacked the capacity or expertise, not to collect the political data, but to analyze and make good use of it.[710] The Obama campaign—which spent $300,000 on digital marketing in one month of 2012[711]—was so successful at using data from Facebook and other social media that its consultants were actually ahead of the private sector—indeed, companies were clamoring to hire them after the campaign.[712]

The 2012 *Times* article quoted Mark LaRow, senior vice president of that company, on the subject of social media: "This is like the biggest focus group someone could ever imagine."[713] In short, if the focus group ever does go away, it will only do so after thoroughly taking over our lives.

Market research industry analysts project that data mining from Facebook and Google—already a huge part of the industry—is likely to continue to grow. Indeed, Trump's 2016 use of such analytics was even more sophisticated than Obama's, despite the Republican candidate's ostentatious rejection of the focus group. This means that our participation in the culture of consultation is becoming less voluntary than ever; in the past I had to sign up to be part of a focus group for the retail industry to learn my habits, but now the industry knows everything, perhaps because I have "checked in" to the Paramus, New Jersey outlet mall with some ironic yet sincere commentary on my love of Black Friday sales.

There are other ways that the trend toward data mining changes the consumer's relationship to market research. While the focus group came to attract "professional panelists" who have managed to leverage their work experience as consumers to make money from the culture of consultation, on the internet, we give our time and insights away for free. Astra Taylor has noted how much the internet depends on—and inspires—free labor, and the serious implications of this giveaway economy for journalism, filmmaking, music, and other endeavors that deserve and require compensation.[714] Similarly, after decades of compensation for participation in focus groups, we now give our opinions away for free on Yelp or Twitter. The internet is a focus group that the elites don't even need to pay us to participate in.

Social media is the "biggest focus group" not only because it gives marketers—and indeed, all political and corporate elites—unprecedented access to our inner lives and habits, but also because it makes us feel heard. And it does a better job of that than the traditional focus group has. It doesn't make us wait to be asked for our opinion. It allows us to hold forth all day long. Through our often honest and impulsive posts and comments on Facebook, Twitter, Instagram, and many other platforms, we the people opine more than ever. We can also, at any moment of the day, know that people are listening. Not only do we know that Big Data is taking and using our information—an uncomfortable knowledge we try to repress—we also get to see that others are paying attention. We anxiously check our feeds for likes and retweets, as well as attacks and objections. Focus group participants have always been drawn—at least in part—to the satisfaction of speaking and being heard. But now we can do that all day—even at work, on the bus, or from the gym. And we take pleasure in expressing our opinions.

Part of the reason that social media is such an addition to the culture of consultation, of course, is that unlike the focus group, its purpose is not only to harvest our opinions so elites can profit from them; it also allows us to connect with our friends, family, and even strangers who share our interests. And it does all those things quite well. But while we are doing that, we are also giving corporate and political elites some of our best insights for free.

Furthermore, in the data-mining era we have far less control over what we are telling them about ourselves; after all, focus group participants reveal, but also take charge of, their own revelations, sometimes outright inventing. The focus group may also allow us to articulate our dreams—a better baby wipe, socialized medicine—while the data collected on social media may simply indicate what we are settling for, as citizens and as consumers.

Some have described social media as a form of mass political empowerment. Clay Shirky, author of *Here Comes Everybody*, is an NYU professor, but also a highly paid consultant who advises clients like Lego, Nokia, and the U.S. Navy on how best to deploy social media to their own ends. No wonder he has cheerfully proclaimed that "everyone is a media outlet."[715]

Observers who are not on the payroll of global multinational corporations have been less sanguine. Evgeny Morozov, the Belarus-born author of *The Net Delusion* and *To Save Everything Click Here*, has pointed out that contrary to the mythology of social media liberating the world from repressive governments—a common theme in 2011 coverage of the so-called Arab Spring—in fact, dictators in China, Belarus, Iran, and elsewhere have learned how to use social media to their own advantage. It lets them know who the political dissidents are so they can monitor them more closely.[716] Political theorist Jodi Dean makes a parallel argument about social media and our relationship to our own rulers here at home, asserting that we are living in a period she has called "communicative capitalism" in which our own drive to connect and to share seduces us into giving up important information to ruling elites[717]—whether the NSA, political campaign consultants, Google, or Walmart.

Dean also questions the quality of internet political conversation, positing that the form of our sharing—and the act of sharing—can become ultimately more important than the content. In other words, the processes of reblogging, liking, retweeting, and posting come to matter more than whatever message it is that we are hoping to convey to the world. In these ways, communicative capitalism can be depoliticizing.

Many other commentators have questioned the value of so-called "hashtag politics." While hashtag efforts like #BlackLivesMatter have certainly put critical social issues into political conversation, they have also enmeshed us more deeply into the culture of consultation, whose biggest paradox is that despite being empowered to speak and to be heard, we still, unless we are plutocrats, have little power or influence. With the decline of unions, and the increasing vise-like grip of money on the political system, ordinary Americans have in some ways less political power than we did before social media, even though in those days, we had to write a letter to a newspaper editor or a politician, put a stamp on it, and take it to the mailbox in order to be heard.

Social media has been hailed by some thinkers as an expansion of the public sphere. And it is. But it should also be thought of as an expansion of the same old culture of consultation, which ultimately serves those in power best of all.

Our corporate elites are, so far, doing an excellent job of using the listening process to seduce our votes and our spending dollars. We the people are, meanwhile, struggling to be heard in ways that actually change anything, because giving voice is not the same as taking power. In this way, the story of social media mirrors that of the focus group, only it has been accompanied by more illusions, as so many commentators have hailed these communication technologies as the beginning of a newly horizontal world.

Yet the culture of consultation—whether in a focus group, a fan fiction blog, or a Yahoo! review—taps into our desire to be creative, engage with others, and to make a difference in the world. If a focus group is what democracy feels like, in the culture of consultation's newer forms we feel it even more. When we are angry at President Trump we can tweet at him.

Even if the incorrigible Tweeter in Chief doesn't respond, millions of our fellow citizens might see it. Our idea might have some impact.

At its best, the culture of consultation has always asked us to imagine what we want and discuss it with others. We can imagine a baby wipe we might like better. But can we envision democracy? Can we talk about it? Can we imagine ordinary people like ourselves having influence that is more meaningful that than the garbled and stuttered input we offer in these airless rooms? Could the culture of consultation give way to something more radically democratic?

Conversation not only drives social media, but some of our forms of street opposition, like 2011's Occupy Wall Street. In sharp contrast to the focus group, which has always been convened by elites and for their purposes, Occupy attempted to prefigure a society without elites, where everyone had power. It is from such experiments in conversation that a better society will grow.

"Mic check!" At Zuccotti Park, while protesters camped there throughout 2011, communication was so important, and normal microphones prohibited, that participants took to amplifying each other's speeches through "The People's Mic": repeating them in unison. People showed up and debated the issues in person. Not everyone agreed with the premise of protesting Wall Street, but people came out nonetheless for the serious discussion. And people came from all over the country to participate in the General Assemblies, the movement's town hall meetings in which decisions ranging from how to keep out the rain to what to eat for breakfast were made—even many who never slept a night in the park.

In the wake of Zuccotti, people formed neighborhood assemblies, from Portland, Oregon, to Staten Island, to work together to solve shared local problems: the need for a park, or a bus shelter. These groups bore some resemblance to focus groups. People engaged in group conversation to figure things out. But at times the Assemblies that grew out of the Occupy movement can be seen as anti-focus groups, in which people talk, not so that a decision-maker outside their group can listen, but to build power and sometimes get their way. The way people continue to gather on the internet, to discuss political issues and to organize, is similar.

Yet these discussions had much in common with our corporate culture of consultation. Some Assemblies at Occupy went on for as long as eight hours about people's feelings. A good deal of internet political conversation, of course, also yields no material challenge to the status quo. Conversation is critical to movements, but conversation without clear thought about building institutions and power can be a dead end.

Though its influence was important, Occupy fizzled out, and that's partly because simply giving voice, simply being heard, is not enough. The People's Mic is a beautiful idea, but the people need much more than a mic. Indeed, as the history of the focus group shows, elites have always been more than happy to give us a mic. To get more, you have to have a strategy, and a theory of how you might take power. The culture of "endless talk,"[718] as Russell Jacoby put it, criticizing the activists of the nineteen sixties, shows how much even our forms of dissent mirror the ritual of the focus group. We cannot remain trapped in the conversation, as pleasurable as it is. I don't mean by this to reinvent that classic Americanism, "Less talk, more action!" I mean that we need to learn to shift our talk, from giving voice to organizing, persuading, and challenging. This kind of talk is harder work, but is where political change actually occurs.

Acknowledgments

It sometimes sounds implausible when writers assert that without these acknowledged people, this book would never have happened. But asserted here, it is absolutely true. The idea for this book came about through many conversations with my editor, publisher, and friend, Colin Robinson, who then waited with heroic patience and just the right amount of nagging as it took much too long to materialize. Early interviews and conversations with Donna Fullerton were also crucial.

The book would never have been completed without the friendship, imagination, rigorous feedback, and enthusiasm of my writing group—Jessica Blatt, Kimberly Phillips-Fein and Caitlin Zaloom—also known as "the Brain Trust." Their ideas have influenced every page, and their intellectual curiosity has been a constant inspiration to me. I may have to write another book just to spend more time with these brilliant women.

I also can't imagine writing this book without Jassica Bouvier. In an incredible piece of good fortune, when I talked about this book on a panel at the Left Forum, Jassica introduced herself and asked if I needed any help. How glad I am that I said yes. Jassica was the most extraordinary research assistant an author could have: not only was she interested in this offbeat subject, she is a deep reader with a wonderfully synthetic mind.

For two of the (many) years that I worked on this project, I was the Belle Zeller Visiting Professor of Public Policy at Brooklyn College. This job was a gift for me in so many ways; I loved my students and my colleagues, and the pay and benefits were excellent. But most materially, the generous research budget and summer vacation were critical to my work on this book. I'm grateful to the political science department for that windfall of time and money.

While working on this book, several institutions were generous and curious enough to invite me to speak about it. I'd like to thank everyone who attended these talks at University of Wisconsin-Madison's Havens Center for Social Justice, Marymount Manhattan College, Caitlin Zaloom's class at New York University, Left Forum, John Jay College's economics department, and the Brooklyn College Historical Society, for enthusiasm and all your excellent questions. I'm especially thankful to economics professor Josh Mason of John Jay for his thoughtful writeup of the talk and the project.

Historians always thank archivists and librarians, and rightly so— what treasures these people are! I relied extensively on those at Columbia University's Rare Book and Manuscript library, especially those over-seeing oral histories and the archives of the Bureau of Applied Social Research and the Oral History Project, as well as on the staff at the Vanderbilt Television News Archive in Nashville, Tennessee. At Duke University, archivists at the John W. Hartman Center for Sales, Advertising, and Marketing History provided not only help navigating the collections, but also a travel grant that made it possible to visit them in person.

Many people generously gave interviews about their experiences in the world of focus groups, and I'm forever grateful for their time and insights. Furthermore, I appreciate everyone who wrote on this subject before I did, especially David Morrison, author of *Search for a Method*, which was probably the most serious book-length history of the focus group before this one.

My agent, Faye Bender, has been so patient with the many interruptions and delays. She is also smart, savvy, and a lovely person; I have been so lucky to work with her for all these years.

All my friends make my life so much better, but on this project, I had helpful conversations with Paisley Currah, Jane Collins, Jodi Dean, Beka Economopoulos, Belén Fernández, Christian Parenti, Michael Pollak,

John Marshall, and Karen Miller, as well as Jim Ledbetter, who also provided generous and incisive feedback on the manuscript. My son, Ivan, now ten, was quite little when I began this book. (Children grow so much faster than books.) I'm grateful for his patience, especially during the many summers I spent writing. My own parents, Jay and Helen Featherstone, deserve the biggest thanks of all, for showing us how to balance love and family with the life of the mind.

Doug Henwood is the love of my life and my greatest intellectual influence. (On this project, he also forced me to finally use an em-dash properly.) Our conversations shape everything I think and write. I wish I could thank him in print, for mass circulation, every single day, but this will have to do for the moment.

.

End Notes

1   Stefan Schwarzkopf and Rainier Gries, eds., *Ernest Dichter and Motivation Research: New Perspectives on the Making of Post-war Consumer Culture* (Palgrave, 2010), 5.

2   Laura Shapiro, *Something from the Oven: Reinventing Dinner in 1950s America* (Viking, 2004).

3   Ibid.

4   Ibid.

5   Alfred Goldman, "The Group Depth Interview," *Journal of Marketing* (July, 1964), 64.

6   Adam Curtis, "Century of the Self," BBC (2002). http://topdocumentaryfilms.com/the-century-of-the-self/.

7   It is also important to note that this story, while widely supported by Dichter scholars and by Dichter's associates, has sometimes been misconstrued. While there is little question that Dichter's work for the Betty Crocker Company in the fifties shaped the marketing of that company's cake mix, he didn't invent the idea of adding the egg. Cake mixes required eggs long before the mass psychoanalysis of consumers. A patent application for cake mix from as far back as the early nineteen thirties noted that "the housewife and the purchasing public in general seem to prefer fresh eggs." (And intriguingly, at least one consumer survey from that period found that some women preferred not to be bothered with the egg.) See Michael Y. Park, "A History of the Cake Mix, the Invention that Redefined 'Baking,'" *Bon Appetit*, September 2, 2013. But Dichter's insight certainly did inform the company's pitch to consumers.

8   Erving Goffman, "On Face Work: Analysis of Ritual Elements in Social Interaction," *Reflections*, Vol. 4, No. 3, 13.

9   Marketing Research Association.

10   Ibid.

11   Ibid.

12   World association for market, social, and opinion research (ESOMAR).

13   Author interview, Andy Tuck, July 7, 2010.

14   Author interview, Nathaniel Wice, June 10, 2011.

15   Ibid.

16   Author interview, Donna Fullerton, November 30, 2009.

17   Lizabeth Cohen, *A Consumer's Republic: The Politics of Mass Consumption in Postwar America* (Knopf, 2003).

18   Richard Fry and Paul Taylor, Pew Research Center, "The Rise of Residential Segregation by Income," August 1, 2012. www.pewsocialtrends.org/2012/08/01/the-rise-of-residential-segregation-by-income/.

19   Author interview, Kara Gilmour, June 8, 2010.

20   Jonathan Bond and Richard Kirshenbaum, *Under the Radar: Talking to Today's Cynical Consumer* (Wiley, 1999). From excerpt in *Brandweek*, December 8, 1997. http://adland.tv/content/under-radar.

21   Now Kirshenbaum, Bond, Senecal & Partners (KBS&P), with the addition of Lori Senecal, who is now president and CEO.

22   Colorism is discrimination not by race but by skin shade. It is common around the globe.

23   Author interview, Donna Fullerton, op. cit.

24   Author interview, Julia Strohm, July 20, 2010.

25   "The Reminiscences of Paul Lazarsfeld," January 20, 1962, 160, in the Columbia Center for Oral History Collection (hereafter CCOHC), Rare Book & Manuscript Library, Columbia University in the City of New York. Photocopied with permission from Robert K. Lazarsfeld.

26   Morton Hunt, "How Does It Come to Be So?" *The New Yorker*, January 28, 1961.

27   CCOHC, , op. cit., 161.

28   Hunt, op. cit. Lazarsfeld corroborates Hunt's account of this evening in his essay, "Working With Merton," Lewis Coser, ed., *The Idea of Social Structure: Papers in Honor of Robert Merton* (Harcourt Brace, 1975).

29   CCOHC, op. cit., 162.

30   Hunt, op. cit.

31   *This Is War*, directed by Norman Corwin, broadcast on CBS, NBC, MBS, and the Blue Network, 1942. Audio of premiere episode: www.otrcat.com/this-is-war-norman-corwin-p-49342.html.

32   Online catalog, Museum of TV and Radio, www.ny.com/cgibin/frame.cgi?url=http://www.paleycenter.org/&frame=/frame/museums.html.

33   James Spiller, "This Is War! Network Radio and World War II Propaganda in America," *Journal of Radio Studies*, Vol. 11, Issue 1 (2004).

34   "This Is War," op. cit.

35   Spiller, op. cit.

36   James Sparrow, *Warfare State: World War II Americans and the Age of Big Government* (Oxford University Press, 2011).

37   Lazarsfeld in Coser, op. cit.

38   "The Focussed Interview and Focus Groups: Continuities and Discontinuities," Robert Merton, talk given to a New York meeting of the American Association of Public Opinion Research (AAPOR), June 1986. Later published in *Public Opinion Quarterly*, vol. 51 (1987): 550–566.

39   Hunt, op. cit., 61.

40   CCOHC, op. cit., 163.

41   Ibid.

42   Merton AAPOR talk, op. cit.

43   Hunt, op. cit., 60.

44   Letter quoted in Lazarsfeld, via Coser, op. cit., 36.

45   Letter from Robert K. Merton to Carl Hovland, July 2, 1943, Columbia University Rare Book and Manuscript Library.

46   Michael T. Kaufman, "Robert K. Merton, Versatile Sociologist and Father of the Focus Group, Dies at 92," *New York Times*, February 24, 2003. www.nytimes.com/2003/02/24/nyregion/robert-k-merton-versatile-sociologist-and-father-of-the-focus-group-dies-at-92.html.

47   Readers will note that Facebook continues this tradition of pressing buttons to indicate whether we "like" or "dislike," while also allowing us to explain ourselves in more nuanced ways.

48   Coser, op. cit.

49   Historian James Spiller has usefully challenged this distinction, but for our purposes the fact that the American architects articulated such a difference is important.

50   Robert Griffith, "The Selling of America: The Advertising Council and American Politics, 1942–1960," *Business History Review* (Autumn 1983): 394.

51   I am indebted throughout this chapter to David Morrison's book, *Search for a Method: Focus Groups and the Development of Mass Communication Research* (University of Luton Press, 1998), which rightly ascribes great importance to Lazarsfeld's personal and historical circumstances in the development of the focus group. Morrison's book influenced my thinking and pointed me to many important sources.

52   Helmut Gruber, *Red Vienna: Experiment in Working-Class Culture* (Oxford University Press, 1991), 87.

53   Ibid.

54   Ibid., 6.

55   Ibid.

56   CCOHC, op. cit., 40.

57   Morrison, op. cit.

58   CCOHC, op. cit., 201–203.

59   Ibid., 240.

60   Ibid, 185–186.

61   Gruber, op. cit.

62   Ibid.

63   Ibid., 140.

64   Ibid.

65   As quoted by Lawrence Samuel in *Freud on Madison Avenue: Motivation and Subliminal Advertising in America* (University of Pennsylvania Press, 2010), 22.

66   Morrison, op. cit.

67   CCOHC, op. cit.

68   Fred Turner, *Counterculture to Cyberculture: Stewart Brand, the Whole Earth Network and the Rise of Digital Utopianism* (University of Chicago Press, 2006).

69   Laura Shapiro, *Something from the Oven* (Viking, 2004).

70   Perham Nahl, "The Snowball Interview," *Printers' Ink*, March 23, 1951.

71   Cohen, op. cit., 112–113.

72   Ibid., 119.

73   Russell Jacoby, *Social Amnesia: A Critique of Contemporary Psychology* (Transaction, 1997).

74   Lawrence R. Samuel, *Freud on Madison Avenue* (University of Pennsylvania Press, 2010), 21.

75   Letter from Herta Herzog to Elizabeth Perse, September 12, 1994. http://outofthequestion.org/userfiles/file/Herta%20Herzog%20(Sept%2012%201994%20to%20Elisabeth%20Perse).pdf.

76   Ibid.

77   Bureau of Applied Social Research Records, 1944–1976. Series I: Project Index.

78   Jonathan Cole, "Paul Lazarsfeld: His Scholarly Journey," keynote address delivered at "An International Symposium in Honor of Paul Lazarsfeld," Brussels, Belgium, June 4–5, 2004. www.columbia.edu/cu/univprof/jcole/_pdf/2004Lazarsfeld.pdf.

79   Ibid.

80   Morrison, op. cit., 97.

81   Jacques Lautman and Bernard-Pierre Lécuyer, eds., *Paul Lazarsfeld (1901–1976): La sociologie de Vienne à New York* (Harmattan, 1998), 142.

82   Morrison, op. cit., 97.

83   Memo to Mr. Reinstrom, sent to all JWT international offices, from Howard Henderson, November 29, 1956. J. Walter Thompson Company Collections. Rare Book, Manuscript, and Special Collections Library, Duke University.

84   Herb Fisher, "The Problems of Research," February 4, 1957. J. Walter Thompson Company Collections. Rare Book, Manuscript, and Special Collections Library, Duke University.

85   Howard Henderson, "J. Walter Thompson Research Is Worldwide," June 17, 1958. J. Walter Thompson Collections, Rare Book, Manuscript, and Special Collections Library, Duke University.

86   Howard Henderson, cover letter to Dr. Donald Longman, with "J. Walter Thompson Research Is Worldwide" attached, June 17, 1958. J. Walter Thompson Collections, Rare Book, Manuscript, and Special Collections Library, Duke University.

87   Henderson, "J. Walter Thompson Research is Worldwide," op. cit.

88   Ralph Goodman, "Freud and the Hucksters," *The Nation*, February 14, 1953. Quoted in Samuels, op. cit.

89   *Printers' Ink*, February 27, 1953. Quoted in Packard's *The Hidden Persuaders*, 63.

90   Goodman, op. cit.

91   Ibid.

92   C. Wright Mills, *The Sociological Imagination* (Oxford University Press, 1959), 65.

93   CCOHC, op. cit., 213.

94   Ibid., 138.

95   Morrison, op. cit., 20.

96   Ibid.
97   Ibid.
98   Kimberly Phillips-Fein, *Invisible Hands: The Businessmen's Crusade Against the New Deal* (W.W. Norton, 2009).
99   Joe Moran, "Mass-Observation, Market Research and the Birth of the Focus Group, 1937–1997," *Journal of British Studies* (October 2008): 827–851.
100   Ibid.
101   Letter from Herta Herzog letter to Elizabeth Perse, September 12, 1994. http://outofthequestion.org/userfiles/file/Herta%20Herzog%20(Sept%2012%201994%20to%20Elisabeth%20Perse).pdf.
102   Ibid.
103   Samuels, op. cit.
104   Elizabeth Perse, "Herta Herzog, 1910–", *Women in Communication: A Biographical Sourcebook*, Nancy Signorelli, ed. (Greenwood Press, 1996).
105   Herzog to Perse, op. cit.
106   Bureau of Applied Social Research Records, 1944–1976, Project Index, http://findingaids.cul.columbia.edu/ead/nnc-rb/ldpd_5012632/dsc/1.
107   "Study on Stomach Distress," 1942, Bureau of Applied Social Research, Columbia University Rare Book and Manuscript Library.
108   Herzog to Perse, op. cit.
109   Ibid.
110   Samuel, op. cit.
111   Ibid., 65.
112   "Interview with Dr. Herta Herzog," Adam Curtis, www.bbc.co.uk/programmes/p009jd1g.
113   Adam Curtis speculates here, but it seems right to me: www.bbc.co.uk/blogs/legacy/adamcurtis/2010/08/madison_avenue.html.
114   This episode makes a composite of Herzog's work with research by Ernest Dichter—the show's creators do not distinguish between Lazarsfeld's students, nor between Freudians and Adlerians.
115   Curtis interview, op. cit.
116   Ibid.
117   Adam Curtis, "Century of the Self," op. cit.
118   Curtis interview, op. cit.
119   Jacoby, op. cit.
120   Ibid.
121   Samuel, op. cit., 65.

122　Ibid.
123　Adam Curtis, "Century of the Self," op. cit.
124　Ibid.
125　Jacoby, op. cit., 51.
126　Ibid.
127　Ibid., 48–49.
128　Adam Curtis, "Experiments in the Laboratory of Consumerism, 1959–1967," www.bbc.co.uk/blogs/legacy/adamcurtis/2010/08/madison_avenue.html.
129　Robin Gerber, *Barbie and Ruth: The Story of the World's Most Famous Doll and the Woman Who Created Her* (HarperCollins, 2009), 106–107.
130　Jonathan Engel, *American Therapy: The Rise of Psychotherapy in the United States* (Gotham Books, 2008).
131　Curtis, "Century of the Self," op. cit.
132　Ibid.
133　Ibid.
134　Robert K. Merton and Patricia Kendall, "The Focused Interview," *American Journal of Sociology* 51, 6 (1946): 541–557; Robert K. Merton, Marjorie Fiske, and Patricia L. Kendall, *The Focused Interview: A Manual of Problems and Procedures* (Glencoe, IL: Free Press, 1956).
135　Merton and Kendall, op. cit.
136　Mark Abrams, "Possibilities and Problems of Group Interviewing," *Public Opinion Quarterly*, Fall 1949.
137　Alfred Goldman and Susan Schwartz, *The Group Depth Interview* (Prentice-Hall, 1987).
138　Abrams, op. cit., 504.
139　Ibid.
140　Ibid.
141　Alfred Goldman, "The Group Depth Interview," *The Journal of Marketing*, Vol. 26, No. 3 (July, 1962): 66.
142　Russell Belk, ed., *Handbook of Qualitative Research Methods in Marketing* (Edward Elgar, 2006), 260.
143　Nahl, op. cit.
144　Goldman, op. cit., 63.
145　Ibid., 62.
146　Ibid., 63
147　Goldman, op. cit., 62.
148　Abrams, op cit.

149 Packard, op. cit., 59.

150 Nahl, op. cit.

151 Ibid.

152 Ibid.

153 Eugene Morris, "The Evolution of Targetting the Black Audience," *Advertising Age*, September 1, 2007. http://adage.com/article/the-big-tent/evolution-targeting-black-audience/120380/.

154 Abrams, op. cit., 503.

155 Nahl, op. cit.

156 Goldman, op. cit., 63.

157 Gruber, op. cit., 103.

158 Kathryn Jay, *More Than Just a Game: Sports in American Life Since 1945* (Columbia University Press, 2004), 55.

159 James D. Thompson and N.J. Demerath, "Some Experiences with the Group Interview," *Social Forces*, Vol. 31, No. 2 (December 1952): 148–154.

160 Ibid., 154.

161 Nahl, op. cit.

162 "Needed: More Research on the Flow from Factory to Consumer," *Printers' Ink*, April 18, 1958. Rare Book, Manuscript, and Special Collections Library, Duke University.

163 Cited in Packard, op. cit., 64.

164 PBS, "The Rise of American Consumerism," www.pbs.org/wgbh/americanexperience/features/general-article/tupperware-consumer/.

165 BBC News, "1959: Khrushchev and Nixon have war of words," http://news.bbc.co.uk/onthisday/hi/dates/stories/july/24/newsid_2779000/2779551.stm. For his part, Nixon offered that the appliances represented the consumer's "right to choose," suggesting that modern conveniences weren't as good if selected by the government.

166 *Twilight: Los Angeles*, 1992. This one-woman play is Smith's reenactment of the jury deliberations for the Rodney King trial.

167 Participant observation.

168 Packard, op. cit.

169 Daniel Horowitz, *Vance Packard and American Social Criticism* (University of North Carolina Press, 1994).

170 Quote Investigator, "Sometimes a Cigar is Just a Cigar: Sigmund Freud? Apocryphal?" http://quoteinvestigator.com/2011/08/12/just-a-cigar/.

171 Packard, op. cit., 109.

172   Ibid., 114.
173   Ibid., 115.
174   Ibid., 153.
175   Ibid.
176   Horowitz, op. cit., 181.
177   Philip Quarles, "Beyond 'Eggheads': Vance Packard Pulls Back the Curtain on Advertising," WNYC, December 5, 2012. www.wnyc.org/story/206678-vance-packard/.
178   Horowitz, op. cit., 180.
179   Ibid., 180.
180   Ann Marie Seward Barry, *Visual Intelligence: Perception, Image and Manipulation in Visual Communication* (State University of New York Press, 1997), 262.
181   Horowitz, op. cit., 182.
182   Pierre Martineau, "Here's a Look at Tomorrow's Consumer," *Nation's Business,* December 1958.
183   Ibid.
184   Ibid.
185   Ibid.
186   Steuart Henderson Britt, *The Spenders* (McGraw-Hill, 1960), 36.
187   Ibid, 6.
188   Ibid, 36.
189   William H. Peterson, "King Customer," *Wall Street Journal,* June 26, 1957.
190   "Consumer King—and Queen—of Retail Marts," *Chicago Tribune,* January 7, 1958.
191   "The Boss," *New Pittsburgh Courier,* May 7, 1960.
192   Stephan Schwarzkopf, "The Consumer as 'Voter,' 'Judge,' and 'Jury': Historical Origins and Political Consequences of a Marketing Myth," *Journal of Macromarketing,* vol. 31, no. 1 (2011): 8–18.
193   Ibid.
194   Ibid.
195   Ibid.
196   Ford Motor Company, Edsel print ad (1957).
197   Ford Motor Company, Edsel commercial (1958), www.youtube.com/watch?v=HpIp_yxaVJI.
198   "History of BASR Edsel Study: 'Project Y Only,'" Bureau of Applied Social Research, Columbia University Rare Book and Manuscript Library.

199 John Brooks, "The E-Car is Looking Out for You, Son," *The New Yorker*, November 26, 1960.

200 "History of BASR Edsel Study: Project Y Only," op. cit.

201 Ford Motor Company, Edsel commercial (1957).

202 Ford Motor Company, "This is the Edsel," print ad, *Ames Tribune*, September 3, 1957. *Ames Tribune* Photo Archive, Ames Historical Society. www.ameshistory.org/tribunearchives/heavy-turnout-see-edsels.

203 Brooks, op. cit., 96.

204 Ibid.

205 Tom Dicke, "The Edsel: Forty Years as a Symbol of Failure," *The Journal of Popular Culture*, Vol. 43, Issue 3 (June 2010): 486–502.

206 Brooks, op. cit.

207 Ibid.

208 Ibid.

209 Cited in Brooks; original is S.I. Hayakawa, "Why the Edsel Laid an Egg: Motivational Research vs. the Reality Principle," *ETC; A Review of General Semantics* 15:3 (Spring 1958).

210 Ibid.

211 Ibid.

212 Steven Bayley, "Car Culture: Trust Intuition, Not a Focus Group," *The Telegraph*, September 13, 2003.

213 Peter Carlson, "The Flop Heard Round the World," *Washington Post*, September 4, 2007. www.washingtonpost.com/wp-dyn/content/article/2007/09/03/AR2007090301419_5.html?sub=new.

214 Paul B. Brown, "Six Solid Marketing Ideas from Those Who Do it Best," *Forbes*, April 28, 2013. www.forbes.com/sites/actiontrumpseverything/2013/04/28/six-solid-marketing-ideas-from-those-who-do-it-best/#5d92153372da.

215 Brooks and Dicke, op. cit., also Thomas E. Bonsall, *Disaster in Dearborn: The Story of the Edsel* (Stanford University Press, 2002).

216 Jesse McLean, *Kings of Madison Avenue: The Unofficial Guide to 'Mad Men'* (ECW Press, 2009).

217 "History of BASR Edsel Study: Project Y Only," op cit.; "History of BASR Edsel Studies: 'Project Y' and 'Edsel,'" Bureau of Applied Social Research, Columbia University Rare Book and Manuscript Library.

218 Brooks, op. cit.

219 "History of BASR Edsel Study: Project Y Only," op. cit.

220 Brooks, op. cit.

221 Bonsall, op. cit., 192.

222 Ibid., 201.

223 Ford Motor Company, Edsel print ad, *Deseret News*, April 17, 1959; Ford Motor Company, Edsel TV ad (1959), www.youtube.com/watch?v=5Cuxkk8dv-c.

224 Brooks, op. cit.

225 Ibid.

226 Ibid.

227 Bonsall, op. cit., 204.

228 Memo from David Wallace to Paul Lazarsfeld, Bureau of Applied Social Research, Columbia University Rare Book and Manuscript Library.

229 Dicke, op. cit.

230 Memo, David Wallace to Paul F. Lazarsfeld, op. cit.

231 Ibid.

232 Bonsall, op. cit.

233 Brooks, op. cit.

234 Memo, David Wallace to Paul F. Lazarsfeld, op. cit.

235 Ibid.

236 Edsel Owners Club, "History," www.edselclub.org/history.html.

237 "Car Crusaders Defend Edsel's Underdog Image," *The Morning Call*, November 12, 1989.

238 Bonsall, op. cit.

239 Dicke, op. cit.

240 Memo from Lee Wiggins to Clara Shapiro, David Sills, Barbara Silverblatt, and David Wallace, Re: Silverblatt Report on Innovation in a Recession, Edsel Project, July 20, 1958. Columbia University Rare Book & Manuscript Library.

241 Confidential Memorandum, from Lee Wiggins, to David Sills and Clara Shapiro, Re: Edsel Project, June 20, 1958. Columbia University Rare Book & Manuscript Library.

242 "Dictators Without Peer," *Wall Street Journal*, November 20, 1959.

243 Dicke, op. cit.

244 George Katona, *The Powerful Consumer: Psychological Studies of the American Economy* (McGraw-Hill, 1960), 9.

245 Ibid., 243.

246 Cohen, op. cit., 125.

247 Ibid.

248 Ibid., 126.

249　At the moderator's request, her name, as well as details about the product, have been withheld to preserve the confidentiality of the study. The year and location have also been changed.

250　George Horsley Smith/Advertising Research Foundation, *Motivation Research in Advertising and Marketing* (McGraw-Hill, 1954), 69–71.

251　The phrase comes from a thriller novel about zombie housewives published in 1972, and a movie of the same name released in 1975. Both book and movie reflect concerns of their own time, as the women's liberation entered pop culture, and the stereotype reflected hostility to fifties images of women.

252　Joanne Meyerowitz, ed., *Not June Cleaver: Women and Gender in Postwar America, 1945–1960* (Temple University Press, 1994).

253　Betty Friedan, *The Feminine Mystique*, originally published by Dell (1963), 206.

254　Kate Forde, "Celluloid Dreams: The Marketing of Cutex in America, 1916–1935," *Journal of Design History*, vol. 15, no. 3 (2002): 183.

255　Ibid., 184.

256　Ibid., 183.

257　Ibid.

258　Erika Rappaport, *Shopping for Pleasure: Women in the Making of London's West End* (Princeton University Press, 2001).

259　Theodore Dreiser, *Sister Carrie* (Doubleday, 1900), 76.

260　Forde, op. cit., 184.

261　Walter Lippmann, *Liberty and the News* (Harcourt, Brace and Howe, 1920), 52.

262　Philip Wylie, *Generation of Vipers* (Rinehart, 1955, originally published 1943), 52.

263　Jonathan Yardley, "'Generation of Vipers' Loses Its Bite," *Washington Post*, July 30, 2005. www.washingtonpost.com/wp-dyn/content/article/2005/07/29/AR2005072902124.html

264　Wylie, op. cit., 53.

265　Friedan, op. cit., 230.

266　Hendrik de Leeuw, *Women: The Dominant Sex* (Arco, 1957), 145.

267　de Leeuw, op. cit., 60.

268　Lucy Key Miller, "Front Views and Profiles: Hidden Persuaders," *Chicago Daily Tribune*, November 5, 1957.

269　Ibid.

270　Samuel, op. cit., p. 106.

271　Thomas J. Fleming, "Why You Buy," *Washington Post*, February 21, 1960.

272 An Italian actress and sex symbol of the nineteen fifties and early nineteen sixties.

273 Elizabeth Ford, "Homemakers Hardening: They're Yearning for Softer Sell," *Washington Post*, May 18, 1960.

274 Britt, op. cit., 229.

275 Meg Jacobs, *Pocketbook Politics: Economic Citizenship in Twentieth-Century America* (Princeton University Press, 2007).

276 Christina E. Bax, "Entrepreneur Brownie Wise: Selling Tupperware to America's Women in the 1950s," *Journal of Women's History*, vol. 22, no. 2 (Summer 2010): 173.

277 Ibid.

278 Susan Vincent, "Preserving Domesticity: Reading Tupperware in Women's Changing Domestic, Social and Economic Roles," *Canadian Review of Sociology/Revue canadienne de sociologie*, vol. 40, Issue 2 (May 2003): 185.

279 Samuel, op. cit., 5; Forde, op. cit.

280 Cole, op. cit.

281 Samuel, op. cit., 64.

282 Ibid., 65.

283 "Jack Tinker & Partners," *Advertising Age*, September 15, 2003. http://adage.com/article/adage-encyclopedia/jack-tinker-partners/98906/.

284 The article was eventually published as a chapter in *Women in Communication: A Biographical Sourcebook*, op. cit.

285 Herzog to Perse, op. cit., September 12, 1994.

286 "Uracell Communication Study, Louisville, Miami, Prepared for Scott Paper Company," Marian G. Schott, Inc., May 1967, Rare Books, Manuscript, and Special Collections Library, Duke University.

287 Ibid.

288 Memorandum to Kyle Felt, from Jerry Ohlsten, re: "Uracell Communication Study," June 19, 1967, Rare Books, Manuscript, and Special Collections Library, Duke University.

289 Ohlsten memo, op. cit.

290 Samuel, op. cit., 146.

291 Friedan, op. cit., 217.

292 Ibid., 218.

293 Ibid., 217.

294 Linda Francke, "See Me, Feel Me, Touch Me, Heal Me: The Encounter Group Explosion," *New York*, May 25, 1970. Her estimate came from the

Manhattan Board of Mental Health. Cited in David Frum's *How We Got Here: The 70s* (Basic, 2000).

295 Morts Davids Infometre Group, "Summary of Results of Golden Lights Focus Discussion Groups," Lorilland, June 1979. https://industrydocuments.library.ucsf.edu/tobacco/docs/#id=mgfx0121.

296 Ibid.

297 Alvin Achenbaum, "Does Advertising Manipulate Consumer Behavior?" Report before the Federal Trade Commission (New York, J. Walter Thompson, 1971), quoted in Stephan Gennaro, "J. Walter Thompson and the Creation of the Modern Advertising Agency," *Advertising and Society Review*, vol. 10, Issue 3 (2009).

298 George J. Szybillo and Robert Berger, "What Advertising Agencies Think of Focus Groups," *Journal of Advertising Research*, vol. 19, no. 3 (June 1979).

299 "Research buyers of major corporations tell how, why they use focus groups, work to avoid or solve problems groups might cause," *Marketing News*, January 16, 1976, vol. IX, no. 13.

300 Thomas Greenbaum, *The Handbook for Focus Group Research* (SAGE, 1998).

301 This continued to be a factor throughout the nineteen eighties; in 1989, a typical quantitative survey could cost $20,000, while a set of three focus groups only cost $7,500.

302 Szybillo, op. cit., and others.

303 Christian Parenti, "Atlas Finally Shrugged: Us Against Them in the Me Decade," *The Baffler*, No. 13 (1999).

304 Howard Zinn, *A People's History of the United States* (Longman, 1980).

305 Parenti, op. cit.

306 Written by David Alan Coe and popularized by Johnny Paycheck.

307 Zinn, op. cit.

308 Ralph Nader, *Unsafe at Any Speed* (Grossman Publishers, 1965), preface. www.naderlibrary.com/nader.unsafeanyspeed.pref.htm.

309 On the other hand, some icons of the counterculture had great talents as admen. Famous yippie Abbie Hoffman was often credited as one of the left's brilliant showmen. As he once explained, "the trick to manipulating the media is to get them to promote an event before it happens . . . get them to make an advertisement for . . . revolution—the same way you would advertise soap." Later on, Jerry Rubin, author of the *Yippie Manifesto* would have a career on Madison Avenue and become the poster child for the popular "hippie-to-yuppie" stereotype.

310   Herbert Marcuse, *One-Dimensional Man* (Beacon, 1964), 5.

311   Christopher Lasch, The Culture of Narcissism (W. W. Norton, 1978), 72.

312   Grace Lichtenstein, "Feminists Demand 'Liberation' in Ladies' Home Journal Sit-In," *New York Times*, March 19, 1970, 51.

313   Margaret Crimmins, "Protesting Advertising's View of Women," *Washington Post*, June 10, 1970.

314   Ibid.

315   Erving Goffman, *Gender Advertisements* (Palgrave, 1979). Cited in Sut Jhally, "Advertising, Gender and Sex: What's Wrong with a Little Objectification?" *Working Papers and Proceedings of the Center for Psychosocial Studies* (1989). www.sutjhally.com/articles/whatswrongwithalit.

316   Jean Kilbourne, "Killing us Softly," 1979.

317   Goldfarb Consultants, "Qualitative Insights on the Women's Market," December 1980. Copy of Material Housed in the Rare Book, Manuscript, and Special Collections Library, Duke University.

318   Ibid.

319   Thomas Frank, *Conquest of Cool: Business Culture, Counterculture and the Rise of Hip Consumerism* (University of Chicago Press, 1998).

320   Sandra Salmans, "Banishing Cliches in Advertising to Women," *New York Times*, July 18, 1982. www.nytimes.com/1982/07/18/business/banishing-cliches-in-advertising-to-women.html?pagewanted=1.

321   Ibid.

322   Myril Axelrod, "Dynamics of the Group Interview," *Advances in Consumer Research* vol. 3 (1976).

323   Lee, op. cit.

324   Ibid.

325   Axelrod, op. cit.

326   "Research buyers of major corporations tell how, why they use focus groups, work to avoid or solve problems groups might cause," *Marketing News*, op. cit.

327   Ibid.

328   Ibid.

329   Ibid.

330   Ibid.

331   "Analysis of Focus Group on Asteroids," June 14, 1979, Strong Museum of Play Archive, www.museumofplay.org/blog/chegheads/wp-content/uploads/2014/12/Focus-Group-Summary-Asteroids-June-14-1979.-Courtesy-of-The-Strong-Rochester-NY.jpg. Cited in Jeremy Saucier, "Video Game Focus

Groups as History," CHEGheads Blog, Museum of Play, December 3, 2014. www.museumofplay.org/blog/chegheads/2014/12/video-game-focus-groups-as-history-2/.

332   Szybillo, op. cit.

333   "Research buyers of major corporations tell how, why they use focus groups, work to avoid or solve problems groups might cause," *Marketing News*, op. cit.

334   Lee, op. cit.

335   Clive Bates and Andy Rowell (Action on Smoking and Health, London, U.K.), "Tobacco Explained," World Health Organization (1998).

336   Raymond Lee, "The Secret Life of Focus Groups: Robert Merton and the Diffusion of a Research Method," *The American Sociologist*, Vol. 41, No. 2 (June 2010): 115–141.

337   "Low-Tar Cigarettes are Not a Safer Choice," Harvard Health Publications, Harvard Medical School, (September 2005). www.health.harvard.edu/family_health_guide/low-tar-cigarettes-are-not-a-safer-choice.

338   Lee, op. cit.

339   Goldfarb Consultants Limited, "Intermediate and Full-size Station Wagon Perspectives," March, 1976. Rare Book, Manuscript, and Special Collections Library, Duke University.

340   Deborah Stewart, "More Than Forty Years of Progress for Child Passenger Protection," *Safe Ride News*, February 2009. http://saferidenews.com/srndnn/LinkClick.aspx?fileticket=NIPfcuqNLlU%3D&tabid=375.

341   Annemarie Shelness and Seymour Charles, "Children as Passengers in Automobiles: The Neglected Minority on the Nation's Highways," *Pediatrics* vol. 56, issue 2 (August 1975). http://pediatrics.aappublications.org/content/56/2/271.abstract.

342   Chevrolet print ad, 1981. www.curbsideclassic.com/wp-content/uploads/2015/04/8fc0bb0185a5c710dc8aaea6c9808171.jpg.

343   Alvin Achenbaum, "Does Advertising Manipulate Consumer Behavior?" Report before the Federal Trade Commission (New York, J. Walter Thompson, 1971), which I first found through Stephan Gennaro,"J. Walter Thompson and the Creation of the Modern Advertising Agency," *Advertising and Society Review*, vol. 10, issue 3 (2009).

344   Szibillo, op. cit.

345   Jacoby, op. cit., vii.

346   Kate Millet, *Sexual Politics*, 1969, 508. (Jacoby cites Millet on Freud as well.)

347   Jacoby, op. cit.

348   Joe Langford and Deanna McDonagh, *Focus Groups: Serving Effective Product Development* (Taylor & Francis, 2001), 47–48.

349   Lee, op. cit.; Samuel, op. cit.

350   Elizabeth Hardwick Research, "Buckshot '3' Focus Groups," Dallas, November 1979. Brown & Williamson. https://industrydocuments.library.ucsf.edu/tobacco/docs/#id=mhvy0139

351   Morts Davids Infometre, op. cit.

352   Elizabeth Hardwick Research, op. cit.

353   Eva S. Moskowitz, *In Therapy We Trust: America's Obsession with Self-Fulfillment* (Johns Hopkins University Press, 2001), 219.

354   Francke, op. cit.

355   Personal conversation with author.

356   Kara Jesella, "'It's Not Therapy': Consciousness-Raising as Identity Creation in the Women's Liberation Movement," unpublished paper, May 2009.

357   Kathie Sarachild, "Consciousness-Raising: A Radical Weapon," in *Feminist Revolution* (Random House, 1978), 144–150. Quoted by Jesella, ibid.

358   Turner, op. cit.

359   "Research buyers of major corporations tell how, why they use focus groups, work to avoid or solve problems groups might cause," *Marketing News*, op. cit.

360   Sarachild, op. cit.

361   Jenny Brown (current Redstockings activist), personal conversation with author.

362   Sarachild, op. cit.

363   Ibid.

364   Cited in Jesella, op. cit.

365   Jacoby, op. cit., 150.

366   Author interview with Wendy, July 8, 2010.

367   "The Focus Group," *Frasier* season 3, episode 23, May 14, 1996.

368   Doris Toumarkine, "Passing the Test," *Film Journal International*, October 27, 2004. www.filmjournal.com/node/12466.

369   Willow Bay, "Test Audiences Have Profound Effects on Movies,"CNN, September 28, 1998. www.cnn.com/SHOWBIZ/Movies/9809/28/screen.test/.

370   Jan Delasara, *PopLit, PopCult, and the X-Files: A Critical Exploration* (McFarland, 2000), 16.

371   Chris Rock, *Big Ass Jokes: School, Platonic Friends and Getting a Man*, HBO, June 16, 1994,

372 Chris Rock, *Married Life*, HBO, April 17, 2004.

373 Some see ethical problems with focus group research on children; market researcher Julia Strohm, who has no children of her own, says she is not comfortable doing this kind of work because kids don't understand what they're consenting to as research subjects. It's also worrisome that with much product research on children, in the area of entertainment, researchers are testing products that are bad for them; no matter how educational a TV show or video is, it's clear that sitting in front of a television for a large part of the day is unhealthy for kids, both mentally and physically.

374 Willow Bay, op. cit.

375 Quoted in Kevin Downey, "Hollywood Ending: Test Screening Takes Over the Directors' Seat," *Change Agent: Market Research Insights Driving Business*, April 2004.

376 Justin Wyatt, *High Concept: Movies and Marketing in Hollywood* (University of Texas Press, 2010).

377 Box Office Mojo.

378 Lester D. Friedman (ed.), *American Cinema of the: Themes and Variations* (Rutgers University Press, 2007), 6.

379 Wyatt, op. cit.

380 Downey, op. cit.

381 Dade Hayes, "H'wood grapples with Third-Act Problems," *Variety*, September 14, 2003. http://variety.com/2003/film/news/h-wood-grapples-with-third-act-problems-1117892369/.

382 Peter Lehman and William Luhr, *Thinking About Movies: Watching, Questioning, Enjoying* (Blackwell, 2003). http://media.wiley.com/product_ancillary/39/14051540/DOWNLOAD/ABO1.pdf.

383 Internet Movie Database (IMDB). www.imdb.com/title/tt0093010/alternateversions.

384 *The Oprah Winfrey Oscar Special*, March 3, 2010.

385 Box Office Mojo, http://boxofficemojo.com/yearly/chart/?yr=1987&p=.htm.

386 Lehman and Luhr, op. cit.

387 Ibid.

388 Catherine Jurca, "What the Public Wanted: Hollywood, 1937–1942," *Cinema Journal* 47, no. 2 (Winter 2008).

389 Leo Handel, "Hollywood Market Research," *The Quarterly of Film, Radio, Telvision*, vol. 7, no. 3, (Spring 1953): 304–310.

390 Ibid.

391   Jonathan Rosenbaum, *Movie Wars: How Hollywood and the Media Limit What Movies We Can See* (A Cappella, 2000), 2.

392   Ibid, 8.

393   Bay, op. cit.

394   Patrick Healy, "Arts, Briefly: More Focus Groups for 'Spider Man,'" *New York Times*, February 12, 2011. http://query.nytimes.com/gst/fullpage.html?res=9905EFD71739F931A25751C0A9679D8B63.

395   Ben Brantley, "1 Radioactive Bite, 8 Legs and 183 Previews," *New York Times*, June 14, 2011. www.nytimes.com/2011/06/15/theater/reviews/spider-man-turn-off-the-dark-opens-after-changes-review.html.

396   Patrick Healy, "Taymor Tries to Reclaim a Reputation," *New York Times*, June 19, 2011.

397   Cynthia Burkhead and David Lavery, eds., *Joss Whedon: Conversations* (University Press of Mississippi, 2011), 16.

398   Christine Birkner, "'Mad Men' Gets Massive Marketing Send-Off," *Marketing News Weekly*, March 31, 2015. www.ama.org/publications/eNewsletters/Marketing-News-Weekly/Pages/mad-men.aspx.

399   http://gametheoryonline.com/2011/06/02/fan-made-video-games-development-designers/.

400   Victor Jordan, "The Embarrassment to the Industry That Is Fan-Made Video Games: AKA When Fans Pay Better Video Game Homage Than You…For Free," *Otaku Dome*, April 16, 2014. http://otakudome.com/the-embarrassment-to-the-industry-that-is-fan-made-video-games-aka-when-fans-pay-better-video-game-homage-than-you-for-free/.

401   Robert Dex, "Viewers want to influence TV show plots," *Independent*, August 26, 2010. www.independent.co.uk/news/media/tv-radio/viewers-want-to-influence-tv-show-plots-2062945.html.

402   "Report on a Focus Group Discussion of the 1980 Presidential Election," Conducted by Peter D. Hart in Canton, Ohio, July 21, 1980. Ronald Reagan Presidential Library, Simi Valley, CA. Thanks to Kimberly Phillips-Fein for sharing her archival findings here.

403   As Erica Fry pointed out in *Columbia Journalism Review*, not many media outlets reported that Walmart had actually paid for the focus groups: www.cjr.org/campaign_desk/watch_out_for_walmart_moms.php?page=all.

404   Four years later, some of the same Walmart moms were interviewed again, even more pessimistic about the future, but with less media attention this time: http://pos.org/walmart-moms-focus-group-video/.

405 For more on that lawsuit see Liza Featherstone, *Selling Women Short: The Landmark Battle for Workers' Rights at Walmart* (Basic, 2004).

406 Joe McGinness, *The Selling of the President* (Simon & Schuster, 1969).

407 Author interview, October 21, 2011.

408 Michael Beschloss, "Never Aired 1976 Gerald Ford Ad Too Emotionally Charged for Its Time," *PBS Newshour*, November 5, 2012. www.pbs.org/newshour/rundown/never-aired-ford-campaign-ad-considered-too-emotionally-charged-for-time/.

409 Author interview with Celinda Lake, op. cit. Also, Dennis W. Johnson, *No Place for Amateurs: How Political Consultants are Reshaping American Democracy* (Routledge, 2007), 286.

410 James Harding, *Alpha Dogs: The Americans Who Turned Political Spin into a Global Business* (Farrar Straus & Giroux, 2009).

411 Author interview, Andy Tuck, July 7, 2010.

412 Author interview, Lily Marotta, June 3, 2010.

413 Author interview, Andy Tuck, op. cit.

414 Ewen, op. cit., 187.

415 Claude Hopkins, *My Life in Advertising* (Harper & Brothers, 1927), 6.

416 Schwarzkopf, op. cit.

417 Harding, op. cit.

418 Dennis Johnson, *No Place for Amateurs: How Political Consultants Are Reshaping American Democracy* (Routledge, 2007), 6–7.

419 Frank Lynn, "Political Consultants' Role is Expanding," *New York Times*, March 28, 1982.

420 Robert G. Kaiser, "White House Pulse-Taking Pollster," *Washington Post*, February 4, 1982. www.washingtonpost.com/archive/politics/1982/02/24/white-house-pulse-taking-pollster/e70a32b5-9fdd-4a1a-9822-13264801748e/.

421 Adam Clymer, "Richard Wirthlin, Pollster Who Advised Reagan, Dies at 80," *New York Times*, March 17, 2011. www.nytimes.com/2011/03/18/us/politics/18wirthlin.html?_r=0.

422 Wynton Hall, "The Invention of 'Quantifiably Safe Rhetoric': Richard Wirthlin and Ronald Reagan's Instrumental Use of Public Opinion Research in Presidential Discourse," *Western Journal of Communication*, vol. 66, no. 3 (Summer 2002): 319–346.

423 Ibid.

424 Ibid.

425 Wynton Hall, "Reflections of Yesterday: George H.W. Bush's Instrumental Use of Public Opinion Research in Presidential Discourse," *Presidential Studies Quarterly* 32, no 3 (September 2002).

426 Clymer, op. cit.

427 Bill Moyers, *The Public Mind* (1989).

428 Ibid.

429 Ibid.

430 Michel J. Crozier, Samuel P. Huntington, and Joji Watanuki, *A Crisis of Democracy: Report on the Governability of Democracies to the Trilateral Commission* (New York University Press, 1975). http://archive.org/stream/The CrisisOfDemocracy-TrilateralCommission-1975/crisis_of_democracy_djvu.txt.

431 Lewis Powell, "Confidential Memorandum: Attack of American Free Enterprise System," August 23, 1971. http://reclaimdemocracy.org/ powell_memo_lewis/.

432 Richard Ullman, "Trilateralism: 'Partnership for What?'" *Foreign Affairs*, October 1976.

433 Dino Knudson, PhD candidate, The Formation of the Trilateral Commission," (unpublished paper), Department of History, Saxo Institute, Faculty of Humanities, University of Copenhagen, Denmark. (2012).

434 Ullman, op. cit.

435 Crozier, Huntington, and Watanuki, op.cit.

436 Ronald J. Hrebenar and Bryson B. Morgan, *Lobbying in America: A Reference Handbook* (ABC-CLIO, 2009).

437 Benjamin Waterhouse, *Lobbying America: The Politics of Business from Nixon to NAFTA* (Princeton University Press, 2015).

438 Joseph A. McCartin, "The Strike That Busted Unions," *New York Times*, August 2, 2011. www.nytimes.com/2011/08/03/opinion/reagan-vs-patco- the-strike-that-busted-unions.html?_r=0.

439 Elizabeth Kolbert, "Test Marketing a President," *New York Times Magazine*, August 30, 1992.

440 Martin Gilens and Benjamin I. Page, "Testing Theories of American Politics: Elites, Interest Groups and Average Citizens," *Perspectives on Politics*, vol. 12, no. 3 (September 2014).

441 Speech to the American Association of Advertising Agencies' Account Planning conference, Chicago (2005). Excerpted by *Advertising Age* in "Focus Groups Should Be Abolished," August 8, 2005. http://adage.com/article/ viewpoint/focus-groups-abolished/104151/.

442   Malcolm Gladwell, *Blink: The Power of Thinking Without Thinking* (Back Bay Books, 2007), 158.

443   Gladwell, *Blink* (Back Bay Books, 2005), 166.

444   Ruth Shalit, "Little Caesars—'Focus Group': Cliff Freeman & Partners, New York," Salon, April 23, 1999. www.salon.com/1999/04/23/little_caesar/.

445   Ibid.

446   In fact, as Slate's Matt Yglesias has pointed out, Pepsi was outselling Coke in supermarkets; Coke merely had a lead in infrastructure (more soda machines and fast food tie-ins). "Sweet Sorrow," Slate, August 9, 2013. www.slate.com/articles/business/rivalries/2013/08/pepsi_paradox_why_people_prefer_coke_even_though_pepsi_wins_in_taste_tests.html.

447   Obviously, things have changed. The total number of women Cosby was accused of raping reached sixty in summer 2016. See Manuel Roig-Franzia, "Two more women allege assaults by Bill Cosby; total now 60," *Washington Post*, August 7, 2016. www.washingtonpost.com/lifestyle/style/two-more-women-allege-assaults-by-bill-cosby-total-now-60/2016/08/07/e8feb1f0-5b1e-11e6-831d-0324760ca856_story.html.

448   Bill Cosby New Coke Commercial. www.youtube.com/watch?v=o4YvmN1hvNA.

449   Thomas Oliver, *The Real Coke, The Real Story* (Penguin Books, 1986), 159.

450   Ibid.

451   Ibid., 167.

452   Frank Bruni, "American the Clueless," *New York Times*, May 11, 2013.

453   Constance Hays, "Soda Flop," *Atlanta* magazine, February 2004. Excerpt from her book, *The Real Thing: Truth and Power at the Coca-Cola Company* (Random House, 2004).

454   The Coca-Cola Company, "The Real Story of Coca-Cola," November 14, 2012. www.coca-colacompany.com/stories/coke-lore-new-coke.

455   Juan Forero, "Union says Coca-Cola in Colombia Uses Thugs," *New York Times*, July 26, 2001. www.nytimes.com/2001/07/26/world/union-says-coca-cola-in-colombia-uses-thugs.html.

456   Harding, op. cit., 74.

457   "The 1985 Launch of New Coke," www.youtube.com/watch?v=W6t7deaplgY.

458   Tom Shales, "New Coke Hater Crusades for the Real Thing," *Chicago Tribune*, June 14, 1985. http://articles.chicagotribune.com/1985-06-14/features/8502070939_1_coca-cola-executive-coke-gay-mullins.

459 Bill Lohmann, "From Jeers to Cheers: Diehards Have New Coke Back," United Press International/*Mohave Daily Miner*, July 12, 1985. https://news.google.com/newspapers?nid=943&dat=19850712&id= 2cRPAAAAIBAJ&sjid=hFMDAAAAIBAJ&pg=1980,1189241.

460 Michael Bastedo and Angela Davis, "God, What a Blunder," December 17, 1993. http://web.archive.org/web/20060515214006/http://members.lycos.co.uk/thomassheils/newcoke.htm.

461 Oliver, op. cit.

462 John Greenwald, "Coca-Cola's Big Fizzle," *Time*, April 12, 2005. www.time.com/time/magazine/article/0,9171,1048370,00.html.

463 Blair Matthews, "Coca-Cola's Big Mistake—20 Years Later,"*Soda Pop Dreams* magazine, vol. 8, no. 2, Issue #36 (Spring 2005). www.sodaspectrum.com/newcoke.html.

464 The Coca-Cola Company, op. cit.

465 Greenwald, op. cit.

466 Matthews, op. cit.

467 The Coca-Cola Company, op. cit.

468 Ibid.

469 Matthews, op. cit.

470 Ryan Gorman and Skye Gould, "This Mistake from 30 Years Ago Almost Destroyed Coca-Cola," *Business Insider*, April 23, 2015. www.businessinsider.com/new-coke-the-30th-anniversary-of-coca-colas-biggest-mistake-2015-4.

471 Robert Schindler, "The Real Lesson of New Coke: The Value of Focus Groups for Predicting the Effects of Social Influence," *Marketing Research*, December 1992. https://archive.ama.org/archive/ResourceLibrary/MarketingResearch/documents/9602193014.pdf.

472 Greenwald, op. cit.

473 Schindler, op. cit.

474 Bob McMath, *What Were They Thinking?* (Times Books, 1998).

475 Douglas Rushkoff, *Get Back in the Box! Innovation from the Inside Out* (HarperCollins, 2005), p. 234.

476 Tanzina Vega, "Focus Groups that Look Like Play Groups," *New York Times*, May 29, 2011.

477 Schindler, *op. cit.*; Oliver, *op. cit.*

478 Oliver, *op. cit.*, p. 126.

479 David Greising, *I'd Like the World to Buy a Coke: The Life and Leadership of Roberto Goizueta*, Wiley (1998). Quoted in Harding, op. cit., 70.

480 Ibid.

481 Oliver, op. cit., 124.

482 Oliver, op. cit., quoted in Schindler, op. cit.

483 Thomas Moore and Michael Rogers, "Old Coke Is It," *Fortune*, August 5, 1985.

484 Schindler, op. cit.

485 Author interview, Kara Gilmour, op. cit.

486 Author interview, Kara Jesella, August 18, 2009.

487 Author interview, Andy Tuck, op. cit.

488 Schindler, op. cit.

489 Ibid.

490 Ibid.

491 Ibid.

492 Harding, op. cit., 78.

493 Christopher Klein, "The New Coke Flop, 30 Years Ago," History Channel (website), April 23, 2015. www.history.com/news/hungry-history/the-new-coke-flop-30-years-ago.

494 Greenwald, op. cit.

495 "Focus Group Research: Premium Salad Dressing," Nottingham-Spirk Design Associates (2007).

496 Malcolm Gladwell, "Choice, Happiness and Spaghetti Sauce," TED2004, February 2004. www.ted.com/talks/malcolm_gladwell_on_spaghetti_sauce.html.

497 Marketing Research Association.

498 Gladwell, *Blink*, op. cit.

499 Gladwell speech to American Association of Advertising Agencies' Account Planning conference, op. cit.

500 Ibid.

501 Morrison, op. cit., 108.

502 Ibid., 111.

503 Susan Cavin, "Adorno, Lazarsfeld and the Princeton Radio Project, 1938–1941," unpublished paper presented at the American Sociological Association Annual Meeting, Boston, MA.

504 Yasha Levine, "Malcolm Gladwell Unmasked," SHAME (Shame the Hacks Who Abuse Media Ethics), May 31, 2012. http://shameproject.com/profile/malcolm-gladwell-2/. Levine expounds on his findings in an ebook, *The Corruption of Malcolm Gladwell* (SHAME Books, 2012).

505 Gladwell, *Blink*, op. cit.

506 Rushkoff, op. cit., 11.

507 Ibid., 38.

508 Ibid., 96.

509 *Mad Men*, "Smoke Gets in Your Eyes," July 19, 2007.

510 Patrick Vlaskovits, "Henry Ford, Innovation and that 'Faster Horse' Quote," *Harvard Business Review* blog, August 29, 2011. http://blogs.hbr. org/2011/08/henry-ford-never-said-the-fast/. (I discovered this marvelous article through a blog post written by marketer Venkatesh Rao.)

511 Ibid.

512 "Interview: Ford's Anti-Semitism" (with Hasia Diner), PBS American Experience (2012). www.pbs.org/wgbh/americanexperience/features/interview/henryford-antisemitism/.

513 Stefan Link, "Rethinking the Ford-Nazi Connection," *Bulletin of the GHI*, Fall 2011. www.ghi-dc.org/fileadmin/user_upload/GHI_Washington/Publications/Bulletin49/bu49_135.pdf.

514 Corey Robin, "Who Really Said That?" *The Chronicle Review*, September 16, 2013. http://chronicle.com/article/Who-Really-Said-That-/141559/.

515 Douglas Martin, "Chuck Jordan, Innovative G.M. Designer, Dies at 83," *New York Times*, December 1, 2010. www.nytimes.com/2010/12/14/business/14jordan.html?_r=0.

516 John Markoff, "Apple's Visionary Redefined Digital Age," *New York Times*, October 5, 2011. www.nytimes.com/2011/10/06/business/steve-jobs-of-apple-dies-at-56.html?pagewanted=all&_r=0.

517 "Last American Who Knew What the Fuck He Was Doing Dies," Onion, vol. 47, issue 50, October 6, 2011. www.theonion.com/article/last-american-who-knew-what-the-fuck-he-was-doing--26268.

518 David Sturt and Todd Nordstrom, "Delight Your Customers By Giving Them What They Didn't Ask For," *Forbes*, January 3, 2014. www.forbes.com/sites/davidsturt/2014/01/03/delight-your-customers-by-giving-them-what-they-didnt-ask-for/#245287ad1e48.

519 Steve Lohr, "Can Apple Find More Hits Without Its Tastemaker?" *New York Times*, January 11, 2011. www.nytimes.com/2011/01/19/technology/companies/19innovate.html.

520 Betsy Morris, "Most Admired Companies 2008: Steve Jobs Speaks Out," *Fortune*, March 2008. http://money.cnn.com/galleries/2008/fortune/0803/gallery.jobsqna.fortune/2.html.

521 David Kiley, "Shoot the Focus Group," *Bloomberg Business Week*, November 14, 2005. www.bloomberg.com/news/articles/2005-11-13/shoot-the-focus-group.

522 Venkatesh Rao, "Product-Driven versus Customer Driven," Ribbonfarm (blog), April 24, 2014. www.ribbonfarm.com/2014/04/24/product-driven-versus-customer-driven/.

523 Morris, op. cit.

524 Leander Kahney, "John Sculley: The Secrets of Steve Jobs' Success," October 14, 2010. www.cultofmac.com/john-sculley-the-secrets-of-steve-jobs-success-exclusive-interview/21572#more-21572.

525 Alain Breillatt, "You Can't Innovate Like Apple," Pragmatic Marketing, August 1, 2009. www.pragmaticmarketing.com/resources/you-cant-innovate-like-apple.

526 David Barboza, "Worker Deaths Raise Questions at an Apple Contractor in China," *New York Times*, December 10, 2013. www.nytimes.com/2013/12/11/technology/worker-deaths-raise-questions-at-an-apple-contractor-in-china.html?_r=0.

527 Michael Beverland, "Right-wing Customers: The Enemy of Innovation," *DMI (Design Management Institute) Review*, September 29, 2010.

528 Morris, op. cit.

529 Breillatt, op. cit.

530 Ibid.

531 Ibid.

532 Beverland, op. cit.

533 Beth Snyder Bulik, "Employees No Longer Baggage But Blessing," *Ad Age*, November 8, 2010. http://adage.com/article/news/marketers-tap-employees-ads-focus-groups-brand-ideas/146943/.

534 "After One Utterance of 'George Bush,' Frank Luntz Focus Group Erupts on Each Other," Grabien: The Multimedia Marketplace, July 29, 2014. https://grabien.com/file.php?id=22354.

535 CBS Evening News, August 12, 1988. Vanderbilt University News Archive.

536 Ibid.

537 "Weekend Prison Passes: Dukakis on Crime," 1988. www.youtube.com/watch?v=Io9KMSSEZOY.

538 "1988: Bush vs. Dukakis," The Living Room Candidate: Presidential Campaign Commercials 1952–2012, Museum of the Moving Image. www.livingroomcandidate.org/commercials/1988/willie-horton.

539   Stefan Forbes, *Boogie Man: The Lee Atwater Story* (documentary), 2014.

540   Ibid.

541   John Sides, "Monkey Cage: It's Time to Stop the Endless Hype of the 'Willie Horton' ad," *Washington Post*, January 6, 2016. www.washingtonpost.com/news/monkey-cage/wp/2016/01/06/its-time-to-stop-the-endless-hype-of-the-willie-horton-ad/.

542   Lloyd Grove, "Focus Groups: Politicians' Version of Taste Testing: Roundtable Talks with Voters Become Candidates' Tool," *Washington Post*, July 6, 1988.

543   Kathryn Dunn Tenpas, PhD, "Words vs. Deeds: George W. Bush and Polling," Brookings, June 1, 2003. www.brookings.edu/articles/words-vs-deeds-president-george-w-bush-and-polling/.

544   Wynton Hall, "Reflections of Yesterday: George H. W. Bush's Instrumental Use of Public Opinion Research in Presidential Discourse," *Presidential Studies Quarterly* vol. 32, no. 3 (September 2002).

545   Adam Clymer, "Once Past Improving the Economy, Clinton's Mandate is Unclear, Poll Takers Say," *New York Times*, May 24, 1993. www.nytimes.com/1993/05/24/us/once-past-improving-the-economy-clinton-s-mandate-is-unclear-poll-takers-say.html.

546   Hall, op. cit.

547   Clymer, op. cit.

548   James Perry, "Clinton Relies Heavily on White House Pollster to Take Words Right Out of the Public's Mouth," *Wall Street Journal*, March 23, 1994.

549   "Interview: Frank Luntz," Frontline, posted November 4, 2004. www.pbs.org/wgbh/pages/frontline/shows/persuaders/interviews/luntz.html.

550   CBS Evening News, October 9, 1992, Vanderbilt Television News Archive.

551   Ibid.

552   Thomas B. Edsall and Mary B. Edsall, *Chain Reaction: The Impact of Race, Rights, and Taxes on American Politics* (W.W. Norton & Company, 1991).

553   CBS Evening News, October 9, 1992, Vanderbilt Television News Archive.

554   Thomas Frank, *One Market Under God: Extreme Capitalism, Market Populism and the End of Economic Democracy* (Anchor Books, 2000), p. 24.

555   "Clinton Speech Re: Lewinsky," NBC, August 17, 1998, Vanderbilt Television News Archive.

556   "Iowa Focus Group on Fox News: Obama is a Muslim," www.reddit.com/r/Iowa/comments/fj4p8/iowa_focus_group_on_fox_news_obama_is_muslim/?.

557   Tactical Gamer, www.tacticalgamer.com.

558   Neal Stephenson and J. Frederick George, *Interface* (Bantam Books, 1994).

559   Ibid., 473.

560   Ibid., 490.

561   Andrew Ferguson, "The Focus-Group Fraud," *The Weekly Standard*, October 13, 1996. www.weeklystandard.com/Content/Public/Articles/000/000/008/078huqnj.asp?page=3.

562   Robert Manning, "The Clinton Doctrine: More Spin Than Reality," *Los Angeles Times*, September 5, 1999. http://articles.latimes.com/1999/sep/05/opinion/op-7008.

563   Acceptance Speech, 2001 John F. Kennedy Profile in Courage Award ceremony, John F. Kennedy Library and Museum, Boston. www.jfklibrary.org/Events-and-Awards/Profile-in-Courage-Award/Award-Recipients/Gerald-Ford-2001.aspx?t=3.

564   Joshua Green, "The Other War Room," *Washington Monthly*, April 2002.

565   Ibid.

566   Ibid.

567   Author interview, Celinda Lake, op. cit.

568   Ibid.

569   Author interview, David Atkins, June 7, 2010.

570   "Americans Support Single Payer. Why Doesn't Celinda Lake?" Physicians for a National Health Program, December 11, 2008. www.pnhp.org/news/2008/december/americans_support_si.php.

571   Author interview, David Atkins, op. cit.

572   Author interview, Celinda Lake, op. cit.

573   "Inside the GOP: Report on Focus Groups with Evangelical, Tea Party and Moderate Republicans," DemocracyCorps, October 3, 2013.

574   Author interview, Morris Fiorina, May 26, 2011.

575   Emily Schulthies, "Hillary Clinton's 2016 Campaign Kickoff Will Look a Lot Like Her 2000 Senate Run," *National Journal*, April 10, 2015. www.nationaljournal.com/2016-elections/hillary-clinton-2016-announcement-20150410.

576   Ibid.

577   Annie Karni, "Hillary's Low-Risk Listening Tour," Politico.com, April 15, 2015. www.politico.com/story/2015/04/hillary-clintons-low-risk-listening-tour-117025.html#ixzz3Zl4CyOed.

578   Walter Lippmann, *Public Opinion* (1922).

579   Karni, op. cit.

580   Rebecca Ballhaus, "Lots of Listening, Little Detail on Hillary Clinton's Listening Tour," *Wall Street Journal*, April 21, 2015. http://blogs.wsj.com/washwire/2015/04/21/lots-of-listening-little-detail-on-hillary-clintons-new-hampshire-listening-tour/.

581   Gabriel Debenedetti and Annie Karni, "Hillary's Dash for Cash," *Politico*, May 21, 2015. www.politico.com/story/2015/05/hillary-clinton-fundraising-goal-2-billion-118183.html#ixzz3ao9nYpOO.

582   Author interview, Nadia, June 4, 2010.

583   Ibid.

584   Lois Gilbert, "How J. Walter Thompson Company Uses Premiums for Its Consumer Panel," Address to the Premium Industry Club, Chicago. Published in *Premium Practice*, June 1945. Distributed as a memo to JWT food and drug representatives August 22, 1945. Rare Book, Manuscript, and Special Collections Library, Duke University.

585   "Needed: More research on the flow of goods from factory to consumer," *Printers' Ink*, April 18, 1958. Rare Book, Manuscript, and Special Collections Library, Duke University.

586   Gilbert, op. cit.

587   Marshall Ottenfeld, "Editor's Note," *Applied Marketing Research: A Journal of the Marketing Research Association*, Volume 30, No. 3 (Third Quarter 1990).

588   Consensus among focus group professionals on American Association of Public Opinion Research mailing list, discussion in late 2010.

589   Jonathan Hilland, "Market Research's 'Dirty Little Secret,'" *Alert* magazine (Marketing Research Association), February 2009. http://old.marketingresearch.org/alert-magazine-february-2009-market-research's-dirty-little-secret.

590   Author interview, Nadia, op. cit.

591   Hilland, op. cit.

592   Rayven Perkins, "Do a Paid Research Study," Stay a Stay at Home Mom, www.stay-a-stay-at-home-mom.com/paid-research-study.html.

593   Ibid.

594   Author interview, Wendy.

595   Ibid.

596   Perkins, op. cit.

597   Ibid.

598   Ibid.

599 Author interview, Lily Marotta, June 3, 2010.

600 Ibid.

601 Author interview, Wendy, op. cit.

602 Author interview, Nadia, op. cit.

603 Ibid.

604 Author interview, Kara Gilmour, op. cit.

605 Author interview, Nadia, op. cit.

606 Ibid.

607 Will Leitch, "Group Thinker," *New York*, June 21, 2004. http://nymag.com/nymetro/shopping/features/9299/.

608 Press release, Market Research Association, October 31, 2004. Besides MRA, the other authors of the statement were Qualitative Research Consultants Association, Council for Marketing and Opinion Research, American Association for Public and Opinion Research, and the Council of American Survey Research Organizations.

609 Ibid.

610 Mark Goodin, "Market Research: How to Avoid Professional Respondents—Part 2," October 15, 2007. http://ezinearticles .com/?Market-Research---How-to-Avoid-Professional-Respondents---Part-2&id=783817.

611 Anne Gonzales, "Average Americans," *Sacramento Business Journal*, April 6, 2003. www.bizjournals.com/sacramento/stories/2003/04/07/focus1.html.

612 Author interview, Kara Gilmour, op. cit.

613 Author interview, Julia Strohm, op. cit.

614 Author interview, Nadia, op. cit.

615 Author interview, Julia Strohm, op. cit.

616 Author interview, Andy Tuck, op. cit.

617 Author interview, Julia Strohm, op. cit.

618 Author interview, Andy Tuck, op. cit.

619 Tracy Smith, "Columbus, Ohio: Test Market of the USA," CBS News, June 24, 2012. www.cbsnews.com/news/columbus-ohio-test-market-of-the-usa/.

620 Gonzales, op. cit.

621 Author interview, Andy Tuck, op. cit.

622 Doug Henwood, "Why TV Sucks," *Left Business Observer* #83, May 1998. www.leftbusinessobserver.com/Why_TV_sucks.html.

623 Jonathan Bond and Richard Kirshenbaum, *Under the Radar: Talking to Today's Cynical Consumer* (Wiley, 1999). From excerpt in *Brandweek*, December 8, 1997.

624 Author interview, Donna Fullerton, op. cit.

625 Mike Savage, "Soft Focus," ResearchLive, September 1999. www .research-live.com/soft-focus/4002663.article.

626 Author interview, Donna Fullerton, op. cit.

627 Bill Carmody, "Why 96 Percent of Businesses Fail Within 10 Years," *Inc.*, August 12, 2015. www.inc.com/bill-carmody/why-96-of-businesses-fail-within-10-years.html.

628 "Interview with Susan Pogash," op. cit.

629 Hilland, op. cit.

630 Author interview, Nadia, op. cit.

631 Damian Lanigan, "The Focus Group Groupies," *Campaign*, September 26, 1997. www.campaignlive.co.uk/news/28582/FOCUS-GROUP-GROUPIES-polite-lying-species–rsquoprofessional-rsquo-focus-group-attendants-seems-leading-researchers-astray-Damian-Lanigan-investigates–rsquogroupie-rsquo-problem/?DCMP=ILC-BETASEARCH.

632 Author interview, Lily Marotta, op. cit.

633 "Interview with Susan Pogash," op. cit.

634 Author interview, Lily Marotta, op. cit.

635 Author interview, Wendy, op. cit.

636 Turi Ryder, "Hear Me Roar: Focus Groups are One Mom's Desperate Attempt to Be Heard," *SF Gate*, March 7, 2004. http://articles.sfgate.com/2004-03-07/living/17419393_1_museum-planning-focus-group-children-s-museum.

637 Author interview, Lily Marotta, op. cit.

638 Author interview, Nadia, op. cit.

639 Ibid.

640 Author conversation.

641 Author interview, Lily Marotta, op. cit.

642 Hilland, op. cit.

643 Bonnie Goebert with Herma M. Rosenthal, *Beyond Listening: Learning the Secret Language of Focus Groups* (Wiley, 2002), 204.

644 Author interview, Julia Strohm, op. cit.

645 Author interview, Nadia, op. cit.

646 Author interview, Andy Tuck, op. cit.

647 "Interview with Susan Pogash," op. cit.
648 Author interview, Nadia, op. cit.
649 Author interview, Julia Strohm, op. cit.
650 Ryder, op. cit.
651 Author interview, Kara Gilmour, op. cit.
652 Author interview, Julia Strohm, op. cit.
653 Author interview, Julia Strohm, op. cit.
654 Author interview, Lily Marotta, op. cit.
655 Author interview, Kara Gilmour, op. cit.
656 Author interview, Wendy, op. cit.
657 Ryder, op. cit.
658 Ibid.
659 Jen Alamilla, "Making and Saving Money from Home," More.com. www.more.com/making-and-saving-money-home.
660 Conversation with a participant in an Advanced Focus group in Manhattan.
661 Stuart Ewen, *Captains of Consciousness: Advertising and the Social Roots of the Consumer Culture* (McGraw-Hill, 1976).
662 Fox News, February 7, 2011. www.youtube.com/watch?v=WiqCCHCD4m8.
663 Author interview, Andy Tuck, op. cit.
664 Ian Martin, Armando Iannucci, Jesse Armstrong, Simon Blackwell, and Tony Roche, *The Thick of It: The Missing DoSAC Files* (Faber & Faber, 2010).
665 Author Interview, Andy Tuck, op. cit.
666 Ibid.
667 Author interview, Julia Strohm, op. cit.
668 Author interview, Kara Jesella, op. cit.
669 Ryder, op. cit.
670 Martin et al., op. cit.
671 "Research buyers of major corporations tell how, why they use focus groups, work to avoid or solve problems groups might cause," *Marketing News*, op. cit.
672 Author interview, Andy Tuck, op. cit.
673 Author interview, Julia Strohm, op. cit.
674 Author interview, Donna Fullerton, op. cit.
675 Author interview, Pat Tobin, June 23, 2010.
676 Fox News, February 7, 2011, op. cit.
677 Thread on NeoGaf, most recent was September 29, 2012. www.neogaf.com/forum/showthread.php?t=493588&page=5.

678 Dennis Glover, "Labor Needs Philosophy, Not Focus Groups," *Australian Financial Review*, January 22, 2014. www.afr.com/opinion/labor-needs-philosophy-not-focus-groups-20140121-iy815.

679 There is an old German social democratic adage: anti-Semitism is the socialism of fools.

680 Fox News, March 7, 2016. http://insider.foxnews.com/2016/03/07/luntz-focus-group-fox-news-democratic-town-hall.

681 Mark Leibovich, "Donald Trump Shares His Opponent-Branding Secrets," *The New York Times Magazine*, May 9, 2016. www.nytimes.com/2016/05/09/magazine/donald-trump-shares-his-opponent-branding-secrets.html?_r=0.

682 From the "Trump: Make America Great Again" Reddit page: www.reddit.com/r/The_Donald/comments/48stzn/graph_trump_has_paid_by_far_the_least_to/.

683 Email conversations.

684 Sam Adler-Bell, "Meet the Democratic Socialist Who's Running for New York State Senate," *The Nation*, March 16, 2016. www.thenation.com/article/meet-the-democratic-socialist-whos-running-for-new-york-state-senate/.

685 Bureau of Labor Statistics, U.S. Department of Labor, *Occupational Outlook Handbook, 2016–17 Edition*, "Market Research Analysts." www.bls.gov/ooh/business-and-financial/market-research-analysts.htm.

686 Dana Stanley, "Focus Groups are Dead: An Interview with Mike Volpe, Hubspot CMO," Researchaccess, November 28, 2011. http://researchaccess.com/2011/11/focus-groups-are-dead-an-interview-with-mike-volpe-hubspot-cmo/.

687 Meenu Sharma, "Is Your Enterprise Well-Designed?" The Center for the Future of Work, June 15, 2015. www.futureofwork.com/article/details/is-your-enterprise-well-designed; Doug Stephens, "Death of the Focus Group: Research Meets Mobility," February 5, 2011. www.retailprophet.com/blog/advertising/death-of-the-focus-group-research-meets-mobility/.

688 "Focus Groups: Are they Still Relevant?" NewFocus. www.newfocus.com.au/focus-groups-are-they-still-relevant/.

689 "Are focus groups still an effective method to gauge consumer insight?" *PR Week*, May 30, 2012. www.prweek.com/article/1279115/focus-groups-effective-method-gauge-consumer-insight.

690 Greg Heist, "5 Things in MR that will become obsolete sooner than you think," GreenBook, July 9, 2013. www.greenbookblog.org/2013/07/09/5-things-that-will-become-obsolete-in-mr-sooner-than-you-think/.

691 Constance Gustke, "Crowdsourcing to Get Ideas and Perhaps Save Money," New York Times, May 11, 2016. www.nytimes.com/2016/05/12/business/smallbusiness/crowdsourcing-to-get-ideas-and-perhaps-save-money.html?_r=0.

692 David Stewart et al., Focus Groups (Sage, 2007).

693 ESOMAR Global Market Research reports 2014, 2007.

694 Greenbook 2014 report, 10.

695 Greenbook 2013 report, 20.

696 Russ Carpenter, "Marketing's Oldest Technique Adapts to the Digital Age," Digital Current, July 14, 2014. www.digitalcurrent.com/digital-marketing/focus-groups-in-digital-age/.

697 On-site observation and interviews, by my research assistant, Jassica Bouvier.

698 Personal conversation with author.

699 Strategic Community Engagement Resource Guide, Gates Foundation.

700 On-site observations and interviews by Jassica Bouvier, op. cit.

701 Richard Edelman, "Our Time to Lead,"November 19, 2012 http://www.edelman.com/p/6-a-m/our-time-to-lead/.

702 Author interview, Celina Su, April 2, 2014.

703 Gianpaolo Baiocchi and Ernesto Ganuza, "Participatory Budgeting as if Emancipation Mattered," Spanish National Research Council. www.iesa.csic.es/publicaciones/040220151.pdf. See also other Baiocchi articles.

704 Author interview, Nathaniel Wice, op. cit.

705 John Nichols, "Not Just the NSA: Politicians are Data Mining the American Electorate," The Nation, June 12, 2013. www.thenation.com/blog/174759/not-just-nsa-politicians-are-data-mining-american-electorate.

706 Sasha Issenberg, "How Obama's Team Used Big Data to Rally Voters," Technology Review, December 19, 2012.

707 Nichols, op. cit.

708 Issenberg, op. cit.

709 Author interview, David Atkins, op. cit.

710 Ruby Roy Dholakia and Nikhilesh Dholakia, "Scholarly Research in Marketing: Trends and Challenges in the Era of Big Data," William A. Orme Working Paper Series, College of Business Administration,

University of Rhode Island (2013). http://web.uri.edu/business/files/Encycl-Communication-DataMining-n-Marketing-.pdf.

711   Associated Press, "Data-mining the New Tool for US Election Campaigns," May 28, 2012. www.dawn.com/news/722025/data-mining-the-new-tool-for-us-election-campaigns.

712   Nichols, op. cit.

713   Stephanie Clifford, "Social Media Is Giving a Voice to Taste Buds," *New York Times*, July 30, 2012. www.nytimes.com/2012/07/31/technology/facebook-twitter-and-foursquare-as-corporate-focus-groups.html.

714   Astra Taylor, *The People's Platform: Taking Back Power and Culture in the Digital Age* (Metropolitan Books, 2014).

715   Clay Shirky, *Here Comes Everybody: The Power of Organizing Without Organizations* (Penguin, 2008).

716   Evgeny Morozov, *Net Delusion: The Dark Side of Internet Freedom* (PublicAffairs, 2012).

717   Jodi Dean, *Blog Theory* (Polity, 2010).

718   Jacoby, op. cit., 150.

Index

douches 107
Douglas, Michael 132, 133
Draper, Don. *See* Mad Men
Dreiser, Theodore 88–89
Dukakis, Michael 183
Dunaway, Cammie 178

eccentrics pretending to be average 211
Edsel 69–76
    focus groups and 72–73
    parallels with New Coke 164, 169
    reasons for failure 72–75
    as vagina 70, 73, 76–77
    see also Ford Motor Company
elites
    declining trust in 105
    degeneration 5
    resentment of focus groups 169
    see also focus groups,
        relationship between elites
        and masses
elitism 234; *see also* Viennese
    socialism/social democracy
encounter groups 120, 122
Engel, Jonathan 49
entertainment industry, focus groups
    and 127–140
    Altman parody of 135
    assignment of blame for bad
        movies 136–137
    Broadway use of 135–136
    children and 130
    creatives beef against 127–128,
        133–134
    drive for more commercial
        success, 1970s 131–132
    gaming industry 138–139
    movie plotting 132
    racial aspects 129
    underestimate audience
        taste 134–135
entrepreneur, everyone is one 214

entrepreneurs vs. focus groups 171–182
    Adorno angle 173
    fake Henry Ford quote 175
    Gladwell on 171–173
    macho contempt for 175, 177
environment 11
ESOMAR 5, 241
EST 120
ethics 205, 274
European Society for Opinion and
    Market Research 33
Ewen, Stuart 224

Facebook 245, 247, 248
false needs 106
false termination 51
fan sites 138
Fatal Attraction (movie) 132–133
fear of client rage 218
feminine guilt 34, 47
Feminine Mystique, The (Friedan) 86, 91
feminism 88, 97–98, 124
    consciousness raising 121, 122
    second-wave 107
    see also women
Fiorina, Morris 196
First National Bank of Denver 112
Fishburne, Tom 215
Fitzwater, Marlin 186
Focused Interview, The (Merton and
    Kendall) 50
focus groupies. *See* professional
    respondents
focus groups
    actors as participants 232
    assembling 203–204, 217
    British origins 40
    changing technology 104
    client hatred of 228–230
    coinage 45
    and community 222
    containing women's

Listerine 145
Little Caesars 160
lobbying, growth in 154
Lobbying America (Waterhouse) 154
Lockheed Corp. 57
Lonely Crowd, The (Reisman) 57
Los Angeles Urban League 56
loss aversion 164
Louis & Brorby 56
Lucky Strike 46, 56
Luntz, Frank 187, 225, 227, 232, 233, 234
Lynd, Helen 41
Lynd, Robert 41
Lyne, Adrian 132

MacLeish, Archibald 17
Macomb County, Michigan 188
Mad Men (TV show) 15, 43, 46, 92, 96,
    135, 138, 175, 275, 281
Marcuse, Herbert 49, 106
Marienthal 34
market immersion 179
Marketing News (magazine) 121, 230
market research
    as tool of democracy 68
    as populist project 232
    scientific pretentions 217
Market Research Association 33, 210, 241
Marotta, Lily 206–208, 216, 217, 223
Martha Stewart Living (magazine) 212
Martineau, Pierre 66
Maslin, Paul 187
Masson-Minock, Megan 244
materialism 59
maternal drinking 30
Mattel 48
Maule, Frances 87–89
McCall's 93
McCann Erickson 38, 42
men, stupidity of 102
Merton, Robert K. 15, 15–22, 16, 18, 19,
    20, 21, 22, 28, 35, 42, 50, 96, 131,

173, 263, 272
    birth name 16
    as father of the focus group 20
    meeting Lazarsfeld 15
    origins 16
Michigan 188
Middletown (Lynd) 41
Millet, Kate 118
Mills, C. Wright 38–39
misogyny 92
Montgomery, Robert 17
Moore, Sara Jane 147
Morozov, Evgeny 249
Morrison, David 260
motivational research 58
Mullen, Cy 55
Mullins, Gay 163

Nader, Ralph 105, 152
Nadia (pseudonym) 204, 208, 209,
    211, 215, 217, 218, 220
Nahl, Perham 56, 58
Nation, The (magazine) 37, 239
Nazis 17, 22, 176, 281
Needham 56
New Deal 9
New Jersey 151, 183, 248
New Left 270
    and corporate culture 121
    see also left
New York (magazine) 120, 209–210
Nichols, John 247
Nickelodeon 136
Nielsen 5
Nielsen Company 179
Nispel, Marcus 131
Nokia 249
Obama, Barack 141, 182
    as blank screen for projection 194
    as Muslim 225
Obama, Michelle 207
Occupy Wall Street 13, 193, 251

Beautiful Rising
Creative Resistance from the
Global South
EDITED BY JUMAN ABUJBARA,
ANDREW BOYD, DAVE MITCHELL,
AND MARCEL TAMINATO

Desperately Seeking Self-Improvement
A Year Inside the Optimization
Movement
CARL CEDERSTRÖM AND ANDRÉ
SPICER

Old Demons, New Deities
Twenty-One Short Stories from Tibet
EDITED BY TENZIN DICKIE

Homeland Security Ate My Speech
Messages from the End of the World
ARIEL DORFMAN

Assuming Boycott
Resistance, Agency, and Cultural
Production
EDITED BY KAREEM ESTEFAN, CARIN
KUONI, AND LAURA RAICOVICH

Swords in the Hands of Children
Reflections of an American Revolutionary
JONATHAN LERNER

The Spread Mind
Why Consciousness and
the World Are One
RICCARDO MANZOTTI

With Ash on Their Faces
Yezidi Women and the Islamic State
CATHY OTTEN

Women of Resistance
Poetry from 50 Activists
EDITED BY DANIELLE BARNHART AND
IRIS MAHAN